THE HONEST MUSE

Oxford University Press, Ely House, London W. 1

GLASGOW NEW YORK TORONTO MELBOURNE WELLINGTON
CAPE TOWN SALISBURY IBADAN NAIROBI LUSAKA ADDIS ABABA
BOMBAY CALCUTTA MADRAS KARACHI LAHORE DACCA
KUALA LUMPUR HONG KONG TOKYO

RACHEL TRICKETT

The Honest Muse

A STUDY IN
AUGUSTAN VERSE

OXFORD
AT THE CLARENDON PRESS
1967

© *Oxford University Press 1967*

PRINTED IN GREAT BRITAIN

TO
DAVID CECIL

PREFACE

THIS book is not in any sense an exhaustive study of Augustan poetry. In it I have tried to consider some of the attitudes and assumptions underlying the poetry of Dryden, Pope, and Johnson, and to see them in relation to the political and intellectual circumstances in which they worked. The strong tradition of verse satire, exemplified in such collections as the *Poems on Affairs of State* and in the work of Rochester and Oldham, has to some extent been neglected in previous studies of the work of the major poets, and I have given it greater prominence to distinguish as far as possible the peculiar characteristics of the school of writers which Dryden helped to establish, of which Pope was the greatest exponent and Johnson the last exemplar.

References to Dryden's poems are taken from *The Poems of John Dryden*, edited by James Kinsley (1958); to Pope's from the single-volume Twickenham edition of the poems, edited by John Butt (1963), and to Johnson's from *The Poems of Samuel Johnson*, edited by D. Nichol Smith and E. McAdam (1941). I have, where possible, quoted from standard modern editions of the minor poets of the age, but when, as in the case of Oldham, such an edition does not exist, I have referred to the first edition of the works. The bibliographical problems of the *Poems on Affairs of State* are notoriously complex. I have used the volumes which were immediately accessible and indicated in each case the date and edition of the individual volume.

My thanks are due to many scholars and friends. I have dedicated the book to Lord David Cecil, who first taught me to love the period. Professor Maynard Mack of Yale University introduced me to methods and ideas of research in this period, and to him and his work I owe a great deal. The late Hugh Macdonald gave me generous and invaluable help in discussing the work of minor authors in the late seventeenth century. Professor Helen Gardner read some of the early chapters of this book and offered helpful and stimulating criticism. Professor Sherard Vines and Mrs. Margaret 'Espinasse of the University of Hull at various times discussed the book with me and gave me advice, and Miss Rosemary Woolf of Somerville College, Oxford, has read most of it and made valuable suggestions. So also, in the early stages, has Professor A. K. Thorlby of the University of Sussex. Miss Betty Kemp of St. Hugh's College, Oxford, has helped me much by discussing the politics of the period with me. I am deeply grateful to Mr. Michael Gearin-Tosh of St. Catherine's College, Oxford, who for the past few years has acted as a research assistant, checking facts and footnotes, and giving me unstinted time and the advantage of his critical perceptiveness. Any faults or errors in the book are entirely my responsibility. Finally I am indebted to Miss M. A. Hennings who has made the index for me.

RACHEL TRICKETT

St. Hugh's College
Oxford

CONTENTS

I

INTRODUCTION

'RISE, Honest Muse! and sing the Man of Ross': with this line
Pope introduces his elaborate compliment to John Kyrle in the
Epistle to Lord Bathurst, Of the Use of Riches (*Moral Essay* III). After
the preceding verse, 'But all our praises why should Lords engross?',
the sturdy tone of challenge sounds either sincere or mildly absurd
according to our sympathy with the attitude behind it. Since Pope
was too well acquainted with the dangers of sinking in poetry to
risk an ambiguous effect at the climax of this 'most laboured' of his
moral satires, and far too conscious a rhetorician not to know the
impressions the lines were likely to convey, we must assume that
the new muse and her everyday material possessed a peculiar significance and authority for him and his readers. They felt no irre-
concilable distance between Kyrle's benevolence, his waterworks
and causeways, his active charity and the terms in which they are
described. These terms themselves are revealing. The muse begins
her flight in the old high style:

> Pleas'd Vaga echoes thro' her winding bounds,
> And rapid Severn hoarse applause resounds.
>
> (ll. 251–2.)

She then descends to rhetorical questions which conceal a bold
religious analogy:

> Who hung with woods yon mountain's sultry brow?
> From the dry rock who bade the waters flow?
>
> (ll. 253–4.)

Next she proceeds to an oblique denial of the ostentation Kyrle's
honesty rejects:

> Not to the skies in useless columns tost,
> Or in proud falls magnificently lost
>
> (ll. 255–6.)

and concludes with a positive statement of his achievement:

> But clear and artless, pouring thro' the plain
> Health to the sick, and solace to the swain.
>
> (ll. 257–8.)

In spite of the echoes of earlier modes in these shifts of style, the culminating praise of the Honest Muse is different in kind from the older vein of panegyric. It points to a new idea of worth and virtue in poetry. Kyrle's goodness is like his reservoir, clear and artless; it has profusion and simplicity; it is real benevolence, concerned with the business of living, with this world rather than the next, and it is very much a matter of use and conduct. The 'pompous enumeration' of his acts of charity which makes up the rest of the passage is a list of actual performances, simple facts dressed in the elevated rhetoric of compliment which emphasizes their dignity and importance without transforming their original material actuality. The false beauty of a fountain or a waterfall is contrasted with the true value of charity, and both are described in a new sort of style which is never entirely figurative in the traditional metaphorical sense. Pope implies the qualities he is attacking and elevates those he admires by a sort of periphrasis, an elaboration of the object which describes it in related terms, or singles out a part for the whole, but which seldom introduces any comparison that might turn the mind away from the thing itself. He does not enrich by transforming; he embellishes and distinguishes at the same time. Two direct statements of Kyrle's activities:

> Whose Cause-way parts the vale with shady rows?
> Whose Seats the weary Traveller repose?
>
> (ll. 259–60.)

are followed by the more oblique and heightened

> Who taught that heav'n-directed spire to rise?
>
> (l. 261.)

where we are shown both the church and the Man of Ross's pious and patient endeavour in building it. We are constantly directed to the thing itself and the intention behind it. For all its formality, there is a realism in this approach which generalizes to achieve its highest point, while it seldom concentrates for an effect of insight or vision. The true value of the theme and the facts of the subject are lucidly presented through every device; nothing is allowed to obscure them.

A fundamental realism—an attempt to see things as they are—is indeed the inspiration of good Augustan poetry, even at its most polished and formal. The artifices which are used to achieve this polish and formality may produce an effect of naïve pomposity in the work of a poet of little thought or feeling. But there were at least three masters of the style who recognized and developed its real resources. Dryden showed how an exuberant amplitude of manner could be matched with unadorned statement of fact; Pope discovered a new kind of complexity to which he was driven by the need to preserve the fact and at the same time give disciplined rein to his imagination and feeling, and Johnson displayed a powerful and even oppressive sense of reality which gives force to the pervasive generalization of his style.

This peculiar and self-conscious idiom of the Augustans has been only partially understood. Its devices were deplored by romantic and Victorian critics, who found them both artificial and prosaic. Twentieth-century critics, on the other hand, have admired its subtleties, ironies, compression, and wit, but their very admiration has tended to isolate these devices from the spirit they reflect. Both the nineteenth- and twentieth-century critics have started from the style rather than from the attitude behind it, and have thus missed the whole by paying too close attention to the parts—a fault which Pope himself singled out as characteristic of pedantry and formal criticism.

The style itself is concerned with certain problems of definition and response. It follows closely changing attitudes and beliefs. So sensitively, indeed, does it mirror the sentiments and assumptions of its time, that we can find it difficult to appreciate a manner which is essentially different from our own because it arises from such different preconceptions. Augustan poetry is not, for instance, 'the unimaginable lodge for solitary thinkings'; it lacks both mystery and passion. Its beauty is melodious, and the limited lucid images in which it abounds have little in common with that metaphorical language Coleridge took to be the hallmark of poetry. The

Augustans were delighted by lines like these so often quoted[1]
from *Cooper's Hill:*

> O could I flow like thee, and make thy stream
> My great example, as it is my theme!
> Though deep, yet clear, though gentle, yet not dull,
> Strong without rage, without ore-flowing full.
>
> (ll. 189–93.)

If we are to enjoy them we must return to a frame of mind where the
idea of strength contained in the limits of moderation, and so exactly
conveyed by the neatly disposed caesura, the punctuation and the
stress, does not sound glib and superficial. One way of doing so is to
isolate the crucial words—deep, clear, gentle, strong, and full—so
that we recognize at once the impression they give of a temperament and a mood that still seems enviable and worth writing about.
Nevertheless, if we are expecting the poet to do more than merely
state them, it is hard to respond to their full associations here. We
have grown to expect him to catch their shades and implications, to
weave them into the work so that the idea of depth, clarity, gentle-
ness, strength, or plenitude is conveyed through a prevailing image
or by the texture of the poem. Thus the simpler style of the Augustans, of which they themselves were so consciously proud, though
it is the perfect mirror of their attitude, is often overlooked or misunderstood by readers accustomed to a different kind of poetry.

Our whole approach since the romantic period has conditioned
us to respond readily to Shakespeare's dramatic language, to metaphysical wit and romantic symbolism—kinds of verse which exploit those metaphorical devices that Coleridge believed to be the
essential nature of the imagination. Poetic language of a different
sort needs more conscious adjustment. Our great tradition consists of Shakespeare, Donne, Coleridge, and Keats. But when Pope
said to Spence 'it is easy to mark out the general course of our
poetry. Chaucer, Spenser, Milton, and Dryden, are the great landmarks for it',[2] Shakespeare's name is conspicuously absent from his
list. Spence, noticing this, observes 'it is plain that he was speaking
of our miscellaneous writers, by his omitting Shakespeare and other

---

[1] See *Poetical Works of Sir John Denham*, ed. T. H. Banks Jr. (1928), pp. 342–50.
[2] Spence, *Anecdotes*, ed. S. W. Singer (1820), p. 171.

considerable names in the dramatic way', but it is just as probable that Pope was defining a tradition based on the narrative, epic, or discursive modes. The Augustans found it difficult to fit Shakespeare into any orthodox category, and, in any case, preferred to think of him as 'the poet of nature', outside the limits of classification. Indeed, within the range of his own work, Shakespeare comprehends many styles of poetry, and the difference between the two we are concerned with can be illustrated from his plays.

These lines from Troilus's farewell to Cressida are an almost perfect example of the dramatic and metaphorical use of poetic language:

> Injurious Time now with a robber's haste
> Crams his rich thievery up, he knows not how:
> As many farewells as be stars in heaven,
> With distinct breath and consigned kisses to them,
> He fumbles up into a loose adieu,
> And scants us with a single famished kiss,
> Distasted with the salt of broken tears.
> (*Troilus and Cressida*, IV. iv. 42–48.)

They are carried along by the impetus of the metaphor; new images are thrown up as the poet's imagination expands, and parting becomes robbery, furtive deception, meanness, starvation, and discord as much as separation. As the figures grow more animated the feelings become more intense and comprehensive. But Shakespeare did not always write in this way. *The Two Gentlemen of Verona* contains a speech in his early style which exemplifies another use of poetic language, nearer to the Augustans'. Julia is telling Lucetta why she means to follow Proteus:

> The current that with gentle murmur glides,
> Thou know'st, being stopped, impatiently doth rage:
> But when his fair course is not hindered
> He makes sweet music with th'enamelled stones,
> Giving a gentle kiss to every sedge
> He overtaketh in his pilgrimage;
> And so by many winding nooks he strays,
> With willing sport, to the wide ocean . . .
> Then let me go, and hinder not my course:

I'll be as patient as a gentle stream,
And make a pastime of each weary step,
Till the last step have brought me to my love—
And there I'll rest, as, after much turmoil
A blessed soul doth in Elysium.
                (*The Two Gentlemen of Verona*, II. vii. 25–38.)

This speech is longer than Troilus's, but its effect is more restricted. Instead of hurrying through the by-ways of an experience, it presents, describes, and persuades in a deliberate, leisurely fashion. But it adds little to the original experience of separation, and it would never lead anyone to remember Coleridge's definition of the imagination as that which 'dissolves, diffuses, dissipates in order to recreate'. On the contrary, it leaves its subject intact, and, by doing so, affirms its importance. Julia's feelings are described by what the Augustans would have called an apt similitude,[1] which acquires no more than a formal and passive beauty, since it has no deeper connexion with the experience than that of an illustration which clarifies and embellishes without transforming it.

Such a style arouses a mixed response. We admire the poet's skill and are moved by the occasion of it. But above all we are invited to reflect on the subject which is so gracefully and exactly supported by the analogy. The appeal is to a meditative frame of mind. The poet who uses this style evokes often a melancholy mood which comes from time and experience remembered, and when he does so his work is, in some sense, like the pictures of the sack of Troy on the walls of the Carthaginian temple, which, by their just representations of the past, moved Aeneas to exclaim 'sunt lacrimae rerum et mentem mortalia tangunt'.

It is false to imagine that deep feelings are not aroused by poetry which limits itself to what is commonly understood or rationally perceived and recalled. Poetry that takes its vision from the mind's eye does not re-create experience in the light of the imagination. It records and broods over whatever is already accepted, leaving the facts in their original state, with all their fundamental appeal to the deepest and often the least sophisticated human instincts. The way

---

[1] The very same simile is used by Cowley, *Davideis*, Bk. I, II. 51–56, and by Rochester, *The Advice*, II. 19–29.

in which mortality and the nature of things impinge on the mind is the subject of much poetry which does not use the language of passion or of the imagination in Coleridge's sense, and Augustan verse is one of the best examples of this. It is poetry in which the subject-matter is peculiarly important and to which a lucid, pointed style is especially appropriate. Some of its strength derives from the narrative manner of the epic, and the epic, which set out to instruct as well as to please, depended inevitably, to some extent, on the art of persuasion. Narrative allows the poet to relate dispassionately, but it can encourage him to command various tones of voice, too, if his intention is to teach. He may assert or persuade while he is telling. Drama, on the other hand, which takes no account of the poet's own person, and forces him to disguise his voice, may contain all these tones incidentally in dialogue, but they can never dominate the whole work. Augustan poetry is closely related to the epic tradition of narrative and discourse: it relates facts or circumstances and displays an attitude of mind towards them.

Obviously such poetry has a palpable design on us, and some people would agree with Keats in hating it on principle. If we are not to resent it, much depends on the integrity and worth of the design and the sincerity of the poet, and these were among the major concerns of the Augustans. They were themselves anxious to draw attention to what they said rather than to the way they said it; their notorious critical metaphor, that the words are the proper dress of the thought, suggests their real respect for the body beneath, and they devised a style which threw the reader back on the substance of the thought and the underlying feelings.

Pope's favourite rhetorician, Quintilian, in his *Institutio Oratoria*, speaking of the emotions which should be used in the peroration to move and persuade the judge, classifies them under the two headings of pathos and ethos. Of these the latter seemed to him the more significant, and his discussion of it illuminates one important aspect of Augustan style. In attempting to define the word *ethos* Quintilian recalls that it had been contrasted with pathos as being moral rather than affective, and as describing the calmer and more subdued emotions. He points out that some critics hold that pathos has a momentary effect, ethos a continuous one: 'Adiiciunt quidam ἦθος perpetuum, πάθος temporale esse.'[1] But Quintilian expands this definition to comprehend a great deal more. He himself sees the moral quality of ethos as a form of goodness which arouses pleasure and approbation, and maintains that its expression should arise naturally from the facts of the subject, and in the process reveal the 'ethical' character of the speaker:

> *Ἦθος, quod intelligimus quodque a dicentibus desideramus, id erit, quod ante omnia bonitate commendabitur, non solum mite ac placidum, sed plerumque blandum et humanum et audientibus amabile atque iucundum, in quo exprimendo summa virtus ea est, ut fluere omnia ex natura rerum hominumque videantur utque mores dicentis ex oratione perluceant et quodammodo agnoscantur.[2]

This epitomizes with extraordinary accuracy the quality of the best Augustan verse both in its treatment of subject-matter and its expression. Ethos as Quintilian describes it is very like the feeling that pervades Pope's later moral satires.

The response the Augustans felt to ideas of virtue and good character is the inspiration that lies behind much of their best poetry. Dryden celebrating his cousin John Dryden, the country gentleman leading a robust and useful life, Pope's Honest Muse singing the Man of Ross, Johnson praising the unobtrusive merits of Levet in verse which has 'the power of art without the show', are all clearly of the same school; they share the same ethos. Every age reconsiders its ideal of the good man, and the Augustans, assessing older styles of writing in the light of their own needs, had first weighed older ideals of conduct against their own experience. Their peculiar mode of writing cannot be properly understood without a close study of their wider attitude—that ethos which expresses itself in a natural exposition of the subject and at the same time reveals a character and a mood which these poets claimed for themselves as well as for their poetry.

There are certain recurrent words in Augustan verse which reveal its predominant ethos. Among these one of the most revealing is the word *honest*, and the Augustan use of it is an important clue in helping to unravel the meaning and estimate the value of their work. As far as I know, the only critic who has

---

[1] Quintilian, *Institutio Oratoria*, VI. ii. 10.   [2] Quintilian, op. cit. VI. ii. 13.

seriously attempted to follow up the various meanings of *honest* in its literary uses is William Empson in *The Structure of Complex Words*.

It has been a rich and shifting but always somehow real and intelligible term of praise, so that it would illustrate, if you could get the performance clear, what people in a given group were prepared to praise, why they were prepared to praise it (that is, what twist of moral feeling made them choose to praise it by this word), and again, perhaps chiefly when different groups meet each other, how far people were able to suggest or impose their moral outlook simply by the way they used the moral word.[1]

In tracing the historical development of the word, Empson is largely concerned with its earlier Elizabethan connotations of frank dealing and good fellowship, with the later touch of patronage it acquires in the seventeenth century, and the ironic overtones with which its Restoration usage (particularly in the work of the wits) suggests a candid admission of vices normally concealed. He touches on Pope's use of the phrase 'an Honest Man' in the eighteenth century—'the man who can recognize and fulfil both his own nature and his duties to society', and remarks how he has become 'the Type of man, the measure of all things'. It is this aspect of the word which particularly concerns us in approaching Augustan poetry. For Empson's analysis of this particular usage can be enlarged and expanded; more than he has time or space to explain in his chapter, the word *honest* in Augustan literature is connected with a whole range of attitudes and assumptions which were closely linked with developments of thought, historical circumstances, and changing literary tastes. For us it is not a word charged with any poetic feeling; for the Augustans it touched on a wide area of emotions.

Throughout the seventeenth century the traditional chivalric conception of honour which had possessed such ample meaning for the Renaissance, with all its implications of nobility, rank, and military glory, was giving place slowly to a humbler private ideal of honesty. In the next century Johnson defined honest as 'upright, true, sincere, just, righteous, giving to every man his due'. It is

[1] W. Empson, *The Structure of Complex Words* (1951), p. 185.

significant that there is no other instance, earlier or later, of such an
extensive and dignified dictionary definition. For Johnson and the
eighteenth century the word in its literary usage had become
weighted with moral considerations that covered a wide field of
human conduct. It suggested especially the just assessment of individual qualities which could be recognized in a man's actual
virtues as they showed themselves to his fellow men, rather than
by his rank and place in society.

The word *honest* appears at one time to have had something of a
Stoic implication. In the sixteenth century it carried overtones of
passive forbearance, a negative rather than a positive virtue. In his
Notebooks Coleridge cites this passage from an essay in *Cottoni
Posthuma*. We shall see at the end of the chapter how the fully
developed Augustan view rejected these ideas.

Honesty is a quiet passing over the days of a man's life without
doing injury to another man. There is required in an honest man not
so much to do everything as he would be done unto; as to forbear
any thing which he would not be content to suffer; for the essence of
Honesty consists in forbearing to do ill. . . . For Honesty doth not
consist in the doing of one, or one thousand acts never so well; but in
spinning on the delicate Threds of Life, tho' not exceeding fine, yet
free from bracks and stains. We do not call him an honest man, but
a worthy man, that doth brave eminent acts; but we give him the title
of an honest man, of whom no man can truly report any ill.[1]

In literature this stoicism shows itself to some extent in the Elizabethan figure of the uncomplaining honest fellow who sees the
world as it is, and in his plain-speaking shows his indifference to it,
such as Kent in *Lear*, or 'honest' Iago—how relevant the phrase
becomes in the light of this meaning and its implications of not
meddling! In these examples the word is associated with plainness
of condition as well as of speech, and from this it is a short step to
the figure of the simple honest man, Empson's patronized pastoral
figure, around whom country associations cluster. These are neatly
and directly described in the seventeenth century in Marvell's
translation of a chorus from Seneca's *Thyestes*:

---

[1] Coleridge, in common with the opinion of his day, falsely attributes this to Sir
Francis Walsingham. See *Notebooks*, ed. Kathleen Coburn, vol. ii (1962), entry 1880.

Climb at *Court* for me that will
Tottering favors Pinacle;
All I seek is to lye still.
Settled in some secret Nest
In calm Leisure let me rest;
And far of the publick Stage
Pass away my silent Age.
Thus when without noise, unknown,
I have liv'd out all my span,
I shall dye, without a groan,
An old honest Country man.
Who expos'd to others Ey's,
Into his own Heart ne'r pry's,
Death to him 's a Strange surprise.[1]

An old honest country man (Seneca has only 'plebeius ... senex')—
here already we have a character slightly different from the bluff
honesty of the Elizabethan drama. The passage was a popular one
in the late seventeenth century: Cowley translated it in his essay
Of Obscurity, where it is openly associated with the idea of retreat,
and the two notions of retirement and honesty were linked throughout the subsequent period, as we shall see. But the passive virtue
of this kind of honesty was not quite enough for men like the Augustans, who were so closely concerned with the life of affairs and
the world.

The value of the ideal of honest, clear-sighted integrity as it
appeared in public life was beginning to be made explicit at the
same time in the seventeenth century as this more private interpretation. Clarendon in his *History of the Rebellion* chose to praise
Charles I for this virtue before proceeding to judge his kingly
qualities: 'He was, if ever any, the most worthy of the title of an
Honest Man.'[2] Sir William Temple in his *Essay upon the Original and
Nature of Government* used the word as a synonym for goodness:
'that which makes men prefer their Duty and their Promise, before
their Passions, or their Interest; and is properly the object of Trust.
In our Language, it goes rather by the name of Honesty.'[3] It is

---

[1] Marvell, *Poems and Letters*, ed. H. M. Margoliouth (1927), vol. i, pp. 54–55.
[2] Clarendon, *History of the Rebellion*, Oxford, vol. iii (1704), p. 197.
[3] Sir W. Temple, *Miscellanea* (1680), p. 56.

remarkable to find this so explicitly stated. Fifty years before
Temple was writing, the name of Honour would have been the
more obvious one for the integrity which prefers Duty and Promise
to Passion or Interest, and even today 'word of honour' has retained
some meaning. But Temple's choice of 'honesty', like Clarendon's,
to suggest 'trustworthy in the widest sense', reveals a shift of attitude and emphasis which helps to explain the growing Augustan
ideal.

Honesty appeared to them above all as an unadorned virtue. In
the same essay Temple enumerates the effects on men of those em-
bellishing graces which should accompany goodness, but he barely
conceals his hint that they only too seldom do: 'Eloquence, As it
passes for a mark of Wisdom; Beauty of Goodness, And Nobility of
Valour (which was its original) have likewise ever some effect upon
the opinion of the People; but a very great one when they are really
joined with the qualities they promise or resemble.'[1] Temple, bred
like the rest of his age to religious and political dissension, was quick
to suspect those occasions and instances where such adornments
were not really joined to the qualities they promised or resembled.
But this distrust of the traditional attributes of virtue as too often
a mere show only threw into greater relief the naked integrity of
honesty. It was not associated with outward graces: rather it was an
inner quality, a state of mind which reason and experience alone
could recognize. As such it was at the opposite extreme from those
great attributes which could be represented by the external signs
of rank, or the natural display of glory or beauty, and thus any poet
who chose to celebrate honesty might find himself rejecting or
modifying the old traditional images of the ideal—the stock conventions of panegyric or even of epic. The Augustans, in their pursuit of honesty, were forced to take into account both the traditional
conventions they held in respect and the new consciousness of virtue that this distrust of outward show encouraged.

Suspicion of the outward trappings of virtue itself leads naturally
to satire of the kind that tears away deceptive appearances from the
reality, and it is as satirists that the Augustans are generally remembered. But this same distrust will force a poet to devise new

[1] Sir W. Temple, *Miscellanea* (1680), p. 57.

ways of presenting that reality, and of recommending the virtue that clear-sightedly takes reality into account. He is likely to reject the preconceptions and the manner of his predecessors even when he is aware of the importance of tradition and authority to his art. This paradox is constantly revealed in Augustan poetry; on the one hand it is conservative, imitative, and formal; on the other it is deeply concerned with the present, with contemporary attitudes, standards of language, and codes of behaviour. Three of the major kinds of poetry which the Augustans inherited—panegyric, satire, and elegy, as we shall see in the next chapter—were all radically affected by the changing ideas and circumstances of the age. Each of these kinds was involved with ideals of conduct and with the reality in face of which such ideals were maintained, so that in their development we can read a brief history of the changing consciousness which was rapidly turning honesty into a cardinal virtue.

Dryden, whose influence more than any other's determined the course of the new verse, came early into the field, before all these changes had been clearly defined or wholly assimilated. His experience as a poet 'betwixt two ages cast', and his position as a professional writer, presented him with peculiar problems; and the way in which he solved them, together with his experiments in finding a tone of voice suitable for his new material, influenced profoundly the whole style of subsequent poetry. He was not alone in pursuing this course. His contemporaries—satirists and wits, scholars, translators, and journalists—were all involved in the same attempt to accommodate their work to new standards of thought, experience, and conduct. Their achievement was the real foundation of Pope's, and his originality can only justly be measured against the great debt he owed to the Restoration writers who preceded him. Pope's imitation of the ancients and of the great poets of his own country has been exhaustively studied,[1] but the whole range of attitudes, conventions, and assumptions he inherited from his immediate predecessors has too often been overlooked. Coming at the end of a brief but vital tradition, he did not share Dryden's opportunities for experiment, but he had all the advantages of the last of a line. He

[1] R. A. Brower, *Alexander Pope, the Poetry of Allusion* (1959).

could see more clearly, perhaps, the essential truth lying behind the manner and the matter of the Restoration poets, and though he was often in sympathy with them, he could afford to eliminate what seemed to him irrelevant in their work, to modify the inadequate or the imperfect, and to impose on the whole school the stamp of his final interpretation. It was Pope who proudly and openly invoked the Honest Muse.

Pope's outlook influenced the whole attitude of the Augustan School. Johnson as a poet shared its preconceptions, and as a man he found that experience bore out many of its favourite moral assumptions, and its prevailing elegiac tone. Essayists and novelists, hymn writers and historians consciously carried on its standards of realism and accuracy, and its ideals of sincerity and general truth. The effect of this concept of honesty, which we shall try to trace in Augustan poetry, in fact extended even beyond the limits of that school. In learning to adopt a new tone of voice while speaking of men and their actions, the Augustans were moulding their art to the needs of a new kind of sensibility, which, for want of a better term, we may call the modern consciousness. However formal and even artificial certain aspects of their style may seem, they were the first authors to be forced to confront the problem of how to accommodate the conventions of poetry—the greatest of all fictions —with the demands of fact, fact as it was now recognized by 'realistic' reason and observation. In some sense this has always been the function of the artist, but the peculiar nature of the problem it presented to Restoration and eighteenth-century writers depended upon their understanding of reality. Much has been written on the philosophical revolution of the seventeenth century, and on the attack by the modernists and the supporters of the Royal Society on the old imaginative structure of thought and literature. It has become fashionable to suggest that the best Augustan poetry, especially Pope's, owes its greatness to a secret affinity with older ways of thought, lingering Renaissance ideas, concepts of order and harmony which can be traced back to the mingled Christian and Platonic notions of a more golden age. But though these vestiges can be found in the poetry of the time, to emphasize them draws attention away from the peculiar quality of Augustan writing—its extreme consciousness of the shift in ideas and terminology which had taken place in the previous century and was now impossible to ignore. The movement from fable to fact in subject-matter, and from myth to history as a mode of understanding and reflecting experience, is as vividly reflected in the poetry of the Honest Muse as in the development of the new literary form of the novel to which these changes gave rise. In some ways the poets were fighting with their backs to the wall, their weapon of defence being satire, but their tactics were seldom aggressive. With a sure instinct of literary caution they moved towards a compromise position between the old and the new, and though they sided for the most part with the ancients, none of them ever attempted to deny the common assumption of the time, that men and manners, matter of fact rather than of fiction, were the true substance of an art which, at its highest, must come home to the business and bosom of every man.

The purpose of this study is to examine some of the ways in which the literary world adapted itself to this situation; to mark some of the changes in conventions and forms it brought about. By the time of Pope and Johnson, the full Augustan ideal of honesty was established. It is discussed in a valuable and neglected periodical *The Tribune*, probably by Patrick Delany. Honesty does 'not consist in abstaining from hurtful and injurious Acts, in paying our just Debts, or in being quiet and inoffensive Members of Civil Society':[1]

... what was called the *Honestum* among the Ancients, from which our Term *Honesty* is most plainly derived, signified the highest Perfection of human Nature, and took in the whole Circle of the moral Virtues. . . . It might be therefore convenient to retrieve the lost Signification of the Word, and restore it to its first Energy and Reverence.[2]

By relating this ideal to the work of Dryden, Pope, and Johnson we may come to share the response of their contemporaries, who were as moved by their approach to truth and virtue as by their artifice.

[1] *The Tribune* (1729), no. 15: collected edition, London (1729), p. 103.
[2] Ibid., pp. 106–7.

II

THE THREE MAIN FORMS

THE moderns, according to Sir William Temple, in his 'Essay upon Poetry', were especially celebrated for certain kinds of verse: *Petra[r]ch, Ronsard, Spencer,* met with much Applause upon the Subjects of Love, Praise, Grief, Reproach.'[1] Love is a constant theme of poetry and has never been confined to a particular genre, but praise, grief, and reproach each had its proper form—the pane-gyric, the elegy, and the satire. In Augustan poetry these three genres, while retaining their old importance, were modified by the new circumstances and the new mood of the times. In particular, panegyric was transformed in a way which vividly illustrates the changes that were beginning to affect every branch of poetry.

There are few poems of praise for public men after the eighteenth century. The romantics liked to show their admiration and affection for friends and fellow poets in private lyric verses—a kind of com-pliment in confidence. But a panegyric proper is not a poem about friendship at all; it is a public celebration of virtue, nobility, and splendour, qualities which can be represented by a monarch, a hero, or a statesman whose private character might not bear a more inti-mate scrutiny. The panegyrist takes it for granted that the em-bellishing graces really are joined to the qualities they promise or resemble, and he removes his subject from personal and individual reality to a more abstract sphere. For, like the epic, panegyric represents an ideal to recall men to a proper sense of elevated dig-nity.

But poets will always need a more intimate tone of address, and alongside the panegyrics an informal style of compliment was de-veloping in the seventeenth century, derived from the Horatian epistle to a friend. Epistles are conversation poems, where formal compliment gives way to an honest exchange of personal views and

[1] Sir W. Temple, *Miscellanea, The Second Part* (1690), 'Essay upon Poetry', p. 46.

information. Thus Ben Jonson's *Epistle to a Friend* is intended to 'persuade him to the warres', but, because of the freedom of the form, it turns into an excuse for Jonson to indulge in some hard-hitting satire against the corruption of city life in time of peace. On the whole, the epistles of his followers, the Tribe of Ben, were less fierce than this, and more consciously Horatian in tone, and they grew in number and range as the century advanced. Many of them, like Carew's to Aurelian Townsend, or Suckling's to D'Avenant, are slight, witty exchanges between courtiers, fellow poets, and friends. Their informality left no mark, however, on the formal eulogy, even though a poet might use the familiar style in jest for a high occasion, as Suckling did in celebrating the marriage of Lord Broghill and Lady Margaret Howard with the *Ballad Upon a Wedding*. The only grave compliments in verse before 1660 which do not belong in any sense to the old panegyric vein are Milton's sonnets, and Milton's view on compliment is expressed directly in *Areopagitica*, where he recommends the instance when 'he who praises, by showing that such his actual persuasion is of whom he writes, can demonstrate that he flatters not'.[1] In his sonnets the great are addressed equally in a style which is neither traditionally ceremonious nor intimate. Cyriack Skinner, Lady Margaret Ley, Fairfax, and Cromwell himself are celebrated nobly, not for their position in the State or society, but for their private virtues and their actual integrity, which alone, in Milton's eyes, justifies the praise. The style, unique in its chaste gravity, is nevertheless an early and exceptional example of something very close to the later Augustan ideal of honest eulogy; it arises from much the same conception of true and intrinsic worth.

Another change takes place with Dryden—a change visible in his complimentary epistles as well as in his formal panegyrics. The epistles are more self-consciously dignified than any of the easy exchanges of the Cavalier poets, and can only be matched by occasional instances of a similar formality in Cowley. They are addressed to people as various as antiquarians, painters, fellow poets, Royal mistresses, and Court wits. The impression Dryden's mode of address creates is of a poet moving in a new and wider world, where the

[1] Milton, *Poems and Major Prose*, ed. M. Y. Hughes (New York, 1957), p. 718.

occupations of the people he is addressing concern him as much as their virtues or their status, and in which he himself is proudly conscious of his own equally dignified trade of verse. These are the poems of a man who is writing as much for profit as for pleasure; they have the unmistakable touch of professionalism.

The graceful complimentary poems of the Cavalier wits were, in a sense, like a Court masque, written and acted by the same group, where writer and performers equally believed in the parts they were playing. But after the Restoration these and the formal eulogies had changed their character. A Restoration panegyric is more like a public show, put on by the best authors with the best materials, the stage elaborately set and the audience always in the producer's mind: a Royal Command performance in every sense. But there is more to such panegyrics than display, for their authors set out to ingratiate and persuade rather than to pay a disinterested compliment. A kind of corruption had set in, which degraded the form and provoked a violent reaction against it in the eighteenth century, for most of the Restoration poets were writing for a living, and the currency of compliment easily becomes debased when it is written for hire. By Pope's time it was a mark of personal integrity and independence and of distinction in the art for a poet to be able to claim that he was 'unplac'd, unpension'd, no man's heir or slave'.

There were other and more fundamental reasons for this change in panegyric, however. The courtly world of the seventeenth century had gone for ever with the Civil War, and the Restoration of the Stuarts could not mean a return to the Silver Age of James I and his son. It was primarily a restoration of three institutions—monarchy, parliament, and episcopacy—and thus it was concerned to re-establish certain political and social conditions with which these institutions were associated. Moreover, the nature of the Royalist party itself had changed, for the men who came back with Charles II were no longer romantic adventurers. They had been forced to learn prudence in their time of waiting, and they knew that the Parliamentarians were too strong and formidable to be treated with the severity that might be used towards irresponsible rebels. When summary justice had been executed on the regicides, the King and his new Parliament soon submitted to the need for placating and winning over the more moderate remnant of the good old cause. And though these were quickly assimilated into society, the republicans and rebels were not easily forgotten by their opponents, for many of the political and religious issues the Civil War had thrown up were still very much alive, and they remained a source of tension throughout the period. Both the panegyric and the satire of the age grew out of this fundamental discord.

The Restoration gave a party impetus to panegyric. An Elizabethan poet singing the praises of Gloriana felt no need to convince his readers, but the poet who welcomed back Charles II was called on to reassert and justify the claims of the monarchy. He could hardly avoid expressing the mood of a party returned to power, and inevitably there was a strong element of persuasive rhetoric in his compliments. He drew on classical allusions to impress a sense of continuity and authority on his readers, and he turned as well to scriptural analogies to support the traditional link between kingship and episcopacy. Charles was hailed as Augustus and as David returned from Hebron. Yet the very skill and contrivance of these analogies incited a rejoinder from the opposition, in the same kind. If David, why not Saul?

> Of a tall Stature and of sable hue,
> Much like the Son of Kish that lofty Jew,
> Twelve Yeares compleat he suffer'd in Exile
> And kept his Fathers Asses all the while.[1]

The new panegyric was a downright provocation to satire in a way unthinkable with the old high compliment, and, in any case, the vein of satire ran near the surface in such factious times. Nourished by the rancours of the Commonwealth, satire was the most spontaneous and popular literary expression of common feeling, perhaps for the first time in the history of English letters. From the demure and sober Evelyn, who was stung to almost satiric vehemence by wilful attacks on the Royal Society, down to the pamphleteers and lampooners whose innumerable broadsides recount with surly realism the rivalries of the moment, satire prevailed

---

[1] These lines were once commonly attributed to Marvell, but Margoliouth inclines to the opinion that they are the work of an anonymous satirist. *Marvell's Poems and Letters*, ed. H. M. Margoliouth (1927), vol. i, p. 325.

as the instinctive literary form. The Restoration poet might feel
convinced of the value of the heroic strain, but he was unusually
conscious of the effort it involved. Satire, on the other hand, came
to him as naturally as leaves to the tree.

There is no period richer in good satire than the Restoration.
Pope and Swift are individually greater satirists than their predecessors, but they stand head and shoulders above their contemporaries, whereas Dryden, for all his great genius, is still comparable
in this vein with men like Butler, Oldham, and Rochester. At the
beginning of the Augustan period satire was the most vital of all
poetic forms, and it retained its force and vigour longer than any
other. But if panegyric was affected by the political situation and
mood of the times, satire could hardly avoid its influence. Inevitably
it was strongly coloured by party feeling, popular opinion, and the
urge for justification. Almost every notable satire of the age is
topical—Butler's *Hudibras*, Marvell's *Last Instructions to a Painter*,
Oldham's *Satyrs upon the Jesuits*, and Dryden's *Absalom and
Achitophel* are all concerned with the affairs of the day. Their subjects are public and political, and, except in the case of *Hudibras*,
their style is rational and persuasive. For men were as eager to show
where their convictions lay as to indulge their spleen, and ridicule
and abuse were tempered by argument.

In argument a satirist will often find it easier to defend an established position than a revolutionary one. The optimism which
generally goes with discovery and change shrivels at the touch of
irony, whereas the conservative instinct which clings to the old and
well tried is frequently sceptical and cautious. Most Augustan
satirists, even when they were not politically conservative, liked
to claim that authority, precedent, and tradition, as well as experience and reason, were on their side. Thus Marvell measures the
degradation of his country against the past glories of the Commonwealth and the example of Republican Rome, and Dryden presents
the Country Party as a rabble of unscrupulous innovators who care
nothing for tradition and the past. Yet there was no limitation on
freedom of opinion in this common appeal to past authority.
Restoration poets in general are much more various in their political
allegiance than their eighteenth-century successors. In the later

writers political disagreements, however genuine, seem superficial in contrast with the deep divisions that separated men like Marvell and Dryden, for the work of the early satirists reflects a sturdy individualism which had its roots in the disturbances and revolutionary changes of the seventeenth century. The same spirit is to be found even in the poetry of an unpolitical writer like Rochester. He directs his irreverent irony against fellow poets and fellow men from the King to the country squire, and the established mode of satire, at once authoritative and personal, suited his restless sceptical nature which loved to strip appearances of worth and respectability from the meaner reality. Satire showed him a way of using reason, observation, and wit to uncover bare and honest facts of experience which it was the poet's duty to reveal to the world.

Even negative and mischievous satire like Rochester's tends to lead the poet and his readers back to first principles of a sort, or to ultimate convictions. No matter how eaten up a man may be by indignation, he is bound to give a reasoned account of it if he wants to make poetry of this kind. Unconsidered rage has no value to poets who do not think of their art as primarily the expression or enjoyment of personal feeling. When the Restoration poet took up his pen it was to produce a poem which his readers would recognize as a contribution to some vital question, or to the understanding and enjoyment of common experience. Satire at its best could effect both. It could argue and persuade for a cause, and yet delight at the same time by witty ridicule; even at its most destructive it supplied the reassurance of a powerful and alert mind at work on realistic material. The satirist could claim authority and display individuality; he could combine morality with passion. But success in this art meant that he must be continually aware of the pressure of immediate circumstances and equally capable of judging them, so that while he was showing things as they are, he was also indicating what they should be. To achieve this he must convince his readers of the honesty of his picture and the sincerity of his attitude. Thus those poets who were born into the contentious world of satire were unavoidably preoccupied with honesty and sincerity, and with the devices, the style, and the tone of voice which would appear to convey these qualities. It was from the practice of satire that 'honest' poetry drew its most immediate inspiration.

Panegyric and satire were both established forms in the critical canon of the Renaissance, and the old theory that there are kinds of literature, with all this implies of the style appropriate to each, lived on in the early Augustan period, though it was interpreted with a characteristic and peculiar bias. Dryden, for example, rebuked Hobbes for his narrow and technical theory of the epic:

> Mr. Hobbes, in the preface to his own bald translation of the *Ilias*, (studying poetry as he did mathematics, when it was too late,) Mr. Hobbes, I say, begins the praise of Homer where he should have ended it. He tells us, that the first beauty of an epic poem consists in diction; that is, in the choice of words, and harmony of numbers. Now the words are the colouring of the work, which, in the order of nature, is last to be considered. The design, the disposition, the manners, and the thoughts, are all before it: where any of those are wanting or imperfect, so much wants or is imperfect in the imitation of human life, which is in the very definition of a poem.
>
> (Preface to the *Fables*, 1700.)[1]

To Dryden the imitation of life in poetry meant more than literary skill. It involved the exercise of imagination and invention in representing the truth of nature. But truth to the order of nature sounds so exalted an aim that it often seems strange that the wide explorations of the Augustans in this field appeared only to lead them to the conclusion that Nature and Homer were the same. Whatever road they took brought them back to the old highway, already so well trodden that no footprint of theirs could leave a fresh mark on its familiar surface. Pope and Johnson were always ready to admit that the best things had already been done, and that their task was to repeat in the context of their own age those facts about life which had long ago been discovered but which were still proved true.

This love of common truth was an important element in the ideal of honesty. The Augustans were not inspired by a blind devotion in their respect for the ancients. When classical forms seemed out of tune with their own ways of life they were remarkably quick to

---

[1] *Essays of John Dryden*, ed. W. P. Ker (1900), vol. ii, pp. 252–3.

discard them. Dryden never attempted the pastoral except in translation; Pope's pastorals were an early exercise never to be repeated;
and once the academic debate between the followers of Rapin and
Fontenelle on the relative merits of the 'ancient' attitude towards
the form and the 'modern' had died down, the old kind gradually
disappeared in favour of a newer, more realistic rural poetry. With
Johnson the last shred of respectability was torn from a form which
had been gradually losing its place in literature as a serious mode of
representing truth for well over fifty years. Attitudes associated
with the pastoral, however, infiltrated other kinds of poetry, and
the old ideal of country retreat was never lost. But the decorum of
the form died in the arid arguments over its validity which soon
ceased to be relevant to the best Augustan practice. On the other
hand the epic, though it proved inimitable, continued to exercise
a powerful influence. Of all its possibilities, none was more attractive to the new age than its elegiac mood.

Elegy itself, the lament over the dead, is a constant poetic theme,
and funeral verse, like panegyric, was a poetic tribute much in
vogue throughout the seventeenth and early eighteenth centuries.
But of the many themes explored by elegiac poetry the Augustans
preferred that of which Johnson spoke when he said: 'To tell of
disappointment and misery, to thicken the darkness of futurity,
and perplex the labyrinth of uncertainty, has been always a delicious
employment of the poets.'[1] The brevity of life and the inevitability
of death are themes that fulfil the strictest requirements of truth,
and simply to state them rouses sentiments that touch a common
chord in every mind. Pastoral elegy had presented them in a more
elaborate way. Beginning with lamentation and ending with consolation, it brought life and death into a new relationship and resolved the poet's grief by an apotheosis. But this is not the elegiac
mood of Augustan verse. Dryden attempted formal elegy in
Threnodia Augustalis, and, with a more metaphysical turn, in
Eleonora, but his most moving elegy, the lines *To the Memory of Mr.
Oldham*, is very different in tone. He offers no apotheosis here, and
no consolation. What begins as a compliment to the young poet's
achievement ends on a note of resigned and melancholy fatalism.

---

[1] Johnson, *Lives of the Poets*, ed. G. B. Hill (1945), vol. iii, 'Life of Pope', p. 224.

Farewel, too little and too lately known,
Whom I began to think and call my own;
For sure our Souls were near ally'd; and thine
Cast in the same Poetick mould with mine.
One common Note on either Lyre did strike,
And Knaves and Fools we both abhorr'd alike. . . .
O early ripe! to thy abundant store
What could advancing Age have added more?
It might (what Nature never gives the young)
Have taught the numbers of thy native Tongue.
But Satyr needs not those, and Wit will shine
Through the harsh cadence of a rugged line.
A noble Error, and but seldom made,
When Poets are by too much force betray'd.
Thy generous fruits, though gather'd ere their prime
Still shew'd a quickness; and maturing time
But mellows what we write to the dull sweets of Rime.
Once more, hail and farewel; farewel thou young,
But ah too short, *Marcellus* of our Tongue;
Thy Brows with Ivy, and with Laurels bound;
But Fate and gloomy Night encompass thee around.

The power of this poem does not simply lie in its noble style. It is present, too, in the quiet change from statement and description to brief lament in the last four lines. By open allusion and an almost literal translation of Virgil's lines on Marcellus from the sixth book of the *Aeneid*, Dryden invokes the spirit of classical epic. The epic does not deal in consolation. Death is the hero's inevitable end, the fate that his actions may defy for a while, but which will eventually overwhelm him. It is the same here. Oldham's poetic achievement is in vivid contrast to his early death, and the ominous associations of fate and gloomy night strike a note of alarm and betray the gulfs beneath the controlled surface of the verse.

This is the characteristic elegiac note of the best Augustan verse. A truly honest appraisal of life and the poet's part in it can be made only in the uncompromising light of the facts of mortality. Pope reminds us that in spite of his fate, he shares a common doom, and he does not always add the consolation that his art remains immortal:

Poets themselves must fall, like those they sung;
Deaf the prais'd ear, and mute the tuneful tongue.
(*Elegy to the Memory of an Unfortunate Lady*, ll. 75–76.)

Transience impresses him more than permanence when he writes to Jervas:

Alas! how little from the grave we claim?
Thou but preserv'st a Face and I a Name.
(*Epistle to Mr. Jervas*, ll. 77–78.)

This mood is inevitably an occasion for moralizing. Dryden is always willing to interrupt the course of his narratives for some general comment, and Pope sees the whole life of man in the perspective of history and overshadowed by 'the black Fear of Death, that saddens all'. Johnson's elegiac sententious vein is recognizable even in the lines he added to Goldsmith's *Traveller:*

How small of all that human hearts endure,
That part which laws or kings can cause or cure.
(ll. 429–30.)

The elegiac tone pervaded Augustan satire and coloured even panegyric, for compliments themselves could only be paid sincerely by a poet who recognized the brevity and tragedy of human life. It was deeply connected with the Augustan love of fact, with reverence for past experience recorded in history or recollected over the span of a lifetime, and with the Stoic ideal of facing reality.

Yet sometimes poetry which cannot escape from the commonplace recognition of death arouses boredom and suspicion. The elderly shade of Polonius seems to haunt it, recalling how easily moralizing can turn to cliché. Why should we accept poetry which seems to begin at the end and is written in the mood Milton ascribes at the close of *Samson Agonistes* to the exhausted spectators of a great tragic event? We can accept it only if we have been convinced that the preoccupation with life and action which these writers presuppose is genuine and worthy, and again we are thrown back on to our judgements of the honesty and sincerity of the work. The Augustans were aware of this; they had created the kind of poetry which requires it. Appetite for life and curiosity seemed to give them, in Milton's words, 'a new acquist of true experience', and their reflections on the human condition share some of the resigned acquiescence which follows strenuous participation in a great event. They saw the poet as in some sort a man of action who, like the soldier retiring to his tent, looks back over all he has experienced in the height of the fray and remembers what he has learned. Even in their satires the Augustans like to recall this situation. Rochester's maim'd debauchee, like an old admiral, watches over the operations in which he once took part, and the souls of women, transformed to sylphs in *The Rape of the Lock*, though they play no more, 'o'erlook the Cards'. Pope studies the great in 'the clear, still Mirrour of Retreat', and boasts of his society at Twickenham:

> There, my Retreat the best Companions grace,
> Chiefs, out of War, and Statesmen, out of Place.
> (*Imitations of Horace*, Sat. 2. 1, ll. 125–6.)

This is the counterpart to the skirmishes and engagements of active life, just as the grave tone of Augustan moralizing is the counterpart to its restless satire and its praise of noble action.

These three major forms of verse, in their new guise, and with the moods and attitudes now associated with them, were predominant in Augustan poetry. During the Restoration satire was supreme, and eulogy, when it was not simply hired flattery, is most commonly to be found in funeral verses, written either in the new high style or as pastoral elegy. But poets were already feeling their way towards a treatment of compliment and elegiac reflection which would not be at odds with the new realistic approach to satire. Dryden especially in this way prepared the ground for Pope's extraordinary achievement; for in Pope we find a new kind of compliment, a pervasive elegiac reflective mood, and such a flexible form of satire that it can move over the whole range of feeling in one poem, from grave to gay, from lively to severe, and seems to contain in itself the other two modes of praise and grief. He could never have accomplished this so perfectly without the work of other poets, in particular Dryden, who showed what could be effected by a powerful genius in these new circumstances, inspired by original and experimental ideas. In Dryden's hands the established and traditional poetic forms had first begun to take their new shape.

III

DRYDEN

I

NO great poet was more completely a man of his age than Dryden
or more powerful an influence on it. The outlines of his career seem
to set a pattern for the professional poets who followed him, and
many of his attitudes as well as his style left their mark on succeeding Augustan verse. As a panegyrist, a satirist, and, in his old age,
a translator and imitator of the ancients, Dryden was the first to try
out seriously new ways of expressing ideas and moods in keeping
with changed circumstances, while yet retaining all that he could of
the older traditions.

Like so many of his literary contemporaries[1] he began his education as a pupil of Dr. Busby at Westminster School, where he received a classical training that helped to form his taste. Later he
remembered making a translation of Persius's third Satire for 'a
Thursday nights' *Exercise*',[2] while he was still there. From Westminster he moved to Trinity College, Cambridge, and took his
B.A. in 1654. A fellow student, Dr. Crichton, left some impressions
of Dryden at college:

[He] . . . was reckoned a man of good Parts and Learning while in
College: he had to his knowledge read over and very well understood
all the Greek and Latin Poets: he stayed to take his Bachelor's degree;
but his head was too roving and active, or what else you'll call it, to
confine himself to a College Life; and so he left it and went to London
into gayer company, and set up for a Poet; which he was as well
qualified for as any man.[3]

---

[1] For example, Stepney, King, Halifax, Rowe, and Prior.

[2] Dryden, *The Satires of Aulus Persius Flaccus*, Argument of the Third Satire.

[3] C. E. Ward, *Life of Dryden* (1961), p. 337, n. 36, disvalues this reminiscence,
published by W. D. Christie, *N. & Q.*, 4th series, x (1872), p. 370. Mr. Gearin-Tosh
has pointed out to me that Ward's argument is weakened by the full transcript of
Christie's source in *N. & Q.*, 6th series, iv (1881), pp. 121–3, which Ward overlooks.

The clever young man setting out to try his fortune in London was
to become the type of the modern poet. In the Augustan Parnassus
University Wits had been exchanged for Town Wits, and when
Addison claimed for the Spectator Papers that they were bringing
philosophy from the schools to the coffee houses, he was following
a trend which had already driven poetry out of the study into the
world. Thus at the very outset of his career, Dryden was anticipat-
ing the Augustan pose.

He does not appear, however, to have set up for a poet immediately. It seems he received payments from Secretary Thurloe for
duties which must have been performed for the Commonwealth
government,[1] so that, like Milton and Marvell, he may at this time
have been a civil servant working for Cromwell. Not inappro-
priately, his first appearance as a poet was in the *Heroique Stanzas* on
the death of the Protector, which were printed in 1659, together
with similar tributes from Waller and Sprat.[2]

Dryden could hardly have appeared before the public in more
respectable company. Sprat, the future historian of the Royal
Society and afterwards Bishop of Rochester, knew Dryden well
enough to be the means of his meeting Cowley, after the unfortunate reception of Cowley's play *Cutter of Coleman-Street*. The two
poets could hardly have been more different. Dryden admired
Cowley, as did every other poet of the age, including Milton, but he
must have recognized in him, even then, more of the old than the
new. For in spirit Cowley belonged to the pre-Restoration world,
and he failed entirely to adapt himself to the conditions of this later
time. He was accused of flattering Cromwell, and his loyal panegyrics at the Restoration brought him no rewards. The Preface to
Cutter of Coleman-Street complains bitterly of an age when literary
success was beginning to depend so much on the vagaries of
politics and public affairs:

We are therefore wonderfull wise men, and have a fine business of it,
we who spend our time in Poetry, I do sometimes laugh, and am often

[1] For details of this period in Dryden's life see J. M. Osborn, *Dryden: Facts and
Problems* (Columbia, 1940), pp. 168–70.

[2] Herringman entered the book in the Stationers' Register as containing poems
by Marvell, Dryden, and Sprat, but it was printed by Wilson with Waller's poem
substituted for Marvell's. See H. Macdonald, *Dryden Bibliography* (1939), pp. 3–4.

angry with my self when I think on it, and if I had a Son inclined by Nature to the same folly, I believe I should bind him from it, by the strictest conjurations of a paternal Blessing. For what can be more ridiculous than to labour to give men delight, whilst they labour on their part more earnestly to take offence? to expose one's self voluntarily and frankly to all the dangers of that narrow passage to unprofitable Fame, which is defended by rude multitudes of the Ignorant, and by armed Troops of the Malitious?[1]

Cowley's fate helps us to understand the delicate situation in which an ambitious poet found himself at the beginning of the Restoration. He was only one of many who joined in the general acclamation at the King's return—Dryden and Waller both contributed their homage. Johnson found it hard to forgive Waller for turning his coat so often—'ascribing the highest degree of "power and piety" to Charles I, then transferring the same "power and piety" to Oliver Cromwell; now inviting Oliver to take the Crown, and then congratulating Charles II on his recovered right'.[2] But of Dryden's change of front, which his detractors never let him forget, he merely observes, 'the reproach of inconstancy was, on this occasion, shared with such numbers that it produced neither hatred nor disgrace; if he changed, he changed with the nation'.[3] Johnson's distinction is just. This was Dryden's last change of interest, as it was his first. From now on he never swerved in his loyalty to the Royal cause. His religious conversion, the sincerity of which can scarcely be doubted, only strengthened his allegiance to the Stuarts.

Thus Dryden's début was in the unexceptional role of the occasional poet and panegyrist, and he remained a master of these forms to the end of his life, at a time when encomiastic verse was the stock-in-trade of every poet who lived by his pen. This still seems the least attractive side of his genius. It is easy to feel contemptuous tolerance of servile hack writers, or to be amused by the story of Elkanah Settle, whose ready-written Elegy and Epithalamium were always to hand, with blanks to be filled in with the names of any promising patron; but not so easy to accept the great poet as a professional flatterer. Our distaste for this is itself an

---

[1] *English Writings of Cowley*, ed. A. R. Waller (1906), vol. i, p. 265.
[2] Johnson, *Lives*, vol. i, 'Life of Waller', p. 271.
[3] Ibid., 'Life of Dryden', p. 334.

Augustan attitude, for by the next century the ideal of honesty involved particularly the refusal to hire out one's talents for gain. Surely Dryden felt degraded by a practice which inevitably encouraged insincerity? Evidently he did not; he enjoyed writing panegyric verse for its own sake, and he had sound poetic reasons for doing so. Johnson recognized these reasons in spite of his dislike of panegyric. He saw that Dryden's habit of mind was admirably adjusted to compliment—'He had all forms of excellence, intellectual and moral, combined in his mind, with endless variation'[1]—and he noticed too the sheer delight Dryden took in exercising this ability —'he considers the great as entitled to encomiastick homage, and brings praise rather as a tribute than a gift, more delighted with the fertility of his invention than mortified by the prostitution of his judgement'.[2] To consider the great as entitled to encomiastic homage is a traditional point of view, belonging to an age which elevated honour rather than honesty, and in so far as he sincerely shared it, Dryden was the hindmost of the last generation. But Johnson, who epitomizes the convention of honesty, recognized that there was a personal and poetic reason for Dryden's success in this genre.

Dryden's pleasure in rising to the occasion of a panegyric was entirely sincere. He spoke of it himself in his Dedicatory Letter to the Earl of Abingdon, which is prefixed to *Eleonora*. When he composed the poem in 1692, he was a sick and ageing man, and the letter pathetically complains of 'ill health, some business and many troubles' which have delayed the work, but he recalls with delight the inspiration under which he wrote:

Let me add, and hope to be believ'd, that the Excellency of the Subject contributed much to the Happiness of the Execution: And that the weight of thirty Years was taken off me, while I was writing. I swom with the Tyde, and the Water under me was buoyant. The Reader will easily observe, that I was transported, by the multitude and variety of my Similitudes; which are generally the product of a luxuriant Fancy; and the wantonness of Wit. Had I call'd in my Judgment to my assistance, I had certainly retrench'd many of them. But I defend them not; let them pass for beautiful faults amongst the better sort of Critiques. . . .[3]

---

[1] Johnson, *Lives*, vol. i, 'Life of Dryden', p. 399.   [2] Ibid., p. 400.
[3] *The Poems of John Dryden*, ed. James Kinsley, vol. ii (1958), pp. 582–3.

Eleonora was a commissioned ode, and Dryden on his own admission never knew the lady it celebrated, but this was no hindrance in a poem intended 'not for an elegie but a panegyric' of which the prevailing tone was to be enthusiastic praise, not grief. The beautiful faults are often metaphysical in style—Donne especially was in his mind when he wrote—but the movement behind them is entirely his own. The metaphysical comparison of Eleonora's virtues to the Milky Way is developed at a dizzying pace:

> For where such various Vertues we recite,
> 'Tis like the Milky-Way, all over bright,
> But sown so thick with Stars, 'tis undistinguish'd Light.
>   Her Vertue, not her Vertues let us call,
> For one Heroick comprehends 'em all:
> One, as a Constellation is but one;
> Though 'tis a Train of Stars, that, rolling on,
> Rise in their turn, and in the Zodiack run.
> Ever in Motion; now 'tis Faith ascends,
> Now Hope, now Charity, that upward tends,
> And downwards with diffusive Good, descends.
>
>   (ll. 143–53.)

This style of panegyric can justly be called heroic, for the heroic to Dryden meant all that was heightened, magnified, and grandiose. In the Preface to *Annus Mirabilis* he had remarked, 'the same images serve equally for the Epique Poesie, and for the Historique and Panegyrique, which are branches of it'. Since both historical poetry and panegyric were equally important as modes of celebrating and describing the people and events of the time, Dryden's idea of the heroic cannot be dismissed as an academic critical notion which has little to do with the originality of his best work. It is especially significant in helping us to understand how he succeeded in bridging the gap between traditional forms and the pressing demands of new tastes and circumstances.

Throughout his life Dryden hoped to compose an epic. He was echoing the sentiments of a long tradition when he wrote in his *Dedication of the Aeneis*, 'A Heroic Poem, truly such, is undoubtedly the greatest work which the soul of man is capable to perform'.[1]

---

[1] *Essays of John Dryden*, vol. ii, p. 154.

Nor was the idea Aristotelian; since the beginning of the Renaissance the instructive exemplary long poem had taken precedence
of tragedy. But Dryden's projected epic, like Pope's, was never
written. The temper of the age to which he was so sensitively
attuned was deliberately unheroic: honesty, unlike honour or magnificence, is not an heroic virtue. His hopes of writing an epic were
not stirred by national events (the warmest partisan of the Stuarts
was unlikely to feel much confidence in the government of Charles
II) so much as by a wish to celebrate the maturity of the English
language. But this could be effected with greater sincerity and point
in writing other forms of poetry. Yet the heroic mood coloured almost every kind of verse Dryden attempted, from panegyric to
satire, its harsh counterpart. A compliment paid to some living
character must be elevated, but it must also take into account the
real and actual circumstances of his life and behaviour, and this—
easy enough in satire—presented a problem in the high style.

In *Annus Mirabilis* Dryden made his first elaborate attempt to
solve this problem in a contemporary heroic poem, where actual
historical incidents are presented in the grand style hitherto
generally confined to legendary or exemplary subjects. Dryden
borrowed his heroic metre from D'Avenant, and the whole idea of
treating a topical subject in this style may well have owed something to Waller, who attempted it in early poems such as *Of the
Danger HIS MAJESTY (being Prince) Escaped in the Road at St. Andere*,
where compliment and the description of an actual incident are
presented in a lofty style of epic dignity. But Dryden deliberately
avoids the traditional epic aid of mythology. He elevates his
material by expanding it with witty figures, or formalizing it
through heroic similes, but he rejects any device which might
transform the subject or remove it from the recognizable world of
reality. His Albemarle is given the epic hero's valiant boast, yet it
is couched in language so direct and natural that, out of context, it
reads like Byron at his best:

> The Moon shone clear on the becalmed floud,
> Where, while her beams like glittering silver play,
> Upon the Deck our careful General stood,
> And deeply mus'd on the succeeding day.

That happy Sun, said he, will rise again,
Who twice victorious did our Navy see:
And I alone must view him rise in vain,
Without one ray of all his Star for me.

Yet like an *English* Gen'ral will I die,
And all the Ocean make my spatious grave.
Women and Cowards on the Land may lie,
The Sea's a Tomb that's proper for the brave.
(Stanzas 99–101.)

Annus Mirabilis is a narrative poem, however, and the heroic style
was no new method for recounting noble actions and events.
Dryden's interpretation of that style is seen equally well with its
peculiar properties in his formal panegyrics. It is here that we can
recognize what he most admired in the epic manner—its magnitude, its being so much larger than life. His own zest and expansive-
ness responded to this kind of amplitude, even though he had little
sense of sublimity or stateliness. These two qualities, in any case,
are often private property and not easy to transmit, as eighteenth-
century imitations of Milton all too clearly show. Unhappily, it was
easy to imitate Dryden's pompous compliments without sharing
the genuine enthusiasm and the genius that produced them.

The dangers of Dryden's heroic style of compliment as well as its
attractions can be seen in his own development as a panegyrist.
Certain themes moved him at once and freed his imagination, as in
Eleonora. The *Heroique Stanzas* have a gravity fitting to their subject, while *Astrea Redux*, celebrating a very different occasion, is
excitable and rapturous, its conceits correspondingly excessive—
Heaven is taken by the violence of the people's prayers, the Saints
lean from their stars with joyful wonder, the land rushes to meet
Charles as he disembarks, and some of the compliments are tinged
with a charming amorous absurdity:

How shall I speak of that triumphant Day
When you renew'd the expiring Pomp of *May*!
(A Month that owns an Intrest in your Name:
You and the Flow'rs are its peculiar Claim.)
(ll. 284–7.)

In spite of the formal heroic conclusion, with its references to Moses and Augustus, the whole poem is floridly gay and very different from the later public odes. Yet it has its peculiar dignity; the fantastic flights are balanced by circumstantial descriptions of actual details of the event—'The wavering Streamers, Flags, and Standart out, The merry Seamens rude but chearful shout'—and this same quality of realism is supported by panegyric allusions to Biblical and historical personages. Moses and Augustus give greater weight to the compliment than Jupiter or Mars. This weight and dignity, however, need expert handling if they are not to become heavy and cumbersome. Lesser imitators of Dryden only too often reproduced the self-conscious Latinate diction, the hyperboles and the far-fetched compliments, but they failed to catch either his lightness of touch or his command of fact.

Threnodia Augustalis and *Britannia Rediviva* were composed when times had changed and the outlook was less fair. Dryden had already used his pen in a party struggle which underlined the insecurity of the succession, and both these subjects—James's accession and the birth of his heir—were delicate. There is little joy in these poems: the elegiac tone of the one precludes it, and Dryden's political defensiveness in *Britannia Rediviva* damps down the sparks of his old enthusiasm. *Threnodia Augustalis*, a Pindaric ode, shows the familiar skill in metre, but its heroic manner is constrained and cold. Conceits are replaced by personifications and large-scale classical images, and while no one could handle the classical allusion better than Dryden, it does not always suit his rhapsodic style so well as the beautiful faults of *Eleonora*. The general effect of these two odes was often reproduced by later imitators—an impression of cold marmoreal solidity, like those effigies, carved in the dress of the period, but cast in a classical pose, which decorate so many Augustan tombs.

Yet these two works still show Dryden's characteristic habit of mingling the elevated with the everyday, which was so evident in *Astrea Redux* and *Annus Mirabilis*. The solemn tone of *Threnodia Augustalis* did not prevent him from inserting a bitter aside on the conditions of poets under Charles II ('Tho little was their Hire, and light their Gain, Yet somewhat to their share he threw'), or an

extended account of the medical treatment given to the King in his
last illness. It is even clearer in *Threnodia Augustalis* than in the
earlier panegyrics that though Dryden accepted the old idea of decorum, a proper form for every subject, and altered his style to suit
his mood, yet there was scarcely anything in the way of reality
that he did not feel capable of handling in this version of the high
style as long as it was a relevant and actual part of the theme. We
have remarked in the Introduction how the kind of verse Waller
brought into favour (which derived so much from the epic) paid
considerable attention to subject-matter without transforming it.
In Dryden, subject-matter is often treated in an almost literal
fashion. Details and circumstances are as much part of his complimentary verse as rhetorical hyperbole and reflection.

This would have been impossible if the high style, as Dryden
understood it, had consisted simply of amplification and elevation.
But he was just as much aware of the reflective generalizing tendency which was always present in the leisurely narrative form of
the exemplary epic. Pindaric odes belong to the lyric kind, and the
lyric itself, particularly classical lyrics and those of seventeenth-
century poets like Jonson who had learned from them, found a
place for sententious commonplaces and generalized reflections. In
Threnodia Augustalis and *Britannia Rediviva* Dryden often pauses to
make simple eloquent statements on themes like the 'frail Estate of
Humane things', and the shifts of fortune, appropriate enough to
funeral verse, but used now to show how every event is part of the
general pattern of experience. Here was a way of elevating the
trivial and exhibiting the great or tragic event in its true perspective in history. This device invests the subject with a dignity which
is different from that conferred by fiction or 'fabling'; it has the ring
of common truth which lends authority to the most trite or grandiose topic. Dryden had perfected the art before he came to write
these public odes. The lines *To the Memory of Mr. Oldham* illustrate
well his power of using it, but even more illuminating is the panegyric elegy on the death of the young Earl of Ossory in *Absalom and
Achitophel*, where he demonstrates how perfectly generalized reflection can be adapted to the heroic panegyric vein.

The peculiar effect of Dryden's style can be understood by

comparing this passage from *Absalom and Achitophel* with Marvell's elegiac compliment to the young Douglas in his *Last Instructions to a Painter*. Both are heroic tributes, but the interpretation in each is entirely different. This is how Marvell describes his hero's death by fire:

> Oft has he in chill *Eske* or *Seine*, by night,
> Harden'd and cool'd his Limbs, so soft, so white,
> Among the Reeds, to be espy'd by him,
> The *Nymphs* would rustle; he would forward swim.
> They sigh'd and said, Fond Boy, why so untame,
> That fly'st Love Fires, reserv'd for other Flame?
>
>   .   .   .   .   .
>
> His shape exact, which the bright flames infold,
> Like the Sun's Statue stands of burnish'd Gold.
> Round the transparent Fire about him glows,
> As the clear Amber on the Bee does close:
> And, as on Angels Heads their Glories shine,
> His burning Locks adorn his Face Divine.
> But, when in his immortal Mind he felt
> His alt'ring Form, and soder'd Limbs to melt;
> Down on the Deck he laid himself, and dy'd,
> With his dear Sword reposing by his Side.
>
>   (ll. 655–60, 679–88.)

Here, in contrast, is Dryden's account of the death of Ossory:

> His Eldest Hope, with every Grace adorn'd,
> By me (so Heav'n will have it) always Mourn'd,
> And always honour'd, snatcht in Manhoods prime
> By' unequal Fates, and Providences crime:
> Yet not before the Goal of Honour won, ⎫
> All parts fulfill'd of Subject and of Son; ⎬
> Swift was the Race, but short the Time to run ⎭
> Oh Narrow Circle, but of Pow'r Divine,
> Scanted in Space, but perfect in thy Line!
> By Sea, by Land, thy Matchless Worth was known;
> Arms thy Delight, and War was all thy Own:
> Thy force, Infus'd, the fainting *Tyrians* prop'd:
> And Haughty *Pharaoh* found his Fortune stop'd.
> Oh Ancient Honour, Oh Unconquer'd Hand,

Whom Foes unpunish'd never coud withstand!
But *Israel* was unworthy of thy Name:
Short is the date of all Immoderate Fame.
It looks as Heaven our Ruine had design'd,
And durst not trust thy Fortune and thy Mind.
Now, free from Earth, thy disencumbred Soul
Mounts up, and leaves behind the Clouds and Starry Pole:
From thence thy kindred legions mayst thou bring
To aid the guardian Angel of thy King.
Here stop my Muse, here cease thy painfull flight;
No Pinions can pursue Immortal height.

                    (*Absalom and Achitophel*, Part I, ll. 831–55.)

Marvell's hero is the kind of figure to be found in any Renaissance
gallery of noblemen, set against a background of familiar poetic
myth. Dryden's, by contrast, has no individual qualities; he stands
as a type of the valiant youth cut off in his prime. His virtues put
him on a level with all good and noble men—'All parts fulfill'd of
Subject and of Son'—and sentiments such as 'Short is the date of all
Immoderate Fame' turn the lament from private grief to public
tragedy. The force of the passage derives from this consistent
generalization. Marvell appears to aim at precision. His hero is celebrated by a final metamorphosis—a transformation, not an apotheosis—and the power of the passage lies in the fantastic emblematic
picture of the youth consumed by flames. Dryden's conclusion is as
far from reality as Marvell's, but in place of an emblem, where
everything is exact and yet mysterious, he presents us with a great
open composition—a heroic canvas by Rubens. The aspiring
movement of the verse follows the upward flight of the hero in his
apotheosis, and has the same effect as the rhythm of some baroque
painting, which lifts the weight of the great figures and disposes
them in a fine flurry of movement. But the figures themselves
remain substantial and recognizable; they have not undergone any
real transformation at all.

The assurance and authority of Dryden's manner in this passage
from *Absalom and Achitophel* reflect his own idea of the dignified
heroic. It was soon to be accepted as the established convention for
all contemporary purposes. Marvell's satire, written probably in

1667, was not published till 1689, and then the elegiac passage,
though admirable in its wit, must have already begun to seem outmoded and uncongenial to the new age. The satire and savagery of
his attack pleased Marvell's readers: Burnet says of him that he was
'the liveliest droll of the age, who writ in a burlesque strain, but
with so peculiar and so entertaining a conduct, that, from the King
down to the tradesman, his books were read with great pleasure'.[1]
But Marvell's serious complimentary manner was out of date.

Literary conventions only succeed when they have some close if
secret relation to the temper of their age, and this dignified style of
Dryden's was no exception. He thought it proper to address the
great in a complimentary style which gave them the satisfaction of
recognizing their own public importance. His was a reassuring
manner, suited to an age insecure but optimistic. The heroic
grandeur of his high style gave a sort of pomp to those mundane
details for which he and his audience had such an appetite—the
circumstances of the City fire, for instance, or the gruesome and
misguided efforts of the doctors attending Charles on his death-
bed. Satire, the love of accurate observation, and the retreat from
speculative thinking all encouraged this delight in realism to an unprecedented extent. Dryden had found a way of satisfying both this
and the desire for pomp and ceremonial at the same time. This combination may seem absurd or incongruous to an age less concerned
with dignity. Often Dryden himself appears to have found his extravagances comic, his hyperboles trembling on the brink of
laughter. Yet he had succeeded in raising contemporary detail and,
without any taint of fiction, linking it to a tradition of epic solem-
nity which still seemed enviable and appropriate. Such a style
shows optimism and satisfaction with the world as the poet finds it.
Unlike Cowley, Dryden never felt out of touch with the temper of
his time.

In writing like this he was also coming to terms with his public.
However much pleasure he gained from exercising his own genius,
the original motive was to satisfy his Royal or noble patrons, and to
strike the right note in doing so. What could be taken for granted
in the old way of writing poetry for private circulation between

---

[1] G. Burnet, *History of My Own Times*, vol. i (1724), p. 260.

friends was now uncertain. Discretion and diplomacy were needed
to negotiate his way successfully through that narrow passage 'defended by rude multitudes of the Ignorant, and by armed Troups of
the Malitious'. This was not the kind of situation in which one might
expect sincere or authentic poetry to arise, and it was easy enough
in his own day to denounce Dryden for dishonest adulation. Yet
his style is itself his defence against such accusations. He loved to
praise, but his praise, however rapturous, is related deliberately to
fact and detail, and set against a background of commonly accepted
truth. Without Dryden's particular skill this kind of eulogy can
quickly become meaningless or affected. Once the vogue had been
established, there was no end to the panegyrics by which poets
hoped to secure a patron. Patrons themselves often seemed pleased
even by the clumsy shadow of magnificence. When Pope and his
friends rejected the grand compliment, they were reacting against
its debasement and all its implications of self-interest. And they had
other reasons. Dryden was confident of his world; they found themselves defensive and critical in their view of the present. Changing
circumstances, political and social, affected their relation with their
public. Pope himself was independent of patronage, and Prior,
Addison, and Swift did not earn their living by their art. It was
easier for them to cultivate the security of a circle of sympathetic
minds and to address their compliments to each other or to personal
friends. In such circumstances, honesty is less a matter of persuasive
public tone and more the virtue of individual integrity.

The honest tone, however, is not to be looked for primarily in the
panegyric. Its traditional place was in satire, and to trace the tone
of Dryden's satire we need to know something of the circumstances
from which it rose and the public to which it was addressed. Alongside the courtly society to which his panegyrics were devoted there
existed the Town, composed of wits and professional people—often
the subjects of his informal complimentary epistles; and the City,
with its different way of life, commercial and aggressively Protestant. Dryden's feelings towards the City are mostly expressed in
satire. As a convinced partisan he wrote for the other party; he
had married into the Howard family and his personal and political
sympathies were entirely with the Court. But he was never

isolated from the other two worlds of Town and City. Merit alone distinguished him from a City poet like Settle, for whom he felt all the scorn of a good poet for a bad; with Shadwell his issue was largely one of party politics. Like them he wrote for his living and to please the same audiences, and he could as easily adapt his style to the rough and tumble of literary and political rivalries. His satires were written at a time when he was most involved with the opposing worlds of Court and City, and, as in his panegyrics, he found it necessary to come to terms with the milieu of his subjects, and to discover a tone of address flexible enough to move from one to the other while giving each world its own substantial reality.

II

The heroic style does not seem likely to be useful to a satirist except in an ironic form, but the occasion arose when Dryden found it both appropriate and indispensable. Charles II demanded from his laureate a poem on the Popish Plot, and *Absalom and Achitophel* was Dryden's answer. The subject was complicated and urgent. Dryden was obliged to make clear his party's convictions without either excusing Monmouth's role or offending the King's fondness for his son. In the Preface to the poem he reveals that his chief anxiety was how to present Absalom, and he took pains to make his own attitude unimpeachable. The Prince is described as 'Half loath, and half consenting to the Ill', while yet being 'Unblam'd of life (Ambition set aside,) Not stain'd with Cruelty, nor puft with Pride', and he is allowed to pronounce a panegyric on his father in answer to Achitophel's temptation. Dryden's solution had been to make Monmouth the misguided hero of a brief heroic episode.

The allegory he chose was not original.[1] Malone, in his edition of Dryden's prose works, refers to the possible influence of Nathaniel Carpenter's *Achitophel or the Picture of a Wicked Politician* (1627), and he suggested other sources in the manuscript additions to his Life of Dryden:

Barten Holiday, during the Civil War, preached four Sermons

[1] Sir Walter Scott refers to the influence of *Naboth's Vinyard* by John Caryll (1679), and I. Jack draws attention to D'Urfey's *Progress of Honesty* (1680), in *Augustan Satire* (1952), pp. 55–57.

against Disloyalty, one of which was on the subject 'of Absolon's Ambition', and was preached before the Prince Charles at Christ-Church in Oxford, Nov. 10 1644. These four sermons were collected and published by Holiday in 1661. That on the subject of Absolon, I suspect, had been read by Dryden. Derrick asserts that 'the application of the story of Absalom *to this part of King Charles the Second's reign* was first made by a clergyman in the pulpit and his sermon was printed with the title of Absolom and Achitophel;' but I have never met with it.[1]

The Biblical allegory not unnaturally brought to Dryden's mind a Biblical epic, and echoes of *Paradise Lost*, and even more frequently of *Paradise Regained*, occur throughout the poem. Milton's example gave Dryden a fine opportunity of setting his attack on rebellious ambition against an epic background, and Dryden's Achitophel is the Satan of his poem, whose temptations are laced with blasphemy, and whose virtues are shown only to reveal from what a height he has fallen. Apart from verbal echoes of *Paradise Lost*,[2] the temptation of Absalom is full of hints of Book III of *Paradise Regained*.[3] Satan's advice to Christ that he should 'on Occasions forelock watchful wait', and Christ's contempt for the 'miscellaneous rabble', are echoed perhaps in Achitophel's exhortation to Absalom to seize his chance while Fortune 'spreads her Locks before her as she flies', and in Dryden's own comments on the 'Headstrong, Moody, Murmring race' of the City men. *Paradise Regained* was an admirable model in many ways. Milton used for it an elevated style, tempered to suit argument and debate, and he had restricted the action to one episode in which a contest of wills took the place of an epic conflict. This was what Dryden needed, since he could not sacrifice the high style which was to dignify the occasion and also provide a worthy setting for the characters of the King and Monmouth. Inevitably the style elevated Shaftesbury too—but to a Satanic eminence in keeping with the enormity of his crime.

Except for Achitophel, the famous character studies which are the immediate attraction of the poem occur in the descriptions of

[1] These additions (Bodleian, Malone E. 61–63, Section VI, p. 141) have been transcribed by Osborn, op. cit., pp. 129–30.

[2] e.g. *Absalom and Achitophel*, Part I, ll. 373 and 598.

[3] Professor Maynard Mack of Yale first suggested this comparison to me.

Shaftesbury's followers, and they are not allowed the same heroic treatment. But Dryden had already shown in panegyric how well his high style could comprehend ironic touches and simple enumerations of detail. Here, when he needed to re-create, in the same poem, in vivid and recognizable terms, an environment very different from the Court, he found the inclusiveness of this style invaluable. Slingsby Bethel, one of the Sheriffs of London, who represents the City and 'the true old Enthusiastick breed', is attacked with familiar contempt for his parsimony, his canting Puritanism, and his hypocrisy. The scriptural allusions which Dryden had used to elevate the truth of his serious compliments in this context turn into one of his favourite satirical devices—blasphemy; the lofty generalizations are exchanged for details, first of the paraphernalia of the Sheriff's office, then of his actual conduct as a magistrate— 'During his Office, Treason was no Crime; The Sons of Belial had a glorious Time'—while the exuberant grandiose rhetoric of his true style of compliment here changes to a mincing delicacy as he describes Bethel's tastes:

> Chast were his Cellars, and his Shrieval Board
> The Grossness of a City Feast abhor'd.
> (*Absalom and Achitophel*, Part I, ll. 618–19.)

But this was not a single character study. It expresses Dryden's quarrel with the whole City, which he reveals by irony as an underworld of meanness, drab hypocrisy, and cunning, where the characters of Oates and Bethel emerge momentarily, only to be lost again in the buzzing confusion of their supporters. Their milieu is as important a part of the satire as the characters themselves.

Dryden was particularly pleased with his portrait of Zimri, the Duke of Buckingham, where individual traits are given epigrammatic clarity, where the verse is as mercurial as the subject, the compliments offensive, and the abuse urbane. Buckingham's temporary exile from Court, as much as his personality, gave Dryden the excuse for refusing him heroic dimensions; yet though he is diminished in contrast to Absalom and Achitophel, he is never lowered to the level of Bethel and Oates. Through his description of Buckingham's dilettantism Dryden contrives to give the impression that his siding with the Whigs was but another instance of caprice and not calculated treachery. The tone of this is exquisitely diplomatic. It is no wonder that Buckingham was 'too witty to take offence' at it; the poet was too witty to provide any open occasion. Zimri is carefully distinguished from his companions in treason; he exists in a happy Limbo of irresponsible wit, cut off alike from the serious world of the Court and the mean life of the City.

Thus Dryden showed himself extremely adept at steering his course through the quicksands of a complex political situation. The very difficulties which proved fatal to many of his contemporaries inspired his genius to fresh feats of discretion and skill. The pleasure of reading a satire like *Absalom and Achitophel* did not lie merely in savouring the irony or admiring the verse, but, to the readers of his day at least, in placing the characters and in recognizing what they stood for, not only from the argument of the poem, but from the way in which they were presented. Once again the real and topical were as unmistakably apparent as the rhetorical flights of panegyric and persuasion.

But Dryden was not always so lucky. He displeased the Court by the anti-Catholic bias of *The Spanish Friar*; and in 1682 *The Duke of Guise*, a play written in collaboration with Lee, which was an open allegory of the situation, presenting Monmouth in the character of Guise as the possible victim of assassination, was refused a licence because of Royal displeasure. It was only performed after the King had ordered Monmouth's arrest, and on this occasion Dryden prudently discarded his original epilogue and substituted for it a truculent piece of party propaganda in defence of his political opinions. There was less chance for subtlety and ironic variation of tone in drama, particularly when the play was written to exploit an immediate public reaction.

The prologues and epilogues composed between 1680 and 1683 help us to understand Dryden's real attitude to the situation, for the change of tone from the grave poise of *Absalom and Achitophel* to the virulence of *The Medal* cannot simply be explained in terms of the different kinds of satire they exemplify. The Restoration poets paid tribute to the traditional doctrine of decorum in criticism, but in practice their tone and manner were more often conditioned by immediate circumstances than by a reasoned choice of poetic form. Indeed their preoccupation with tone and presentation reflects this dependence upon the contemporary situation and the public for whom they were writing. More than anything else it taught them to use a mode of address which drew attention to their own point of view. Dryden's occasional prologues and epilogues reflect his reaction to the growing political crisis and the intensity of the situation. Contempt for the City was, of course, fashionable, indeed traditional, even before its political associations became important. The earlier prologues and epilogues are full of jokes at the expense of the cits who are born to be the dupes of the witty world:

> But the poor Cuckold seldom finds a friend.
> Since therefore Court and Town will take no pity,
> I humbly cast myself upon the City.
> (Epilogue to *Marriage à la Mode*, ll. 30–32.)

But Dryden first mentions the violent Protestantism of the City in the prologues and epilogues of 1678 and 1679, after the murder of Sir Edmund Berry Godfrey, when anti-Catholic feeling was so high that the King had been reluctantly forced, in December 1678, to exclude Roman Catholic peers from Parliament. Hints of the situation are present in the Prologue to *Oedipus* (1678), where captious critics are compared to dissenters:

> But, when you lay Tradition wholly by,
> And on the private Spirit alone relye,
> You turn Fanaticks in your Poetry.
> (ll. 29–31.)

The Epilogue to the same play concludes with an allusion to the more dangerous tastes of a City crowd:

> Their Treat is what your Pallats rellish most,
> Charm! Song! and Show! a Murder and a Ghost!
> We know not what you can desire or hope,
> To please you more, but burning of a *Pope*.
> (ll. 31–34.)

After the dissolution of Parliament in January and the ensuing election, it became clear how closely popular anti-Catholic feelings had become associated with the anti-Royal policy of the Opposition. Shaftesbury and Russell, who were anxious to secure a Protestant succession and limit the Royal prerogative, were both made members of the new Privy Council devised by Sir William Temple as a temporary intermediary between Parliament and the Crown, and their policies achieved the passing of the Exclusion Bill in May 1679. The Duke of York had already been banished to Brussels, and Monmouth's successes at Bothwell Brig against the Covenanters in June so terrified the Royal party that Charles was induced to dissolve Parliament in July. It was not recalled until January 1680. In the meantime the Council broke up, and the King, free from the influence of more moderate councillors, proceeded to act on his own initiative. The agitations to declare Monmouth legitimate forced him to proclaim that he recognized only his brother James as his successor. Such a crisis seemed likely to precipitate another civil war, but Charles, waiting for public feeling to turn by a natural reaction, summoned Parliament to meet at Oxford, out of the influence of the City, and, with unexpected firmness, dissolved it in 1681 just at the moment when Shaftesbury and his supporters, who had come up to Oxford as if for a military triumph, were convinced that they had won the day.

During this period the licensing restrictions of the Press Act had expired,[1] and the result was a war of journalists which involved the literary world in the political struggle. Dryden's first contributions at this time were restricted to comments of growing severity in his prologues and epilogues. The Prologue given at Oxford in 1680 attacked Dissenters again, and the Prologue to *The Loyal General* in the same year remarked on the growing popularity of party pamphlets:

> The Rest may satisfie their curious Itch
> With City Gazets or some Factious Speech,
> Or what-ere Libel for the Publick Good,
> Stirs up the Shrove-tide Crew to Fire and Blood!
>
> (ll. 4–7.)

But in 1681, the year of *Absalom and Achitophel*, the tide had turned, particularly after the arrest of Shaftesbury at the end of the Oxford

---

[1] See Macdonald, op. cit., pp. 18–19.

Parliament, and this change accounts for the mildness of tone of Dryden's satire. It explains too the serious presentation of Shaftesbury's crime—an attempt to prejudice the jury against him in the forthcoming indictment. The general feeling of easiness is shown by the fact that the only comment in the prologues of the period is a light reference in that to *The Princess of Cleves*, where a perjured lover is insulted by the comparison, 'Achitophel's not half so false to David'. But in November 1681 something occurred which roused the furious anger of the Court and its poet. The result of Shaftesbury's indictment before a London Grand Jury was a complete acquittal; the Bill was sent back with *ignoramus* written across it; Shaftesbury was released on bail, and the City struck a medal to celebrate its victory.

It was at this point that the tone of Dryden's political satire changed. No doubt, with his fellow Tories, he smarted under the mortification of frustrated revenge, particularly since *Absalom and Achitophel* had failed of its purpose. Spence maintained that *The Medal* was also commissioned by the King, but, whatever its occasion, the poem clearly reflects Dryden's feelings in its violent tone, its lowered picture of Shaftesbury, and its anxious and emphatic restatement of a political argument which is the main thread of the poem. The prologues and epilogues which belong to this period are remarkable, too, for their viciousness.[1]

For us it is hard not to see this outburst of fury as the result mainly of pique rather than genuine fear, for the situation, in fact, was well in hand. The King took revenge on the City of London by the unprecedented measure of issuing a writ of *quo warranto* to inquire into the rights whereby the City held its special liberties and prerogatives. Meanwhile the election of a Tory Lord Mayor, Sir James Moore, and of two Tory Sheriffs, and the flight and death in exile of Shaftesbury, strengthened the Royal position. Some panic was caused by the Rye House plot, for which Russell and Algernon Sidney were unfairly tried and executed, but with the surrender of the charter of the City of London in 1683, the monarchy was in a more powerful position than at any time since the early years of

---

[1] See among others the Prologues to *The Duke of Guise*, *The Unhappy Favourite*, and *Constantine the Great*, and the Prologue and Epilogue to *The Loyal Brother*.

Charles I's reign. Cities throughout the country, either compelled
by threats or through voluntary submission, surrendered their
charters,[1] and in the general enthusiasm the University of Oxford
distinguished itself by a servile exhibition of misguided loyalty in
passing a decree which laid down that, as members of the Church of
England, the whole body subscribed dutifully to the doctrine that
submission was to be 'clear, absolute and without exception of any
state or order of men'.[2] In view of this it is hard to feel much sympathy with Dryden's aggressive attacks on his enemies. His rage
seems to be at its highest when the danger was at its lowest. But
this may not have been apparent to him, and for a man who lives by
his pen nothing is more natural than to find quarrel in a straw when
security is at stake. Besides he had Shadwell and Settle, personal
rivals, in the Whig camp to aggravate his irritation. In such a position poets on both sides were clamorous in their protestations,
bullying and cajoling the public to their point of view, and using
every weapon of persuasion or abuse in the process.

The Medal is in fact an argumentative poem, in which the satire
serves as a powerful accessory to the argument but no more. No
time is spent on elaborate analogies like that in *Absalom and Achitophel*, where the original surrender of liberties to a ruler is compared
to the binding effects of Adam's original sin. Here the case is openly
and plainly stated, in a manner of strong personal conviction:

> That Kings can doe no wrong we must believe:
> None can they doe, and must they all receive?
> Help Heaven! or sadly we shall see an hour,
> When neither wrong nor right are in their pow'r!
>
> (ll. 135-8.)

The theme of the poem is the same as that of the prose *Epistle to the
Whigs* which prefaces it, and both are equally forthright and violent.
The Medal is a piece of declamation, but it is also a versified

---

[1] Contemporary accounts of these events are to be found in N. Luttrell's *Brief
Historical Relation of State Affairs 1678–1714* (vol. i, 1857), and, though biased from
the Whig point of view, in G. Burnet's *History of My own Times*, vol. ii (1734).

[2] Oxford reaped its reward for this when James II exercised the absolute right
they had bound themselves to obey by putting his own Catholic candidates into
office as Fellows and Heads of Houses. It was this more than anything else which induced Oxford to accept William of Orange.

pamphlet—the first of any poetic value to have been written in English. Dryden uses no obvious disguises in it; he thrusts himself forward, openly abusive and unashamedly enraged, but, even at his angriest, always ready with the weapon of laughter. In contrast with *Absalom and Achitophel* this is personal utterance and, for that reason, nearer to the familiar tone of the prologues and epilogues. Many of these share the pamphleteering style, but although they are topical and full of the raw material of political reference, they were written to be spoken, not read. This eliminates any attempt at reasoned argument, just as their occasion—the performance of a play—prevented them from being grave in tone. But their intention is as persuasive as that of *The Medal*, and they exhibit the variety of resources Dryden had at his disposal for this kind of effect. If he could not argue openly in them he could dazzle and trick by the witty sophistry of his similes and employ all his powers of description. The picture of the Pope burning on Queen Bess's night in the Epilogue to Southerne's *Loyal Brother* uses the easy freedom of the form for an exercise in substantial realism, animated by all the satirical verve of Dryden's narrative style. No further comment is needed on the City's traditional Protestant celebration when Dryden has finished his ironic picture of it:

> Sir *Edmond-berry*, first, in wofull wise,
> Leads up the show, and Milks their Maudlin eyes.
> There's not a Butcher's Wife but Dribs her part,
> And pities the poor Pageant from her heart;
> Who, to provoke revenge, rides round the fire,
> And, with a civil congee, does retire.
> But guiltless blood to ground must never fall:
> There's *Antichrist* behind, to pay for all.
> The Punk of *Babylon* in Pomp appears,
> A lewd Old Gentleman of Seventy years.
> Whose Age in vain our Mercy wou'd implore;
> For few take pity on an Old-cast Whore.
> The Devil, who brought him to the shame, takes part;
> Sits cheek by jowl, in black, to cheer his heart:
> Like Theef and Parson in a *Tyburn*-Cart.
> The word is giv'n; and with a loud Huzzaw
> The Miter'd Moppet from his Chair they draw:

On the slain Corps contending Nations fall;
Alas, what's one poor Pope among 'em all!

(ll. 20-38.)

In these prologues and epilogues Dryden learned to combine the
vigour of popular material with a conversational cadence. He had
discovered all he needed to know from this form about the varied
emphasis of the speaking voice, and the author who had seized the
chance to exploit the characters of actresses like Nell Gwynne[1]
could assume a bewildering variety of manners. He uses the accents
of the demagogue persuading his audience to sneer:

Make *London* independant of the Crown:
A Realm apart; the Kingdom of the Town.
Let *Ignoramus* Juries find no Traitors:
And *Ignoramus* Poets scribble Satyres.
(Prologue to *The Duke of Guise*, ll. 41-44.)

or the truculent swagger of the bully, in this dialogue between
a timid Trimmer and a hearty royalist:

Lenitives, says he, suit best with our Condition.
Jack Ketch, says I, 's an excellent Physician.
I love no Bloud.– Nor I, Sir, as I breath;
But hanging is a fine dry kind of Death.
(Epilogue to *The Duke of Guise*, ll. 29-32.)

Some of his poses, like the last, are ugly enough; others are more
engaging. But in all of them Dryden takes the opportunity of forthright address and a popular form to suggest the busy various world
of affairs in which the poet and his audience are equally at home. He
is setting up a new kind of relationship between himself and them,
which demands an air of candour and honest raillery, and the consequences of this were far-reaching in Augustan poetry.

Dryden himself found that he could use the accents he had learned
here in more formal and serious works. A tone of good-humoured
contempt was often his most useful weapon in argument. It would
not do, even in *Absalom and Achitophel*, always to speak in the
accents of the epic poet. The feminine rhyme was one of his favourite
devices for lowering the tone and turning rebuke to laughter. It

---

[1] See the Epilogue to *Tyrannic Love*.

recalls Butler's burlesque style, and, in the prologues, it conveys the mocking voice of the actor:

> His various modes from various Fathers follow,
> One taught the Toss, and one the new *French* Wallow.
> (Epilogue to *The Man of Mode, or Sir Fopling Flutter*, ll. 21–22.)

Dryden used it in the Zimri passage in *Absalom and Achitophel* for its touch of vapid lightness. In the second part of the poem it gives force to his contemptuous easy abuse of Doeg:

> Spightfull he is not, though he wrote a Satyr,
> For still there goes some *thinking* to ill-Nature.
> (ll. 421–2.)

This device has a suggestion of improvisation which was particularly useful in conveying a tone of easy confidence to win the reader round to the poet's point of view. Rallying irony was often what Dryden needed in more seriously argumentative work. Both the Hind and the Panther speak in a colloquial fashion from time to time, the Panther more offensively than her opponent, especially when she accuses her of having fled like a coward before persecution:

> Not trusting destiny to save your head.
> For, what e'er promises you have apply'd
> To your unfailing church, the surer side
> Is four fair leggs in danger to provide.
> (Part II, ll. 11–14.)

Dryden had mastered all these devices in his occasional theatrical verse, and they inevitably give the effect of a personal presence and address. Whenever he uses them he seems to confront his readers, graciously or aggressively, but with an effect of immediacy which can scarcely help suggesting some sort of sincerity. The art of the prologue is to achieve this, but Dryden found it as important to command the same tone in commissioned satire as in playhouse verse. There is something of the same feeling for authenticity and direct communication which was to become the aim of the poetry of the Honest Muse, even in those prologues on graver occasions, where decorum demanded a more elevated style, and where vivid details and popular reference would have been out of place. The

Prologue and Epilogue spoken at the University of Oxford in 1674 are fine examples of this. Objective as they are, they are still monologues, and the reflective style in which they are written is transformed by this into a fluent personal expression which touches with intimacy the sober generalized statements and at once commands our confidence:

> Poets, your Subjects, have their Parts assign'd
> T'unbend, and to divert their Sovereign's mind;
> When tyr'd with following Nature, you think fit
> To seek repose in the cool shades of Wit,
> And from the sweet Retreat, with Joy survey
> What rests, and what is conquer'd, of the way.
> Here free your selves, from Envie, Care and Strife,
> You view the various turns of humane Life:
> Safe in our Scene, through dangerous Courts you go,
> And Undebauch'd, the Vice of Cities know.
>
> (ll. 1–10.)

The Epilogue, spoken by a woman, shows even more clearly this union of the familiar and reflective styles:

> Oft has our Poet wisht, this happy Seat
> Might prove his fading Muses last retreat:
> I wonder'd at his wish, but now I find
> He sought for quiet, and content of mind;
> Which noisfull Towns, and Courts can never know,
> And onely in the shades like Laurels grow.
> Youth, e'er it sees the World, here studies rest,
> And Age returning thence concludes it best.
> What wonder if we court that happiness
> Yearly to share, which hourly you possess,
> Teaching ev'n you, (while the vext World we show,)
> Your Peace to value more, and better know?
>
> (ll. 1–12.)

How vivid here is Dryden's awareness of the situation! The actor, speaking to this learned audience, constantly balances his showing of the busy active world in which Dryden's poetry is so involved against his admiration for the sweet retreat from which the wise observer innocently reviews the progress of his own struggle for truth, and the turmoil of the rest of mankind. Already the most informal, topical, and occasional poetry of the new age was beginning to find expression for the favourite attitudes which that age was to breed. Involvement in the world was not to preclude detachment and reflection, just as the vivid realism of satire was not incompatible with a more elevated style. In different prologues and epilogues Dryden practised each. In his formal satires and argumentative verses he combined them, setting one off against the other, and suggesting a more comprehensive attitude in which both could find their place.

III

Dryden's satire was never confined to politics. Much of it is personal, and as such concerns poetry and poets. The professionalism of the poets of the Restoration meant that one of the recurrent subjects of their work was the craft of letters itself: they wrote about it either directly or by attacks on their rivals or by compliments to their fellow poets. Most of Dryden's literary and social comment is to be found in his prologues and epilogues—descriptions of the manners of his audiences, comments on their taste and their pretensions to wit. These audiences belonged to that section of society which, in the Restoration, went by the name of the Town. Ever since the growing importance of London in Elizabeth's reign, 'the Town' had begun to stand for high life, polished manners, literary and intelligent society and fashion. Herbert, in *Affliction* I, had complained that his vocation tempted him from his original preference for 'the way that takes the town', but he was one of the few who had turned their backs on it. By the time the Court was re-established at Whitehall after the Restoration, the educated and professional men of London were very keenly aware of their position between the two extremes of aristocracy and mercantilism. But it would be wrong to think of the Town as in any way a middle class. Men from each of the other groups might find themselves part of it. The Town was rather a way of life, and Dryden does not give it a local habitation (like the City's—'from *Leaden-hall* to *Ludgate*'): for him it is the society of the coffee house and the theatre, the haunt of wits and men of public affairs, in which he felt himself most at

home. This was his world, and his literary and personal satire grew
out of it.

The only quarrel Dryden had with the men of the Town was that
of the poet who lived by pandering to their tastes and was naturally sceptical of them. He may not have felt any distaste at paying
court to the great and soliciting their indulgence, but he was quick
to resent criticism from equals who might more justly be called in-
feriors. At first he wrote with contemptuous disregard for professional critics and authors, relying on the fashionable element of
the Town to support him—'the greatest Wits and Beauties of the
Town' whom, in his Epilogue to *The Wild Gallant*, he calls 'too grateful to become severe'. But in the 1674 Prologue to the University
of Oxford he shows irritation with these same wits and beauties:

> Poets must stoop, when they would please our Pit,
> Debas'd even to the Level of their Wit.
>
> (ll. 32–33.)

From this time his attacks on his audience grow more serious. Inde-
fatigable purveyor of popular indecency as he was, he hints in the
Prologue to the most drearily obscene of all his comedies, *Limberham,
or the Kind Keeper*, that true comedy has long since died and this
is the level his audience deserves. The ghost of Shakespeare who
speaks the Prologue to *Troilus and Cressida* accuses the fashionable
drama of the time of dullness, though more often Dryden's anger is
provoked by the new vogue for sensationalism. 'Non-sence is the
new Disease that reigns', he declares in the Prologue to *The Loyal
General*.

The Town then, and not the City—that vulgar, simple world of
commerce and stupidity—was most to blame for false taste and bad
poetry. Yet it happened that two of Dryden's rivals, Elkanah Settle
and Thomas Shadwell, were both poets of the City faction. Settle,
a Vicar of Bray among authors, was put in charge of the Pope-
burning ceremonies in 1680, turned Tory at the election of Sir
James Moore as Lord Mayor, changed again with the accession of
William III, and retained his post of City Poet, the last of the line,
only to be damned to everlasting fame in *The Dunciad*. Shadwell's
career was considerably more respectable. He had criticized Dryden's

heroic plays (being himself an imitator of Jonsonian comedy), but in his Preface to *The Humorists* (1671) he admitted the power of Dryden's elevated style: 'His Verse is smother and deeper, his thoughts more quick and surprising, his raptures more mettled and higher . . . than any other Heroick Poet'.[1] Dryden, too, had obliged Shadwell with a prologue to his play *The True Widow* in 1678, but later in the same year *MacFlecknoe* itself was composed and circulated in manuscript.[2] There seems no doubt that Dryden's dislike of Shadwell was personal, prompted by irritation at his literary pretensions, his criticism of Dryden's own poetry, and his popularity, and confirmed by his political convictions. When Shadwell appeared as the supporter of the Whigs, Dryden had all the excuse he needed for an open attack, and the publication of *MacFlecknoe* and of the character of Og in the second part of *Absalom and Achitophel* coincided with the political campaign in which he took such a leading part.

Dryden clearly felt no need to revise *MacFlecknoe* to give it a political bias when he published it. It suited him better to retain the picture of his rival as the supreme dullard, an accusation which, as it was manifestly unfair, yet of its nature was unanswerable. When Shadwell tried to defend himself in his Dedication of the tenth Satire of Juvenal to Sir Charles Sedley (1687), he reiterated his denial with a helpless insistence which only seemed to add point to the accusation of dullness. He did succeed, however, in presenting Dryden in a singularly unpleasant light by maintaining that he refused to own his authorship of the satire: 'It is hard to believe that the supposed *Author* of *Mack-Fleckno* is the real one, because when I taxed him with it, he denied it with all the Execrations he could think of'.[3]

MacFlecknoe is Dryden's only essay in the mock-heroic proper, and of its kind it is perfect. Heroic declamation as much as heroic narrative is the foundation of the style. The enthusiasm of the declamatory panegyric style he had used so seriously in other works produces the tremendous comic effect of the poem. The main part

[1] *Works of Thomas Shadwell*, ed. M. Summers, vol. i (1927), p. 187.

[2] For a full account of Dryden's dealings with Shadwell up to this time, and for details of the dating of *MacFlecknoe*, see Macdonald, op. cit., pp. 28–31.

[3] Shadwell, *Works*, vol. v, p. 292.

of the work is taken up with Flecknoe's congratulatory address to his successor, which not only gives exquisitely ironic point to the rapturous account of triumphant stupidity, but allows Dryden to exercise all his own effusive vigour. With it he blends a homely colloquialism from time to time—'here stopt the good old *Sire*', 'Let father *Flecknoe* fire thy mind with praise, / And Uncle *Ogleby* thy envy raise'—as a reminder of the vulgar simplicity of that City world he chose as the perfect setting for Shadwell's duncery.[1]

Shadwell's associates and the setting in which he is placed are an integral part of the satire. Richard Flecknoe, an Irish priest turned poet (hence the appropriateness of 'father Flecknoe'), had done little to deserve Dryden's enmity. Once, indeed, he had hailed Dryden in a halting epigram as 'the Muses' darling and delight',[2] but he was a notoriously bad poet, a fault to which good poets are seldom charitable. The forebears Dryden gives Shadwell are most carefully chosen to form a genealogy of hacks, all in some way connected with the City and its spectacles. Thomas Heywood[3] was City Poet from 1631 to 1633 and again from 1637 to 1639. James Shirley the dramatist probably finds a place here on account of the story Wood records in *Athenae Oxoniensis*[4] that he worked as a drudge for Ogilby in his translations. Ogilby himself, the dancing master who, having sprained his foot while executing a particularly high leap at a Court revel, turned to poetry and publishing, was put in charge of the public ceremonies and celebrations at the coronation of Charles II. These are the types who precede the Messiah of Dullness, and fall short of his absolute perfection.

The idea of vulgar ceremony and spectacle lies behind the whole

---

[1] This anticipates Pope's use of a similar setting for Bks. I and II of *The Dunciad*. For a full account of Pope's use of the City see A. Williams, *Pope's Dunciad* (1955).

[2] For details of Flecknoe's references to Dryden see Macdonald, op. cit., pp. 190-1. Langbaine accused Dryden of plagiarizing Flecknoe's *Demoiselles A la Mode*: see Osborn, op. cit., pp. 219 ff.

[3] For a list of City Poets see Nichols, *Literary Anecdotes of the Eighteenth Century*, vol. i (1812), p. 43. Pope also mentions Heywood in a similar context as a 'city swan' or laureate, but in a note applies the reference to John Heywood, the author of some of the Tudor Interludes (*Dunciad*, Bk. I, l. 96). He may have misunderstood Dryden's reference; if so it is a clear case of his dependence on Dryden as a source of this City mythology (a point which Williams ignores when denying the influence of *Mac-Flecknoe* on *The Dunciad*). Pope repeats the allusion and compares Heywood to Cibber in the *Epistle to Augustus* (*Imitations of Horace*, Ep. 2. 1), l. 88.

[4] Wood, *Athenae Oxoniensis*, vol. ii (1692), column 262.

poem, from Shadwell's water progress to the final catastrophe, taken from his own play *The Virtuoso*. Following the tradition of Jonson and the bourgeois place-name comedy writers of the Jacobean age, Shadwell's other plays, *The Squire of Alsatia* and *Bury Fair*, were realistic comedies of low life, set in the City or the suburbs, and depicting with considerable gusto the life and festivals of this kind of society. Dryden appropriately places his coronation in the Barbican, near the City boundary, at a nameless theatrical booth, where 'unfledg'd actors' and 'the suburbian Muse' delight the tastes of the crowd.

Deliberate though these details are, and interesting to follow up, they only make a small part of the final effect. Dryden did not spend as much of his ingenuity as Pope was to do in *The Dunciad* exploiting the associations of stupidity and spectacle. It was not his intention to expose a false scale of values in literature or life: his purpose was simpler—to annihilate Shadwell. Morally indefensible though this may be, the result has always been contrasted with Pope's on account of its unexpected geniality. The famed good humour of *MacFlecknoe* is partly a result of the panegyric style, and partly of Dryden's obvious delight in creating a comic figure. His brilliance drives the reader along with him, from the irresistible couplet:

> The rest to some faint meaning make pretence,
> But *Sh*—— never deviates into sense
>
> (ll. 19–20.)

to the swelling hyperbole:

> But *Sh*——'s genuine night admits no ray,
> His rising Fogs prevail upon the Day:
>
> (ll. 23–24.)

and on to the next line, where the very first word suggests the new idea just rising in the poet's mind, the addition he could not resist:

> Besides his goodly Fabrick fills the eye,
> And seems design'd for thoughtless Majesty.
>
> (ll. 25–26.)

Even when he resorts to physical abuse, Dryden's fertility does not grow less. He squeezes the last drop of meaning from the line by pointing out the pun on 'thoughtless', as if, after using the word to its full heroic extent, he had just been struck by its alternative meaning:

> Thoughtless as Monarch Oakes, that shade the plain,
> And, spread in solemn state, supinely reign.
>
> (ll. 27–28.)

Shadwell is more ruthlessly destroyed than any of the fools in *The Dunciad*, yet he receives one sort of poetic justice, for Dryden has taken him to pieces only to re-create him in a new comic form, and his delight in the process is so completely communicated that few who have entered into the spirit of the poem have not concluded it with a feeling of affectionate tolerance towards the absurd figure of the hero. Shadwell himself can have derived no comfort from this, nor would it have been so obvious when it was written and the characters of the opponents were well known to everyone. But time, which has left so many of Pope's victims the proper prey of scholars and annotators, has veiled Dryden's malice and softened Shadwell's fate. For *MacFlecknoe* exists as a great comic creation to readers to whom Shadwell's name means nothing, and the reflected glow of Dryden's genuine delight in his own powers plays so warmly over the poem that we find ourselves praising what was, after all, a brutal lampoon in origin for its good humour and gaiety.

For all its contrivances and comic devices, *MacFlecknoe* is a realistic poem. It makes its point by appealing to an audience to whom the topography of the City, the race of City poets, the references to places and people, were matters of immediate and topical interest. The style and the setting create a recognizable world in which the poet and his readers both know their place. There is thus a peculiar bond between them: the poet uses their common knowledge to make his satire more persuasive, in a curious way more intimate; while the reader is able to judge the authenticity of the detail and the authority of the tone. Confidence is the keynote of this kind of poetry, since it seems as if the mysterious division has been torn down between the reader's world and the poet's, which is usually private and only communicable through the transforming devices of metaphor and myth. This, of course, is an illusion of the style, for the use of a style itself marks the same basic division, but more than any mode of writing, other than drama, it creates the effect of a direct contact between poet and reader.

This style suited personal indignation admirably, and personal feeling often inspired Dryden's satire. There is nothing Horatian about it, for he is seldom moved by objective rage, and makes no pretence to a moral intention. In the Prologue to *Amphitryon* (1690) Dryden grumbles about his inability to use the old freedom since the change in the political situation:

> The lab'ring Bee, when his sharp Sting is gone,
> Forgets his Golden Work, and turns a Drone:
> Such is a Satyr, when you take away
> That Rage, in which his Noble Vigour lay.
> What gain you, by not suffering him to teize ye?
> He neither can offend you, now, nor please ye.
> The Honey-bag, and Venome, lay so near,
> That both, together, you resolv'd to tear;
> And lost your Pleasure, to secure your Fear.
>
> (ll. 1–9.)

The rage Dryden speaks of always originated as a personal emotion. 'Self-love is a busy prompter', Johnson remarks, commenting on the poignancy of the satire in the characters of Og and Doeg in the second part of *Absalom and Achitophel*.[1] Yet when we remember how his contemporaries were struck by the unexpected diffidence and taciturnity of Dryden the man, it becomes clear that the final impression of a robust and lively personal attack delivered by a vigorous speaker is a skilful illusion of the style.

> Nor Love nor Wine cou'd ever see me Gay,
> To writing bred I knew not what to Say

wrote an anonymous satirist on the laureate,[2] and men of letters were surprised to notice Dryden's awkward manner in company.[3]

---

[1] *Johnson, Lives*, vol. i, 'Life of Dryden', p. 437.

[2] See Macdonald, op. cit., p. 234.

[3] Colley Cibber also recalled Dryden's unimpassioned delivery of his verses when he was reading them to the actors: 'in which, though it is true, he deliver'd the plain Sense of every Period, yet the whole was in so cold, so flat, and unaffecting a manner, that I am afraid of not being believ'd, when I affirm it'. *An Apology (for the Life of Mr. Colley Cibber, Comedian, and Late Patentee of the Theatre Royal)* (1740), p. 68.

Yet a poet's style, however much it may differ from his own manner, must bear some relation to his way of thinking and deepest preconceptions. In his theories about satire Dryden often expresses admiration for the moral tone and even temper of Horace, but he is forced to admit that Juvenal's strength and energy is more truly congenial to him: 'Juvenal is of a more vigorous and masculine wit . . . I have the pleasure of concernment in all he says; he drives his reader along with him.'[1] In this preference he was not entirely at one with his age. The Juvenalian mood was traditional rather than modern. Even Oldham, the most truly Juvenalian of the Restoration satirists, was sufficiently influenced by the prevailing taste of the time, and probably by his admiration for Rochester, to claim in his Preface to an imitation of the *Ars Poetica* that he was devising a new style in English verse, in which 'I have been careful to avoid stiffness, and made it my endeavour to hit (as near as I could) the easie and familiar way of writing, which is peculiar to *Horace* in his Epistles . . .'[2] The intention of the Horatians was essentially the same as Dryden's—to give the impression of a direct communication between the poet and his readers—but Dryden could achieve an effect of honest forthrightness by a different method. Rather than experiment in conversational idiom, he chose to vary the older declamatory style of Juvenal, allowing it the traditional roughness of satire as well as the eloquence of oratory, and tempering it with the familiar devices he had learned in writing prologues for the theatre, so that his utterance is both intimate and authoritative.

The Revolution and the defeat of Dryden's political hopes and his private fortune forced him to abandon satire. Even before this he had begun to show signs of dissatisfaction and remorse. His conversion to Roman Catholicism brought a new seriousness into his verse that is evident in the gravity and intensity of some of the passages in *The Hind and the Panther*. But Dryden's alarm at the attacks on James II prompted in this poem one of his last pieces of public satire—the character of the Buzzard, Bishop Burnet. This is made up of a variety of his satiric styles. The robust comic opening:

[1] *Essays of John Dryden*, vol. ii, p. 84.
[2] John Oldham, *Some New Pieces* (1681), p. ii.

> He came, and Crown'd with great Solemnity,
> God save King *Buzzard*, was the gen'rall cry
> (Part III, ll. 1139–40).

turns to the measured manner of *Absalom and Achitophel*:

> A Theologue more by need than genial bent,
> By Breeding sharp, by Nature confident.
> Int'rest in all his Actions was discern'd;
> More learn'd than Honest, more a Wit than learn'd.
> (Part III, ll. 1147–50.)

He concludes with a catalogue of qualities, some of which are expressed in pointed antitheses, and some in characteristic tones of open contempt:

> Prompt to assayle, and careless of defence,
> Invulnerable in his Impudence;
> He dares the World, and eager of a name,
> He thrusts about, and justles into fame.
> Frontless, and Satyr-proof he scow'rs the streets,
> And runs an *Indian* muck at all he meets.
> So fond of loud Report, that not to miss
> Of being known (his last and utmost bliss)
> He rather would be known, for what he is.
> (Part III, ll. 1183–91.)

The old vigour and skill are there, but the character has no context. In the animal-fable world of *The Hind and the Panther* Burnet seems to lack the substantial immediacy of the characters of *Absalom and Achitophel* and *MacFlecknoe*, supported as they are by their vividly realized environment. The result is that this character study seems more like a brilliant collection of disagreeable traits than a consistent portrait. Its isolated merits were easier to imitate, however, than the unified effect of his earlier satirical sketches, and more than one line of this piece looks forward to Pope in its neat exactitude. But the haphazard combination of so many satirical styles itself, perhaps, suggests the work of a man no longer certain of his line of attack, and we may infer that Dryden was not now wholly in sympathy with his task.

The same year as the publication of *The Hind and the Panther*, 1687,

Dryden renounced the personal vindictive motive that had so often inspired his satire. In the epistle to Henry Higden he wrote:

> *Revenge* wou'd into *Charity* be chang'd,
> Because it costs too Dear to be *Reveng'd*:
> It costs our *Quiet* and *Content of Mind*;
> And when 'tis compass'd, leaves a Sting behind.
> Suppose I had the better End o' th' Staff,
> Why shou'd I help th' ill-natur'd World to laugh?
> 'Tis all alike to them, who gets the Day;
> They love the Spight and Mischief of the *Fray*.
> No; I have Cur'd my Self of that *Disease*;
> Nor will I be provok'd, but when I please.

(ll. 25–33.)

But Dryden's position after the Revolution was such that revenge would have cost him more than his content of mind, and his later moderation was perhaps as much forced as voluntary. His very last works—the Prologue and Epilogue to *The Pilgrim*, which was performed for his benefit in 1700—showed him responding when he was pleased to be provoked, this time to Sir Richard Blackmore's scurrilous attack on the indecencies of his earlier comedies. The old man could still rouse himself to defend his reputation as a poet; his sting had not been drawn. There is a consistency that is entirely convincing in the story of his irritation when Tonson was quarrelling with him over a request for money: he turned to the printer's boy who had brought Tonson's message and handed him the following verses:

> With leering looks, bull faced and freckled fair,
> With frowsy pores poisoning the ambient air,
> With two left leggs, and Judas coloured hair . . .

with the words 'Tell the dog that he who wrote these can write more.'[1]

But there is little doubt that Dryden's misfortunes after his conversion mellowed his controversial opinions. Already in *The Hind and the Panther* he had modified the vindictive spirit which possessed him for a short time in the early 1680s. James II himself, of course, was anxious to conciliate the Dissenters for the sake of the Catholics at the beginning of his reign, but it is hard to believe that

---

[1] *John Dryden's Works*, ed. Scott and Saintsbury, vol. i (1882), p. 327. See also Kinsley's note, *Poems of Dryden*, op. cit., vol. iv, pp. 2084–5

expediency alone prompted the lines where Dryden pleads for tolerance:

> Of all the tyrannies on humane kind
> The worst is that which persecutes the mind.
> Let us but weigh at what offence we strike,
> 'Tis but because we cannot think alike.
>
> (Part I, ll. 239–42.)

Such an example raises the problem of sincerity which the new poetry forces on the reader. The poem is persuasive, and needs at least an assumed tone of sincerity, which Dryden, with his skill in adapting his manner to argument and in claiming forthright honesty, could easily command. But whereas in satire the new style induces a confident relation between the poet and his reader, in argument it can do exactly the opposite and put the wary reader on his guard. May not the effect of candour here be simply a rhetorical device? So Dryden's enemies who held him up as the supreme example of the time-serving turncoat tried to suggest:

> *Great Truckling Soul!* whose *stubborn* Honesty
> Does with all Revolutions still comply

wrote one, *To Mr. Dryden, upon his declaring himself a Roman Catholick,*[1] and another:

> Tell me, for 't is a Truth you must allow;
> Who ever chang'd more in one Moon, than thou?
> Ev'n thy own *Zimri* was more stedfast known;
> He had but one Religion, or had none.[2]

Yet there is some evidence of sincerity in this case, for the same sentiment is to be found in Dryden's *Life of Lucian*,[3] where he applies the argument boldly to abuses in the Roman Catholic Church itself:

We have indeed the highest Probabilities for our reveal'd Religion; Arguments which will preponderate with a reasonable Man, upon a long, and careful Disquisition; but I have always been of Opinion, that we can demonstrate nothing, because the Subject-matter is not capable of a Demonstration. 'Tis the particular Grace of God, that

---

[1] *Poems on Affairs of State*, vol. ii (1703), p. 221.
[2] Ibid., 'The Laureat', vol. i (1716) (second part), p. 129.
[3] Written in 1696 but published in 1711; see Macdonald, pp. 177–9.

any Man believes the Mysteries of our Faith; which I think a con-
clusive Argument against the Doctrine of Persecution in any Church.
And tho' I am absolutely convinc'd, as I heartily thank God I am,
not only of the general Principles of *Christianity*, but of all Truths
necessary to Salvation in the *Roman* Church; yet I cannot but detest
our Inquisition as it is practis'd in some foreign Parts, particularly in
Spain, and in the *Indies*. . . . To instruct, is a charitable Duty; to com-
pel, by Threatenings and Punishment, is the Office of Hangman, and
the Principle of a Tyrant.[1]

Intense sincerity is present in all those parts of *The Hind and the
Panther* where the poet speaks in his own person, and, perhaps, with
his new-found faith, Dryden could no longer feel free to indulge in
personal satire. Nor was this the only sacrifice that might be required. The most moving passage in the poem is that in which the
Hind speaks of the worldly losses necessary to salvation, in words
that tell of Dryden's own struggle to make some final renunciation
of his poetic reputation:

> Be vengeance wholly left to pow'rs divine,
> And let heav'n judge betwixt your sons and mine:
> If joyes hereafter must be purchas'd here
> With loss of all that mortals hold so dear,
> Then welcome infamy and publick shame,
> And, last, a long farwell to worldly fame.
> 'Tis said with ease, but oh, how hardly try'd⎫
> By haughty souls to humane honour ty'd! ⎬
> O sharp convulsive pangs of agonizing pride!⎭
> Down then thou rebell, never more to rise, ⎫
> And what thou didst, and do'st so dearly prize, ⎬
> That fame, that darling fame, make that thy sacrifice.⎭
> 'Tis nothing thou hast giv'n, then add thy tears
> For a long race of unrepenting years:
> 'Tis nothing yet; yet all thou hast to give,
> Then add those *may-be* years thou hast to live.
> Yet nothing still: then poor, and naked come, ⎫
> Thy father will receive his unthrift home, ⎬
> And thy blest Saviour's bloud discharge the mighty sum.⎭

(Part III, ll. 279–97.)

[1] *The Works of Lucian . . . with the Life*, vol. i (1711), pp. 17–18.

It is easy to imagine that when the poet writes like an orator with pomp and persuasion, or argues, or exchanges banter over the foot-lights, his verse reduces itself to empty rhetoric. But in Dryden's poetry the public tone mingles imperceptibly with personal feeling, and its peculiar principle of honesty sometimes extends from public declamation to private confession. Later poets, particularly Pope, were to display this flexibility more fully, but it is established already in Dryden's verse. The rhythms of the final lines in the passage quoted above have an emotional intensity that recalls Donne, and before them Dryden alludes to Shakespeare in his echo of Wolsey's farewell. But the foundation of the whole effect is that even, lucid style of verse introduced by Waller. Long practice in conciseness, openness, and hard factual clarity has simplified the reflections and left the emotion to stand bare and innocent of any complication or adornment except for the harmony of the line. And this verse, which could be hard-hitting and direct in satire, de-scriptive and terse in narrative, and pointedly persuasive in argu-ment, could also convey the subtlety of emotional sincerity.

In spite of the confession in *The Hind and the Panther*, however, Dryden never entirely renounced his pride in poetry. The last years of his life, when he had retired from politics, disgraced and de-prived of his laureateship, were occupied by the translations and *Fables*, poems written for no particular audience, but for his own pleasure. They show him at the height of his powers, employing that style which had been forged as an instrument of public argu-ment and persuasion for more intimate, private, and traditional purposes.

IV

Dryden had always been an experimenter in poetry, and his ver-satility did not leave him when, after his enforced retirement from public life, he could write ostensibly for his own pleasure. But his position was not enviable. He was still writing for his living, and the pressure on him was as great as it had ever been. Even if it is true that Dorset allowed him a pension, he was poorer than in his early years, and his letters of this period often refer to the amount of work he was forced to undertake. It is ironic to find him at the end of his career in the Dedication of the *Examen Poeticum* (1693) echoing the bitterness of Cowley, and complaining of the follies and hypocrisies which had discouraged the older poet:

'Tis a vanity common to all writers, to overvalue their own productions; and 'tis better for me to own this failing in myself, than the world to do it for me. For what other reason have I spent my life in so unprofitable a study? why am I grown old, in seeking so barren a reward as fame? The same parts and application which have made me a poet might have raised me to any honours of the gown, which are often given to men of as little learning and less honesty than myself. No Government has ever been, or ever can be, wherein timeservers and blockheads will not be uppermost. The persons are only chang'd, but the same jugglings in State, the same hypocrisy in religion, the same self-interest and mismanagement, will remain for ever.[1]

When he wrote now to solicit patronage, it was not in the old terms of grateful flattery, for even before the death of Charles II he had known what it was to demand his due reward. A letter in 1683 to Laurence Hyde, Earl of Rochester, requesting the advance of half a year's pension, suggests that Dryden had received little for *Absalom and Achitophel* and *The Medal*. There was no servility in his appeal, but a great deal of bitterness: '... I onely think I merite not to sterve ... I have three sonns growing to mans estate, I breed them all up to learning, beyond my fortune; but they are too hopefull to be neglected, though I want. .... 'Tis enough for one Age to have neglected Mr Cowley, and sterv'd Mr. Buttler.'[2] His need for money for his family haunted him to the end, and in 1697 he wrote to Jacob Tonson: 'Now I have the surgeons answer, wch I have inclosed in my letter to my Sonn: this is a business of the greatest consequence in the world: for you know how I love Charles ... and if it please God that I must dye of over study, I cannot spend my life better than in saving his.'[3]

The greatest poet of the age thus found himself in a position scarcely better than that of the meanest hired writer. He was supported only by pride in his art, which grew stronger in his later

---

[1] *Essays of John Dryden*, vol. ii, pp. 1–2.
[2] *Letters of John Dryden*, ed. C. E. Ward (1942), p. 21.   [3] Ibid., p. 99.

years, and softened the humiliations that envious rivals heaped upon
him. In his disgrace he seemed to have joined the ranks of the hacks,
and contempt mingled with harsh pity informs the numerous
satires of the period in which Dryden is mentioned. He and Oldham
had begun to suggest the idea of a pantheon of unfortunate great
writers from Spenser to Cowley and Butler who had been neglected
by their age, but hostile satirists lowered the position of the dis-
tressed genius by returning again and again to the contemporary
type of the starveling muse—Settle, Brown, and Ward:

> *Brown* their chief Leader, whom the Mob adore,
> A pigmy Poet, scandalous, and poor.
> *Pettis* to him succeeds, and trifling *Ward*,
> A frolick Writer, and a *Smithfield* Bard.
> Next *Settle* shews, amidst the rhyming Throng,
> Unhappy Poet to have liv'd so long!
> A Play-wright once; for Profit and for Praise,
> He drudg'd: But vanish'd are those golden Days.
> Expel'd the Stage, he met unhappy Times;
> And now for Bread composes Bellman's Rhymes.[1]
>   (ll. 448–57.)

Cowley's sober complaint is more brutally echoed by these minor
and anonymous satirists to whom poverty or neglect becomes a
source of scorn. The background of *The Dunciad* is already roughly
sketched out in the works which make up the short but vigorous
tradition of satire at the expense of the writer's new trade. In
Prior's *Satyr on the Poets. In Imitation of the seventh Satyr of Juvenal*[2]
the range of contemporary poets is covered to demonstrate the folly
of writing without the security of a patron or a place:

> *Shadwell* and starving *Tate* I scorn to Name;
> Poets of all Religions are the same:
> Recanting *Settle*, brings the tuneful Ware,
> Which wiser *Smithfield* damn'd to *Sturbridge* Fair:
> Protests his Tragedies and Lybels fail
> To yield him Paper, penny Loaves and Ale;

---

[1] *P.O.A.S.*, vol. iv (1707), 'The Grove: Or, the Rival Muses', p. 361.
[2] *Matthew Prior: Literary Works*, ed. H. B. Wright and M. K. Spears (1959), vol. i,
p. 28.

And bids our Youth, by his Example fly
The love of Politicks, and Poetry.

(ll. 10–17.)

The familiar details of the Grub Street environment are recalled
again:

When Age, and Poverty comes faster on,
And sad Experience tells thou art undone:
May no kind Country Grammar School afford
Ten Pound a year, for Lodging, Bed and Board,
Till void of any fix'd Employ, and now
Grown Useless to the Army, and the Plow,
You've no Friend left, but Trusting Landlady,
Who stows you in hard Truckle Garret high,
To dream of Dinner, and Curse Poetry.

(ll. 69–77.)

Prior singles out Dryden for special scorn, and the great poems of
his maturity when he could successfully boast 'the love of politics
and poetry', are simply the occasion for a sneer:

But shou'd Drudge *Dryden* this Example take,
And *Absaloms* for empty Glory make,
He'd soon perceive his Income scarce enough,
To feed his Nostrils with Inspiring Snuff,
Starving for Meat, nor surfeiting on Praise,
He'd find his Brain as barren as his *Bays*.

(ll. 149–54.)

But 'Drudge Dryden' was at least free now to choose his own subjects and themes for poetry, though money was still his immediate
object. His confidence in his powers had not failed. To Mrs.
Steward, his cousin, he wrote wryly that he was 'still drudging on:
always a Poet, and never a good one',[1] but, though he complained
to his sons that his promise to write a St. Cecilia Ode (*Alexander's
Feast*) was 'troublesome and no way beneficiall',[2] he was under no
illusion, when it was done, as to its greatness. He wrote to Tonson:
'I am glad to heare from all Hands, that my Ode is esteemd the best
of all my poetry, by all the Town: I thought so my self when I writ
it but being old, I mistrusted my own Judgment.'[3] His partiality

---

[1] *Letters*, p. 109.   [2] Ibid., p. 93.   [3] Ibid., p. 98.

for the work is understandable. All the enthusiasm of the panegyric style without any of the limitation of a panegyric subject glows through the verses, and the simple classical commonplaces resolve themselves into the murmurous repetition of the refrains:

> Bacchus *Blessings are a Treasure;*
> *Drinking is the Soldier's Pleasure;*
> *Rich the Treasure,*
> *Sweet the Pleasure;*
> *Sweet is Pleasure after Pain.*
>
> (ll. 61–65.)

Dryden once spoke of music as 'inarticulate poetry', and the poetry of *Alexander's Feast* might well be called, in a more familiar phrase, 'articulate music'.

Of all English poets Chaucer influenced him most at this time. In the *Preface to the Fables* (1700)[1] Dryden admitted that for many years he had planned to make a verse translation of the tales, but was dissuaded by the Earl of Leicester, who thought that Chaucer should be read in the original or not at all. Dryden believed he had found a kindred spirit in Chaucer, praising him in comparison even with his favourite Ovid. He may not have understood Chaucer's metre, or some of the ironies that depend for their effects on the conventions of Chaucer's art and times, but he recognized a deeply congenial spirit in the elder poet's interpretation of life. 'God's plenty' was the imaginative breadth which displayed itself in Chaucer's understanding of men and 'the various turns of human life'. Of Chaucer and Ovid Dryden said that they 'understood the manners, under which name I comprehend the passions and, in a larger sense, the descriptions of persons, and their very habits . . .'. Both 'writ with wonderful facility and clearness', and Dryden found in them both a courtly and learned background which made them worthy of imitation in a polite age. But above all, Chaucer possessed the quality which Dryden admired most and which is the foundation of 'honest' poetry of the new kind—a lively interest in real circumstances, which, though it need not preclude poetic contrivance, conventional rhetoric, or wit, communicated itself to the reader directly in the speed of the narrative, the authenticity of the

[1] *Essays of John Dryden*, vol. ii, pp. 246–73.

descriptions, and the open exhibition of the 'passions' or of those feelings commonly recognized in the ordinary situations of life.

Dryden's own love of the manners had already shown itself in his satires, but it is displayed with new breadth and delicacy in the *Fables* and the translations of the later period. He could scarcely hope to improve on Chaucer, but what he added to his original was not always unworthy. The widow's cottage in *The Nun's Priest's Tale* is enlivened by small vivid details from Dryden's own observation:

> Her Parlor-Window stuck with Herbs around,
> Of sav'ry Smell; and Rushes strew'd the Ground.
> A Maple-Dresser, in her Hall she had,
> On which full many a slender meal she made:
>
> (ll. 15–18.)

Another devoted student of the manners—Samuel Pepys—suggested to Dryden that he should imitate Chaucer's character of the Good Parson, though, in doing so, he hardly chose the best subject for Dryden's skill. He did not resent, either, the long passage of historical analogy at the end of which Dryden hinted his disapproval of the Revolution, as if such a real and lively style could comprehend, without any indecorum, topical political material and the poet's own attitude towards it. The result satisfied Pepys enough to suggest a party on the strength of it:

SIR,

You truly have oblig'd mee; and possibly in saying so, I am more in earnest then you can readily think; as verily hopeing from this your copy of one good Parson, to fancy some amends made mee for the hourly offence I beare with from the sight of soe many lewd originalls.

I shall with great pleasure attend you on this occasion, when ere you'l permit it; unless you would have the kindness to double it to mee, by suffering my coach to wayte on you (and who you can gayne mee ye same favour from) hither, to a cold chicken and a sallade, any *noone* after Sunday, as being just stepping into the ayre for 2 days.

I am most respectfully
Your hono^rd and obed^nt Servant,
S. P.[1]

---

[1] *Letters of John Dryden*, p. 116.

To put Chaucer into modern dress meant, however, exchanging some old conventions for new. The spirit Dryden recognized and admired in Ovid or Chaucer or Shakespeare appears in different guises in every period. Dryden's interpretation of it in his versions of Chaucer and of poets like Boccaccio is an indication of the new ideals and preconceptions of his own age. In *The Knight's Tale*, which he described as 'of the epic kind', Dryden substituted the code of love and honour, familiar from heroic drama, for the courtly and chivalric spirit of the original. The two had much in common, but the Restoration fashion for declamatory disputations on themes of love and loyalty creates a completely different impression from the medieval conventions of courtesy. *The Knight's Tale* and *Sigismonda and Guiscardo* are permeated by what Van Doren disparagingly calls 'the false dignity of Almanzor and Aurung-Zebe'.[1] But this style represents one of the Augustan ideals of truth to nature, and cannot be appreciated without a knowledge of what that truth meant to Dryden.

Wordsworth was severe about Dryden's treatment of the love theme of *Sigismonda and Guiscardo*, but he preferred the work to the other fables and described it as a noble poem. It is treated as a heroic episode, and the heroic mood was Dryden's peculiar form of romanticism. In *Sigismonda and Guiscardo* this romanticism exists side by side with a sceptical realism at times amounting almost to brutality, which makes no concession to the emotions or the imagination. The contrast is exaggerated in the poem by Dryden's insensitivity to all but the sensual aspect of love, but it is latent in every one of his works. He saw human life as crude but susceptible of refinement; absurd, but on occasion capable of rising to dignity and heroism. Both sides of the picture were real to his imagination. Sigismonda, the prey of a peculiarly mundane passion, can respond heroically to a tragic situation:

> She said: Nor did her Father fail to find,
> In all she spoke, the Greatness of her Mind;
>
> (ll. 582–3.)

A mind more sensitive and subtle than Dryden's might have found

[1] M. Van Doren, *John Dryden* (1946), p. 223.

it difficult to reconcile these views of human nature, but in doing so he was not out of tune with the feeling of his time. For this attitude was based on a hard sense of reality and a simple enthusiasm for dignity—a feeling for the authentic and the obviously important. Dryden's love of the real drew him to narrative and description—to all that he meant by 'the manners': his faith in heroic dignity led him to use not only conventional rhetoric, but also that reasoned commentary on experience through which the Augustans chose to express the deep seriousness of their inspiration.

Dryden's poems suggest that he saw all tragic or heroic occasions in life as part of a common and inevitable human fate. He repeats this truth with a personal conviction which was confirmed and strengthened by his reading in classical literature. The magnitude of such occasions demanded a language raised from the common level. But something more was needed: a context, an atmosphere which would affirm this universality while yet being as validly authentic as that contemporary world he used in topical satire. For this purpose Dryden exploited the past—in various ways. He refers to real historical events, traces the growth of a branch of knowledge, alludes to classical literature, or introduces sentiments whose first expression no one can trace, but which had passed from the Greeks and Romans through the Middle Ages into proverbial wisdom. The effect is that 'the mind is to be transported, as Shakespeare expresses it, *beyond the ignorant present*, to ages past'.[1] In his high style it is by this ranging through history that Dryden achieves universality.

The use of history in the poetry of the time was widespread, and derived from the need for historical precedents in political satire which has been discussed, and also from the pervasive influence of the epic. There were two main historical forms—the poem on contemporary events, like *Annus Mirabilis*, written in epic manner, and the survey poem, which could be either topographical, like *Cooper's Hill*, or a political panegyric. Dryden does not use the topographical form, but he develops the complimentary epistle to include an historical survey of the growth of an art, painting in the *Epistle to Kneller*, poetry in that to Congreve. These are the only

---

[1] Sir Joshua Reynolds, *Discourses on Art*, ed. R. R. Wark (San Marino, 1959), pp. 235–6.

poems in which he universalizes by direct reference to historical events and by tracing the growth of a branch of knowledge. It is by the other two means that he consistently universalizes and elevates his style in the later works—the general habit of allusiveness, and the use of sententious reflection. Their effect is to capture the pervasive spirit of the past, in particular of 'ancient Rome, with all the objects which a literary education makes so precious and interesting to man'.[1] It achieves a kind of grandeur by establishing a relationship between Dryden and the epic masters, Virgil, Tasso, Spenser, and Milton. The sensibility of the Augustans was excited by this continuity, this great sweep of history; it was not the appeal of the rules, or the desire for precedent which came first in their response to it. Dryden's successors were deeply satisfied by the style and its mood, and adopted it enthusiastically for their elevated verse.

Because of this style, *The Knight's Tale* in Dryden's version differs from its original. Chaucer had given Saturn these simple lines:

> My cours, that hath so wyde for to turne,
> Hath more power than wot any man
>
> (ll. 2454–5.)

but Dryden expanded and elevated them in a passage whose sombre verses reverberate with the sense of the past and move with a weight and gravity which suggest Virgil:

> Wide is my Course, nor turn I to my Place
> Till length of Time, and move with tardy Pace.
> Man feels me, when I press th' Ethereal Plains,
> My Hand is heavy, and the Wound remains.
>
> (Bk. 3, ll. 397–400.)

The accents are not entirely new in English literature; they recall Sylla's ghost in Jonson's *Catiline*:

> Do'st thou not feele me, *Rome*? not yet? Is night
> So heauy on thee, and my weight so light?
>
> (I. i. 1–2.)

but if Jonson was early to recognize their power in drama, Dryden was the first to exploit them fully in narrative and discursive poetry.

---

[1] Reynolds, op. cit., Discourse 13, p. 237.

In the same way, he changed the tone of Arcite's death. Instead of exclaiming simply

> Allas, the wo! allas, the peynes stronge,
> That I for yow have suffred, and so longe!
>
> (*Knight's Tale*, ll. 2771–2.)

Dryden's Arcite takes his leave of Emily with a well-turned compliment and a general reflection that understates his personal grief deliberately so that the irony of the situation is emphasized:

> This I may say, I only grieve to die
> Because I lose my charming *Emily*:
> To die, when Heav'n had put you in my Pow'r,
> Fate could not chuse a more malicious Hour!
>
> (Bk. 3, ll. 788–91.)

Arcite speaks like a hero and a gentleman, not a lover, and to the end Dryden missed the personal tenderness and poignancy of Chaucer. He understood Ovid's temptation to turn passion into wit, but when he observed that if Ovid had written the poem he 'would have made Arcite die wittily', he clearly felt that he himself had avoided the fault. There is no hint that he suspected any false politeness in his hero's last words, for, though the style was part of that wider context which constituted the ideal, it had to bear also a close relation to reality if it was to succeed in moving his readers. Men were still polite on their death-beds in Dryden's age. Charles II himself apologized for being an unconscionable time in dying, with 'a last glimpse of that exquisite urbanity, so often found potent to charm away the resentment of a justly incensed nation'.[1]

The other attributes Dryden admired in Chaucer and Ovid—facility and clearness—were integral to the development of the simplicity and propriety of sentiment which he most desired in his later works. The Prefaces to *Sylvae*, the *Fables*, and the *Examen Poeticum*, which, in spite of their rambling freedom—'never wholly out of the way, nor in it'—contain his best criticism, are full of examples of these qualities from classical and native poets. In the Preface to *Sylvae* (1685) Dryden betrays the envy of a naturally copious writer for the 'succinct and grave majestic' style of Virgil,

---

[1] Lord Macaulay, *History of England*, vol. i (1849), p. 439.

and his inimitable 'exact propriety'. Then he proceeds to make a
distinction which is revealing with regard to his own style: 'Tasso
tells us, in his letters, that Sperone Speroni . . . observed of Virgil and
Tully, that the Latin orator endeavored to imitate the copiousness
of Homer, the Greek poet; and that the Latin poet made it his
business to reach the conciseness of Demosthenes, the Greek
orator'.[1] The copiousness of Latin oratorical style came to Dryden
more naturally than the terseness of great Latin poetry, and he
always admitted that he preferred Homer's vigour to Virgil's
suavity. Similarly, though Ovid is not praised when compared with
Virgil, Dryden reveals a secret fondness for the more careless poet
whose faults were so like his own—facility and an over-luxuriant
fancy. He loved the speed and gaiety of Ovid's wit, his mastery
of 'the manners', which, together with the 'curiosa felicitas' of
Horace's odes, were the qualities he most wished to imitate. 'For,
after all,' he remarked in the dedication of the *Examen Poeticum*, 'our
language is both copious, significant, and majestical, and might be
reduced into a more harmonious sound.'[2]

Dryden's aim was to rival the ancients by using the English
language for the effects they achieved. Under their influence he began to look for new kinds of expression, more natural and 'correct',
which might match the classical principles of simplicity and propriety. The style he perfected was the source of that manner which
it is easy to condemn in the minor Augustans as artificial and stulti-
fying in its imitation of the ancients. How a poet who, when he
chose, wrote so vigorously and persuasively in language which still
seems realistic and natural could have turned to this deliberately
contrived manner is a question which demands a serious answer.
A paradoxical aspect of the poetry of the Honest Muse is that it
turns so often when not satirical to what may look like a dead convention and an apparently falsifying poetic diction. But Dryden's
original purpose in devising this imitative idiom had been to harden
and refine the language, to give it greater compression and accuracy
without sacrificing its general intelligibility. Thus the intention
was well in keeping with the ideal of honesty. By following the
'naturalness' of the ancients, Dryden meant to make poetry simpler

---

[1] *Essays of John Dryden*, vol. i, p. 256.   [2] Ibid., vol. ii, p. 12.

and truer as well as to harden and stabilize the language. He had succeeded already in the *Lines to the Memory of Mr. Oldham* (1684) in drawing out the latent power of classical allusion and combining it with an account of the young man's work which was both natural and correct, though enlivened by wit, and from this point onwards simplicity and propriety become increasingly important in his style. 'The beautiful faults', as he called the conceits in *Eleonora*, grow less. From his many translations he learned something of Virgil's succinctness, of Ovid's sweetness, and the calm temper of Horace's lyric mood. Out of these materials he created an eclectic style which combined the sinewy vigour of the old with a new and limpid beauty.

Dryden's later miscellaneous poems are so full of peculiar beauties that it is hard to know where to single out examples. The audacity with which, in the *Fables*, he mingles heroic, dramatic, and lyric styles with the plain telling of a story delighted and astonished succeeding generations of poets and critics. The lyric mood predominated in these later poems. All the tenderness so lacking in his earlier work finds expression in the enchanting metrical effects of his later years. The triplet, which he had so often used for emphasis in satire, now points intensity or lingering suspense. In the opening lines of *Cymon and Iphigenia* it carries all the eloquence of sentiment:

> Old as I am, for Ladies Love unfit,
> The Pow'r of Beauty I remember yet,
> Which once inflam'd my Soul, and still inspires my Wit.
> (*Cymon and Iphigenia*, ll. 1–3.)

In his translation of Virgil, Dryden discovered the exquisite modulation which the triplet could give to a long verse paragraph, and in the passage describing the sea-nymphs in the fourth Georgic he creates the effect of three short lyric stanzas by introducing an alexandrine at regular intervals of four lines, and concluding the whole with a triplet.[1] But some of his most beautiful effects can scarcely be explained by technicalities. 'All the graces a good ear affords' went to the making of the voluptuous simplicity of verses like the song in *King Arthur*, in which the most trite and conventional sentiments are transformed:

[1] Lines 477–89.

How blest are Shepherds, how happy their Lasses,
    While Drums and Trumpets are sounding Alarms!
Over our Lowly Sheds all the Storm passes;
    And when we die, 't is in each others' Arms.[1]

Dryden never lost the art of transforming the decasyllabic line by a wide range of subtle metrical variations. In one lovely lilting passage from the translation of Virgil's seventh Eclogue, it is hard to know whether he was imitating Chaucer,[2] who more than once had struck out the same dancing rhythm, or whether he was influenced by Latin lyric measures:

Fair *Galathea*, with thy silver Feet,
O, whiter than the Swan, and more than *Hybla* sweet;
Tall as a Poplar, taper as the Bole,
Come charm thy Shepherd, and restore my Soul.

                            (ll. 52–55.)

Waller's new style had taken more account of the music of numbers than of the beauty of images. In this Dryden followed him. Wit might 'strike out new sparkles of her own' (and wit was with difficulty suppressed by Dryden), but truth and sincerity lingered over the sentiments with a musical delight in the harmony of their expression. Dryden's later poems and translations lack the easily identified personal vigour of his satires, but they are alive with the emotion that rose quickly to the surface when poetry itself was his theme. No subject moved him more. He had never before felt such delighted confidence in his own powers. Like Yeats, he knew that the years which had taken away his youth had brought him greater strength of imagination and skill. His interest in life and letters was as strong as ever, and it was sustained by summer visits to the country and by the warm friendship of his relations and of admiring young men like Congreve and Walsh, who sought out the old man's company and advice. The *Epistle to My Honour'd Kinsman*,

---

[1] *King Arthur, or The British Worthy*, Act 2. Dryden, *The Dramatic Works*, ed. M. Summers, vol. vi (1932), p. 258.

[2] Dryden himself had quoted as an example of Chaucer's skill 'the rude sweetness of a Scotch tune', a couplet which shows this rhythm:

     Winsing she was as is a joly colt,
     Long as a mast and upright as a bolt.

John Driden declares his new pride in the family, which mingles happily with confidence in his own poetic worth:

> Nor think the Kindred-Muses thy Disgrace;
> A Poet is not born in ev'ry Race.
> Two of a House, few Ages can afford;
> One to perform, another to record.
>
> (ll. 201-4.)

Dryden described his latest performances in superlatives: he could not conceal his pleasure in them. His translations of Ovid seemed to him 'the best of all my endeavors in this kind', though he admits that this may be 'the partiality of an old man for his youngest child'. In the Preface to the *Fables* he exults in 'the vigour of the faculties of my soul': 'What judgment I had, increases rather than diminishes; and thoughts, such as they are, come crowding in so fast upon me, that my only difficulty is to choose or to reject, to run them into verse, or to give them the other harmony of prose: I have so long studied and practised both, that they are grown into a habit, and become familiar to me.'[1] This combination of a vigorous poetic old age with his appreciation of the society of friends and family is distinctly Horatian. It implies an attitude the Augustans were quick to associate with poetic wisdom, and Dryden was able to enjoy, then if ever, those advantages he had attributed to the scholars of Oxford:

> When tyr'd with following Nature, you think fit
> To seek repose in the cool shades of Wit,
> And from the sweet Retreat, with Joy survey
> What rests, and what is conquer'd, of the way.
>
> (Prologue to the University of Oxford, 1674, ll. 3-6.)

His varied career and his experience of success and disappointment left him resigned rather than resentful, for he had learned that the struggles and difficulties of the professional poet were hardly different from those of other men who live in the world.

No poem is more characteristic of Dryden's latest mood than his translation of the twenty-ninth Ode of the third Book of Horace, of which he wrote in the Preface to *Sylvae*: 'One Ode which infinitely

---

[1] *Essays of John Dryden*, vol. ii, p. 249.

pleased me in the reading, I have attempted to translate in Pindaric verse . . . and I have taken some pains to make it my masterpiece in English. . . .'[1] In this Dryden mastered more than the Pindaric style. He made it a full expression of the classical spirit which had tempered heroic defiance to wise resignation and the hard perspicacity of the satirist to a genial acceptance of what is best in life. His old virtuosity is still present: octosyllabics alternate with iambic pentameters, now in the form of the triplet, now in regular couplets, and, as the poem gathers momentum in the description of the avalanche of fortune, the lines expand to a final alexandrine. With this familiar impetus the climax is approached and the poem moves easily into the fine stanza of simple direct assertions which reach the secret happiness he so much admired in the original. Nowhere else in Augustan poetry is there a more successful mingling of succinct gravity with lyrical grace:

> Happy the Man, and happy he alone,
> He, who can call to day his own:
> He, who secure within, can say
> To morrow do thy worst, for I have liv'd to day.
> Be fair, or foul, or rain, or shine,
> The joys I have possesst, in spight of fate are mine.
> Not Heav'n it self upon the past has pow'r;
> But what has been, has been, and I have had my hour.
>
> (ll. 65–72.)

The calm conclusion is matched by the same ease and directness of style:

> In my small Pinnace I can sail,
> Contemning all the blustring roar;
> And running with a merry gale,
> With friendly Stars my safety seek,
> Within some little winding Creek;
> And see the storm a shore.
>
> (ll. 99–104.)

This was the poetry Dryden chose to write for himself. It is coloured by a reflective mood and strengthened by allusion in a way which recalls the elegiac strain of the great epic. Its hard simplicity is

---

[1] *Essays of John Dryden,* vol. i, p. 267.

suited particularly well to express the wisdom of experience seen against a background of history or general reflection, and it established for the Augustans a poetic ideal of wisdom and eloquence happily blended.

V

Dryden was hailed by his successors as the originator of a school of poetry, and the title would have pleased him. Although he saw himself as 'betwixt two ages cast, the first of this and hindmost of the last', he was not consciously a trimmer in his art. He thought of himself as a modern but not as a revolutionary, for the conservative instinct which saw political innovation as 'the blow of fate' was at work in his poetry. He was always conscious of tradition, classical or native. His own contemporaries, moreover, did not always think of him as in the van of the new movement. When Rochester, in his *Allusion to Horace*, put him in the position of Lucilius, he suggested by the analogy that Dryden was to be thought of as a powerful but rather outmoded forerunner. To the new young poets some old-fashioned qualities may have been more apparent than they are to us—the Juvenalian vigour, for example, the love of conceits, and of witty speculations and digressions. Yet Dryden himself was openly critical of the period from which many of his characteristics derive. He believed that during the seventeenth century the style and subject-matter of poetry had degenerated, and to reform this he set up a standard of truth to nature which, though personally expressed, was in keeping with the philosophical and commonplace ideas of the Restoration.

Truth to nature was not only a matter of the imitation and interpretation of life; it extended to style. If a poet thought remote and ingenious reflections proper material for a poem, his style was likely to be contrived and obscure. If, on the other hand, he believed that the most natural sentiments were those which men would commonly and spontaneously feel, his language would tend to be generalized, but simple, direct, and exact. Dryden's use of the conceit illustrates how he transformed one of the conventions he inherited. Johnson, in his *Life of Cowley*, observed that metaphysical images, when 'expanded to perspicuity and polished to elegance may give lustre to works which have more propriety though less copiousness of sentiment'.[1] This is the effect that Dryden achieved by those devices which were still congenial to him, for more propriety and less copiousness of sentiment were among his ideals, though he found it hard to curb the luxuriance of his fancy.

No convention, old or new, ever seems to limit Dryden's poetry. When he was choosing words to reproduce another poet's effects, as in his translations, his personal genius intruded and stamped the finished work with the impression of an original hand. He was censured for this by the more academic generation of translators of the next age. But Dryden's language was all his own, whether he chose to recall the dignity of Latin, whether he turned his style to narrative or argument, assumed his singing robes, or railed in the accents of satire. Nor was it merely a written language. The spoken word is always present in Dryden's poetry. He is declamatory or discursive or familiar, but his own voice is always audible in the emphasis behind the verse. 'The long majestic march and energy divine' were only possible to a poet 'gifted with so fine an ear' as Dryden, and the sounding qualities of his verse died with him.

Much else, though, was transmitted to his followers. A great poet usually leaves his mark, but his influence is likely to be especially extensive when he has been affected himself by contemporary circumstances. Poets who, like Dryden, wrote for their living and took part in public affairs found themselves facing the same problems and adopting instinctively his tone and attitudes. The man who lives by his pen and is willing to join in public arguments and professional quarrels draws attention to his own point of view—in a sense makes himself public property and asks to be judged by the effect of honest sincerity which his work produces. The question arises rarely in objective forms like the drama, or in conventional lyric poetry; but the didactic poet, the satirist, the recorder of the events of his own time, must give an impression of conviction. In this Dryden was eminently successful. Attacks on his change of faith matter little here. We are not required to judge whether Dryden's private opinions were always scrupulously honest, but, from his life, and the significant evidence of his poetry, we can discover a general

---

[1] *Lives*, 'Life of Cowley', vol. i, p. 22.

principle of sincerity which sprang from his convictions and was
a matter of his sensitivity to the manner best suited to their expression. He warmed to panegyric and satire, and he was lucky to
be able to combine such genuine delight in his own poetic powers
with feelings that were roused easily on a wide range of topics.
Honesty is the traditional plea of the satirist, especially if he claims
a moral purpose. Dryden made that plea in other roles. The honest
layman is the spokesman in *Religio Laici*, the honest Tory, anxious
for the welfare of the State, presents the serious arguments in the
political satires. Sincerity has to be taken for granted in a defence of
the poet's religious faith like *The Hind and the Panther*.

'Honesty' was closely involved with truth, and though Dryden
himself has little to say on this particular issue, he was enough of
a modern to accept by implication many of the new emphases on
the nature of truth which, by the early eighteenth century, had
transformed the idea of the proper subject-matter of poetry. He
shared his age's optimistic belief in the enlightened new philosophy
that had swept away the obscure and tangled superstitions associated
with Aristotle:

> The longest Tyranny that ever sway'd,
> Was that wherein our Ancestors betray'd
> Their free-born *Reason* to the *Stagirite*,
> And made his Torch their universal Light.
> So *Truth*, while onely one suppli'd the State,
> Grew scarce, and dear, and yet sophisticate.
>
> (*Epistle to Dr. Charleton*, ll. 1–6.)

Truth unsophisticate was the ideal of the new poets, as of the new
philosophers. Dryden did not join the literary battle between the
ancients and the moderns which, particularly in the issue between
Temple and Bentley, had such a strong influence on later Augustan
satirists, but in spirit he was on the optimistic side which Swift and
Pope were to reject. Yet though the subjects of most of his poems
are rational, clear, and relevant to the times or to human nature in
general, Dryden, unlike his followers, did not limit the possible
themes or devices of poetry according to whether they could be

accounted true in a simple and literal way. Pagan mythology, for instance, is introduced into his formal odes, as an occasional reference, but without any feeling of embarrassment. Yet by the middle of the eighteenth century it was almost entirely discredited on those grounds of truth to nature which Dryden himself had expounded more liberally and traditionally. To Pope, even a heroic epistle like *Eloisa to Abelard* gained by being historically 'true', and Johnson based many of his literary judgements on a criterion of truth which was moral and historical rather than literary in the old sense. This was no blind personal bias, but an acceptance of the natural conclusions of the Augustan tradition of truth which, in a wider sense, Dryden had helped to initiate.

Dryden and his successors were equally concerned to be true to poetry as an art. In their position this had a peculiar significance. Because of the widespread misuse of poetry for propaganda and the unavoidable competition with hack writers, serious poets were unusually sensitive about the dignity of their art. They were conscious of their craft as a part of the high tradition of poetry, which set them apart from amateurs and journalists in verse alike. Dryden's prologues and epilogues, which are his main forms for literary comment in verse so relaxed in tone, however, that they give the impression that he is turning familiar topics over in play as often as seriously. His prose criticism shows a similar tendency to mould language nearer to the cadences of direct speech, and to aim at polite intelligibility as well as argument, but there is no doubt about his intense pride in his work and his concern for poetry. Rochester, Oldham, and later Pope were more openly defensive and introduced the literary apologia so often into their poems that it assumed the importance of a major theme in their work. To them, as to Dryden, it represented the need to be sincere about poetry itself. Dryden seldom discusses this, but it is implicit in his experiments, his devotion to his craft, and in those labours of love, the translations of his later years. After his death, a full acquaintance with the ancients and with the native tradition began to be expected of any true poet. What Dryden had chosen to read and write for pleasure in his old age had become a *sine qua non*.

For general purposes then, Dryden's style became the important

model. Writing as a man for men, he found himself naturally adopting the tone we expect in the conduct of everyday life—not that of
a scrupulous accuracy, but a tone which, however partisan, is
recognizable as that of a man saying what he means in the simplest
and most common sense. The result of this was far-reaching.
Although the romantics rejected the idiom of the Augustans, their
freedom to write as individuals, about their private convictions and
emotions, owed more than they admitted to the discovery of this
tone of open sincerity. If the poets who preceded them, like Cowper
and Goldsmith, could say what they felt and thought directly and
personally in poetry, they could do so because a manner of address
different from the old conventions had already been evolved in this
earlier period, whereby a writer could express himself not only as
a poet but as a man.

This tone was adopted, though sometimes less convincingly, by
Dryden's contemporaries, because persuasive satire, argumentative
verse, and witty lyrics generally require an assumption of sincerity,
however traditional the forms on which they are based. Like Dryden, other writers of the age preserved convention in both form and
attitude, but new influences revealed themselves through that
realism of detail and tone which is characteristic of Augustan verse.
The mingling of these two apparently contradictory qualities of convention and realism lies at the heart of Dryden's poetry, and it is
perhaps the most important clue to understanding the whole attitude of the Augustan school. More and more he found himself
bringing together in one poem moods and manners of address which
previously had been kept decorously apart—satire and panegyric,
the realistic and the heroic, the argumentative and the elegiac. It is
characteristic of a new age to attempt this kind of eclecticism in the
search for an original means of expression. But Dryden's genius, like
that of most great poets, achieves such a unity of style that it is
sometimes difficult to discern where he is expressing new attitudes
and where he is modifying older ones. His lesser contemporaries
show more clearly the typical assumptions of the period. Through
their imperfections the new tone and rapid changes of attitude reveal themselves clearly. A whole school of writing develops with
Oldham and Rochester, through the minor and anonymous satirists

of the Restoration and the early eighteenth century, to the point at which certain conventions had become so generally accepted that Pope, at the culmination of this tradition, could not avoid using them. It is these conventions which constitute a great part of the attitude to life and literature of the poetry of the Honest Muse.

IV

THE CONVENTIONS OF SATIRE

THE school which Dryden established is often discussed as if it consisted solely of himself and Pope. Pope was an imitator, but, on his own reckoning, the ancients—Spenser, Shakespeare, Milton, and Dryden—make up the count of his sources. Besides, it is easy to forget that an imitator who is also a great poet can exist only at a time when there is a flourishing tradition of good minor verse, written in the same vein and on similar assumptions. Imitation is a social, almost a communal art. Subtle allusions are wasted on a public that is unable to recognize or even to expect them. The imitator depends on what others have done to prepare the ground, and his originality can only be appreciated in relation to his literary environment. Pope, however original a poet, was aware of himself as the polisher and perfecter of a living tradition.

The peculiar circumstances of the Restoration and the early eighteenth century had created a hierarchy among writers, dividing the hack from the gentleman amateur, and both from the dedicated man of letters. It was for this reason that Pope was willing to acknowledge his debt to Dryden and other great poets of the past, while he was perhaps over-anxious to conceal less distinguished influences. In any case, there was no need for him to indicate where he was doing better what Oldham or Rochester or Dorset or Garth had done before him, when it was self-evident to his readers. In his conversation he made a few slighting references to the Restoration wits—'holiday writers', 'gentlemen that diverted themselves now and then with poetry'. But his poems remind us continually how intimately he knew their work and how much he owed to it. Two branches of Restoration literature particularly influenced his own poetry—the various satiric conventions, and the vogue for translation and imitation of the ancients.

Dryden had not exhausted the satiric vein of the Restoration.

There were certain kinds of satire he had not touched, notably the imitation which was often used to attack literary conditions and the debasement of poetry, and the social epistle, the town eclogue or the Horatian satire. Of these forms Rochester and Oldham were the masters, followed by a number of minor imitators, from Court wits to the versifiers in the miscellanies. Such themes as the attack on women and the follies of the fop were repeated by the same group of wits in the lyrics and comedies of the age, and established the tone of a closed society which set out to arbitrate the taste of the time. Outside this coterie the contest of political opponents, poetic rivals, and literary scavengers flourished in verses which pick up the tone of the wits, but more often fall back on the abusiveness of lampoon or the more respectable tradition of Juvenalian scorn. It was fashionable, indeed, for the poet to appear bored by this profusion of satire, and he might recommend his own contribution by suggesting that he was goaded from modish indifference by the confusion of the time and the badness of its poetry. One of the most scurrilous satires in *Poems on Affairs of State* declares:

> I who from drinking ne'er could spare an hour,
> But what I gave to some obedient Whore,
> Who hate all Satire, whether sharp or dull,
> From *Dryden* to the Governour of *Hull*;
> Provok'd at length to a Poetick Rage,
> Resolve to share in railing at the Age.[1]

> (ll. 1–6.)

Provocation was the prevailing inspiration as well as the prevailing tone of satire.

After 1688 a gradual change becomes apparent. Topical and religious matters still inspired satire, and political sentiments might be expressed in the disingenuous guise of street ballads, like Prior's *The Orange*. But much of the impetus had disappeared. Horror at the possibility of civil war and relief that it had been avoided recommended prudence to the writers of the time. The tendency to a more general politeness, a spreading sense of public decorum,

---

[1] *P.O.A.S.*, 'Satire; *Quem Natura negat dabit Indignatio Versum*', vol. iii (1716), p. 110.

coloured even satire, the most popular form of verse writing. For whatever reason, the best satire after 1688 is graver on the whole, more argumentative and less abusive.

Some old conventions remained. Among the most popular were the 'dream' or 'ghost' satires, which were generally political. In his *Last Instructions to a Painter* (ll. 885 ff.) Marvell had introduced the apparition of degraded England brought to Charles II's bedside to rebuke him as he rouses himself to receive what he believes to be yet another mistress. None of the lesser poets could match Marvell's power in describing such an episode, but they enjoyed the Juvenalian indignation of the tone which this kind of satire encouraged. Oldham made use of the convention in his *Satyr concerning Poetry*, which is spoken by the ghost of ill-used Spenser, but on the whole the more reputable satirists avoided it. Possibly Marvell's use of it stamped it as old-fashioned, but more likely he had appropriated the form for the anti-Royalists, or for anyone who needed a convention for attacking the *status quo*. In anonymous political versions it is dangerously associated with sedition. For such poems pretended to reveal the horror of the present situation, using a Senecan ghost motif to suggest revenge and impending disaster. A powerful late example of the form is to be found in the first volume of *Poems on Affairs of State* in a work entitled *Caesar's Ghost*, by an anonymous supporter of James II. His description of the army at Hounslow Heath, their dissipation and their irresponsibility towards the King they were pledged to defend, is seen through the eyes of Caesar's ghost—an apparition of Charles II, who watches the scene with horror as a portent of his brother's doom and the downfall of his house. In a rather more sophisticated way than is common in such satires, the poem combines political indignation and violent personal attack with topical detail in character study and description:

> By chance the Poet *Elkanah* was there
> To make them sport, for 'twas not yet the Fair;
> With many more too scandalous to name,
> Whose Talents are to Swear, Whore, Drink and Game.
> At a large Table they were seated round,
> With Bottles, Snush, foul Pipes and Glasses crown'd,

> Boxes and Dice—but whether false or true,
> I leave it to the Fools that Night shall rue;[1]

For obvious reasons the form did not recommend itself to Dryden
either when he was laureate or when he had withdrawn from politics. But Pope, though he rejected its conventional outlines, did not
forget it when he came to write *The Dunciad*. Its vulgar associations
of prophecy and doom are present, mingled ironically with the epic
source, in the vision of future dullness which the familiar apparition
of Settle displays to the hero in Book III.

Conventions of specifically literary satire were more to Pope's
purpose, and he had a wide variety to choose from. Serious accounts
of the growth or technique of the art of writing, based on Horace's
Ars Poetica, were offset by popular ballad forms like the 'Sessions'
poems, jog-trot satires, imitating Suckling's original version of the
type, which were a favourite excuse for lampoon. Vulgar though the
form was, it became a favourite with the wits, who enjoyed its
jaunty improvised manner and its tradition of insolent personalities
and tit-bits of literary gossip.[2] Rochester, who could satirize his
fellow poets seriously in an imitation like the *Allusion to Horace*, was
equally at home in his *Session of the Poets*, while Prior, who as a young
man adopted the attitudes of the wits, employed it with all the
assurance of a fashionable versifier. Yet it was as limited in its way
as the vision satires were to the political poet. It suggested all the
cameraderies of a small literary set and was as partisan in its own
sphere as many of the topical satirical forms.

The danger of this situation was that too many forms were beginning to be associated with passing fashion, cliques, or political
parties. The topicality which animated Restoration satire inevitably
limited it too. Though the ground had been thoroughly prepared,
any new poet with serious ambitions of maintaining the dignity and
honesty of his role would have to choose his area very carefully.
Pope himself, cut off from public life and from gayer fashionable

---

[1] *P.O.A.S.*, vol. i (1716), Part II, p. 169.

[2] For example this reference to Denham in 'Session of the Poets', ibid., Part I, p. 210.

> But *Apollo* advis'd him to write something more,
> To clear a Suspicion which possess'd the Court,
> That *Cooper's*-Hill, so much brag'd on before,
> Was writ by a Vicar, who had forty pound for 't.

society, was predisposed to look for more permanent conventions, and ones which were more complex and serious. He found much of value, however, in the poems of Oldham and Rochester, for these two poets had caught most of the contemporary attitudes and wrote with all the contemporary vigour. And each of them did so in a detached and independent fashion which showed how a poet with no particular political allegiance could make good use of topical material. Neither was primarily attached to a party or a cause, yet nothing lay outside the range of their satire—not the Court, the country, the Town, politics, religion, or human nature in general. They claimed the freedom of the serious satirist to treat every kind of subject.

Rochester, the centre of an admiring clique of friends and imitators, led a life too notorious to need any fresh description. From time to time scholars have succeeded in exonerating him from some charges—the Rose Alley attack on Dryden, for instance—but the escapades attributed to him are as various and unsifted as the obscenities which were printed under his name after his death. What remains clear is that while he shared many inevitable aristocratic prejudices—contempt for cits, and a modish taste in light wit which led him to over-estimate his courtly friends as poets—Rochester owed no allegiances and considered himself a champion of free thought and conduct. Having a keen mind and considerable sensibility, he composed poetry that was alternately satiric and lyrical, but always serious under the occasionally wearisome tone of cultivated fashionable contempt. He was more gifted, more concerned with his art, and of a more interesting cast of mind than his friends Buckingham, Etherege, Sedley, or Dorset, and his personality and privileged position of independence left a mark of genuine originality on his work which impressed his contemporaries. Marvell thought him the only writer of the age with the true vein of satire, Rochester half returned the compliment in his poem *Tunbridge Wells*[1]

[1] He being rais'd to an Arch-deaconry,
By trampling on Religious Liberty;
Was grown so fat, and look'd so big and jolly,
Not being disturb'd with care and melancholly,
Tho' *Marvel* has enough expos'd his Folly.

(*Tunbridge Wells*, ll. 65–69.) *Poems by John Wilmot, Earl of Rochester*, ed. V. de S. Pinto (1953), p. 89.

by referring to Marvell's witty triumph over Parker. But his strongest and most lasting influence was on Oldham, whose masculine and original genius was fascinated by his brilliant flexibility.

Oldham's personal connexion with Rochester is still obscure, though his poetry makes it clear that he was a warm admirer. Two of his works purport to be monologues spoken by Rochester, and his lament for Bion is confessedly an elegy on his friend. An early biographer of Oldham, in the Memoir prefaced to the 1722 edition of his poems, relates the story of how Oldham, an usher at a school at Croydon, first received a visit from Rochester and his associates:

> Here it was he received a Visit from the Earl of *Rochester*, the Earl of *Dorset*, Sir *Charles Sedley*, and other Persons of Distinction, merely upon the Reputation of some of his Verses, which they had seen in Manuscript. His Superior, or Head-Master was not a little surprized at such a Visit, and would have taken the Honour of it to Himself, but was soon convinced that he had neither Wit or Learning enough to make a Party in such Company. We have been told that this Adventure was of some Length, and brought him to the Acquaintance of some other Persons of Note.[1]

It did not bring Oldham any advancement, however. He was always in poor circumstances. When he had taken his degree, he left his home in Northamptonshire, where his father was a dissenting minister, and was forced into schoolmastering. The alternative was to become chaplain in some noble family, a dependent position for which he expressed unreserved contempt in the *Satyr address'd to a Friend*, and he chose instead to accept the place of tutor, first in the family of Sir Edward Thurland, and later with Sir William Hicks. As soon as he had saved a little money, he set up independently as a poet in London, where he attracted Dryden's notice and the patronage of William Pierrepont, the young Earl of Kingston, at whose country house he lived for a brief time, dying there of smallpox at the early age of thirty.

In view of this it is surprising that Oldham's poetry is so free from flattery and hired pamphleteering. He was determined not to sell his talents, and proud enough of his determination to advertise his last work, the *Poems and Translations* of 1683, in these words: 'This at

[1] Oldham, *Works* (1722), vol. i, pp. v, vi.

present is content to come abroad naked, Undedicated, and Un-prefac'd, without one kind Word to shelter it from Censure; and so let the Criticks take it amongst them.' The recurrent theme of Oldham's satire is the importance of independence and the disgrace of sycophancy—a common pose of the satirist, but one that was obviously genuine in a writer whose own position must often have tempted him to prostitute his muse. Rochester could afford to laugh at the City hack—the 'Trader in Wit'—for his own security made it a matter of detached interest to him. But Oldham flaunted his honest poverty and exploited his own position to add strength and sincerity to a commonplace satirical theme. For all Pope's comments to Spence on the Billingsgate quality of Oldham's rage, he could scarcely have been unmoved by a spirit of poetic integrity akin to his own.

The *Satyr address'd to a Friend*, with its vivid picture of the humili-ations of a chaplain's life, concludes with a version of Aesop's fable of the dog and the wolf to underline Oldham's views on inde-pendence. The *Satyr concerning Poetry* is even more relevant, for it presents us with a picture of the professional writer in his day. Its details were often imitated, notably by Prior in *A Satyr upon the Poets*, but in Oldham they have all the freshness of observation of a man involved in what he is describing. The ghost of Spenser comes to grieve over the state of literature. He contrasts the gentleman writer with the man who lives by his pen:

> *Sidly* indeed may be content with Fame,
> Nor care should an ill-judging Audience damn:
> But *Settle*, and the Rest, that write for Pence,
> Whose whole Estate's an ounce, or two of Brains,
> Should a thin House on the third day appear,
> Must starve, or live in Tatters all the year.
> And what can we expect that's brave and great, ⎫
> From a poor needy Wretch, that writes to eat? ⎬
> Who the success of the next Play must wait ⎭
> For Lodging, Food, and Cloaths, and whose chief care
> Is how to spunge for the next Meal, and where?[1]

The apparition looks at the golden age of Greece, when 'poets by

[1] John Oldham, *Poems and Translations* (1683), p. 175.

the State were held in pay', as a contrast to the contemporary
example, which haunted the age and which Dryden in his letter to
Hyde had bitterly recalled—the fate of Samuel Butler:

> On *Butler* who can think without just Rage,
> The Glory, and the Scandal of the Age?
> Fair stood his hopes, when first he came to Town,
> Met every where with welcomes of Renown. . . .
> But what Reward for all had he at last,
> After a Life in dull expectance pass'd?
> The Wretch at summing up his mis-spent days
> Found nothing left, but Poverty, and Praise:
> Of all his Gains by Verse he could not save
> Enough to purchase Flannel, and a Grave:
> Reduc'd to want, he in due time fell sick,
> Was fain to die, and be interr'd on tick:
> And well might bless the Fever that was sent,
> To rid him hence, and his worse Fate prevent.[1]

The age of professional poets was already creating its own myths,
based on fact, and fit, in their eyes, to be used as serious examples of
human vice, folly, and ingratitude. The poverty of great poets is
as constant a theme in the literature of this period as the degradation of hacks like Settle is in its satire. Charles Gildon in *The Laws of
Poetry* (1721), speaking of the fate of professional authors, observes,
'Spencer and Butler starv'd', and forty years later Goldsmith's
Citizen of the World in Letter LXXXIII cites the examples of Spenser,
Dryden, Butler, and Otway.

But in Oldham's satire the mention of Butler has a conventional
as well as a realistic power. Specific example is a familiar device for
rousing rage in satire, and Oldham liked to use contemporary instances to sharpen indignation. This device is not the same as the
illustrative character sketch which Dryden used so often. It is more
immediate and emotional in its effect, the typical weapon of the
ardent satirist to drive home his point more deeply and to afford
momentary relief from the tension of direct attack. Pity as well
as indignation is aroused by it, and the whole range of the subject
is deepened.

[1] John Oldham, *Poems and Translations* (1683), pp. 173–4.

Oldham had found a somewhat similar example in Rochester, which may have influenced him. In *A Letter from Artemisia in the Town to Cloe in the Country* (one of the two poems of Rochester's which we possess in Oldham's transcript), the character of Corinna is thus described, before and after her downfall:

> Gay were the hours, and wing'd with joy they flew,
> When first the Town her early Beauties knew:
> Courted, admir'd, and lov'd, with Presents fed;
> Youth in her Looks, and Pleasure in her Bed:
> 'Till Fate, or her ill Angel, thought it fit
> To make her doat upon a man of Wit:
> Who found 'twas dull to love above a day
> Made his ill-natur'd jeast, and went away.
> Now scorn'd of all, forsaken and opprest,
> She's a *Memento-Mori* to the rest;
> Diseas'd, decay'd, to take up half a Crown
> Must Mortgage her Long Scarf, and Manto Gown;
> Poor Creature, who unheard of, as a Flie,
> In some dark hole must all the Winter lye;
> And want, and dirt, endure a whole half year,
> That, for one month, she Tawdry may appear.
>
> (ll. 193–208.)[1]

Just rage is not involved here. Corinna takes her revenge by capturing a foolish country gentleman, and no pity is shown for her victim, who is written off as one of 'those kind-keeping Fools' nature provides 'to patch up Vices, Men of Wit wear out'. Rochester is far from indignant at the characters in this sordid little social comedy; he makes his ill-natured jest and goes away, so that there is no hint of moral disapprobation about it. And yet the old device of comparing the past with the present cannot help reminding us of the grave theme of the vanity of human wishes; it brings genuine seriousness even for a moment into the poem. 'Look here upon this picture and on this', the satirist seems to say, displaying briefly the buoyant hopes of the beginning, and then, in ruthless detail, the horrors of the end.

To look for a particular source for this habit of contrasting the changes of fortune would be idle. The greatest example is Juvenal's

[1] Rochester, *Poems*, op. cit., p. 85.

tenth Satire, but sermons and satires through the centuries had employed it, and narrative poems and tragedies. Pope was to make even more effective use of the device, choosing, like Oldham, a precise contemporary example to illustrate a general theme, where in the past conventional types might have been used to support traditional authoritative ideas. In contrast to Atticus and Sporus, satiric character sketches, the one restrained, the other vituperative, in the style of Dryden, are his pictures of Philip, Duke of Wharton in the first *Moral Essay*, and of the second Duke of Buckingham (Dryden's Zimri) in the third. Both are moral *exempla* appealing to the pity of the reader as well as to his censure; in the case of Wharton particularly, Pope arouses a more reasoned if more restrained compassion than the moral indignation Oldham feels for Butler's fate. From Rochester Pope learned the art of selecting vivid detail to imprint a situation clearly on the reader's mind, but in his description of Buckingham's death he inverts the usual sequence of events to stress the elegiac note in this favourite moral and satiric device. The squalor of the 'worst inn's worst room' comes first, and then, in the antithesis of that enormous but perfectly constructed sentence of which the whole passage consists, he turns back to the reflected glory of the past,

> —— alas! how chang'd from him,
> That life of pleasure, and that soul of whim!
> Gallant and gay, in Cliveden's proud alcove,
> The bow'r of wanton Shrewsbury and love;
>
> (*Moral Essay* III, ll. 305–8.)

Pope brought to perfection the art of mingling together in varying proportions, according to the subject or tone of his satire, contemporary realism like Rochester's, Juvenalian indignation like Oldham's, and the elegiac note of Virgil's *quantum mutatus ab illo*. The elegiac mood, as we have seen, is never far away from Augustan satire; it is one of the characteristics of the Honest Muse. Donne, Jonson, and Hall have scarcely any of it, but those brief reminders in Oldham and Rochester were enough to teach Pope how subtly and movingly it could be used to deepen the range and complicate the wit of satire.

One of the most profound and lasting influences on Pope was the whole attitude that Oldham and Rochester professed towards poetry. They both looked back to classical satirists for their example. Horace, Persius, and Juvenal had all written about themselves as poets, their hatred of the versifiers of their age and their distaste for the general literary situation. The theme recommended itself naturally to Restoration writers; the new growth of poetic journalism, the new academic interest in criticism, the inevitable self-consciousness of poets in approaching their craft, encouraged them to take Latin satire as a model. Oldham's apology for the violence of his *Satyrs upon the Jesuits* is an imitation of Persius' prologue to his satires. The tone, however, is just as close to Persius' first Satire, where he explains his anger against bad poetry and debased literary values. Much of the violence of Oldham's attacks on bad poetry (in works like the *Letter from the Country to a Friend in Town, Upon a Printer*, or the *Satyr concerning Poetry*) depends on the same source, and on the opening of Juvenal's first Satire. Both Persius and Juvenal felt that something harsher than Horace's fine raillery was needed to expose the vices of their degenerate age. Persius himself obliquely criticized Horace in this description of his ironic style:

> Unlike in method, with conceal'd design,
> Did crafty *Horace* his low Numbers joyn:
> And, with a sly insinuating Grace,
> Laugh'd at his Friend, and look'd him in the Face:
> Wou'd raise a Blush, where secret Vice he found;
> And tickle, while he gently prob'd the Wound.[1]

In contrast to Lucilius' open attacks on vice, Horace practised a timid skill, and surely, says Persius, he can imitate this, even if he has to whisper his satire to the reeds, like Midas' wife. Juvenal, too, refers to Lucilius rather than Horace when he explains how the craze for poetry and the degeneracy of the age have forced him into satire.[2] Beyond a reference to Persius in his Advertisement to the *Satyrs upon the Jesuits*, Oldham makes no suggestion that he was influenced either by him or by Juvenal: he tries hard to give the

---

[1] Persius, *Satire* I, ll. 231–6, Dryden's translation.
[2] Juvenal's first Satire, Dryden's translation, ll. 26–27.

fashionable impression that Horace is his true master. But both Oldham's rage, which Pope found too strong, and the claim he makes in the Prologue to the *Satyrs upon the Jesuits*, are completely Juvenalian:

> Nor needs there *art* or *genius* here to use,
> Where *indignation* can create a *muse* . . .

Like Dryden, Oldham seems to have felt an instinctive sympathy for the satirist whose faults were of the kind that occur when 'poets are by too much force betray'd'.

Rochester's attitude towards the Roman satirists is harder to judge because the canon of his work is so uncertain.[1] The poem known as *Rochester's Farewell*[2] is written in the saturnine Juvenalian manner, while the *Satyr* beginning 'Must I with Patience ever silent sit'[3] is a sketch of an imitation of Juvenal's first Satire. Yet most of the time he was consciously affecting the Horatian attitude, not only in his *Allusion to Horace* but also in *Timon*, a version of Boileau's imitation of Horace's Satire I, 9, and in the conversational idiom of *Artemisia*. In spite of his familiar and lively interpretation of the 'slip-shod muse', however, Rochester falls into a defensive attitude when he tries to exploit his own personality, a manner of deliberately cynical Machiavellian indifference to the world's opinion, which is scarcely Horatian in its aggressive confidence:

> But I who am of sprightly Vigour full,
> Look on Mankind, as envious, and dull.
> Born to my self, I like my self alone;
> And must conclude my Judgment good, or, none:
> For cou'd my Sense be naught, how shou'd I know
> Whether another Man's were good or no.
> Thus I resolve of my own Poetry,
> That 'tis the best; and there's a Fame for me,
> If then I'me happy, what does it advance,
> Whether to Merit due, or Arrogance?
>
> (*An Epistolary Essay*, ll. 71–80.)[4]

---

[1] It is a safe guide to assume that only poems included in Tonson's 1691 edition are actually by Rochester.

[2] De Sola Pinto (*Poems of Rochester*, pp. 230–1) attributes to Rochester, but not with certainty.

[3] See H. F. Brooks, 'The Imitation in English Poetry . . .', *R.E.S.*, vol. xxv (1949), pp. 132–4 *et passim*.   [4] Rochester, *Poems*, op. cit., p. 94.

This impudent parodying of serious argument is neither Horatian nor Juvenalian; it is more like the earlier metaphysical conception of wit, and it shows that for all his skill in social commentary or conversational repartee, Rochester himself can hardly be claimed as an Horatian. His strength, like Oldham's, lies in his originality, but it is tinged, too, with a darker colour of rhetoric that recalls Juvenal.

Juvenal had always been a more powerful influence on English poetry than Horace, and it would have been hard for the Restoration satirists to avoid his morose and savage tone. That tone had already entered the tradition, for Donne and Hall both had a blunt Juvenalian strength, and Jonson, the English satirist most admired by the Restoration poets, anticipated them in his critical admiration for Horace and his poetic likeness to Juvenal. Clearly the period from Elizabeth to Anne, in spite of the traditional gloom of the moralists, was not so degenerate as to account for this preference for the Neronian satirists over the Augustan Horace. It seems rather that the earnest and passionate temper of the English poets found a closer counterpart in Juvenal than in his smoother predecessor. And the vigorous vein of popular satire in burlesque and lampoons had strengthened the tendency to roughness and force as opposed to smoothness and restraint, for Restoration satire was close to the vulgar tradition. This and its Juvenalian background of feeling saved it from a pedantic and artificial formality which the critical precepts of the age might well have imposed. But it was this, too, which disgusted Pope. Oldham's Billingsgate and Rochester's faulty numbers were both symptoms of an attitude towards satire which was at once too old-fashioned and too casual to be taken seriously. Not that he misunderstood their purpose or underestimated their vitality, but he felt that they were talented enough to deserve censure for their faults. For Pope was not their direct heir. He had been conditioned by his immediate predecessors, the polite circle of pseudo-classicists, Congreve, Garth, Walsh, and Granville, who had finally established the cult of Horace to which Pope was committed from the start.

Yet Pope's use of Horace, like Oldham's, has always been something of a red herring. Though he followed Rochester in developing an appropriate style of easy familiarity for the Horatian Epistle, the spirit behind his satire was at once more personal, more indignant and passionate than the Latin poet's. In the first Dialogue of the Epilogue to the *Satires*, where he explains in traditional style his reasons for anger, Pope deliberately recalled Dryden's version of Persius' description of Horace[1] by putting it into the mouth of a friend who is advising him to be cautious:

> His sly, polite, insinuating stile
> Could please at Court, and make AUGUSTUS smile:
> An artful Manager, that crept between
> His Friend and Shame, and was a kind of *Screen*.
> (ll. 19–22.)

Pope gives another reason, besides the impossibility of raising a smile in the English Augustus, for suggesting that Horace's method is inadequate to the situation. In a note to the last line he glances lightly at its wider application—'a metaphor peculiarly appropriated to a certain person in power'. So he identifies Horace's caution with Walpole's, whose cunning moderation in shielding Stanhope and Sunderland on the matter of the South Sea Bubble, in which they were deeply implicated, had earned him the nickname of the Screen-Master General. Neither Horace nor Walpole is dignified by the comparison.

By these oblique means Pope indicated his dissatisfaction with mere urbanity. In the *Epistle to Arbuthnot* he found it impossible to avoid alluding to Persius' and Juvenal's first Satires, already so widely imitated, but he did his best to disguise the references. Codrus, who sits unconcerned amidst the peals of laughter at his folly, is referred in a note to a source in Horace's third Ode, though in this context one inevitably recalls his appearance in Juvenal's first Satire. But if Pope did not wish to return to the open Juvenalian vigour of Oldham, he was not blind to other aspects of the earlier poet's work which might be adapted more easily to his own purposes. Nor were those aspects entirely separate from the influence of Juvenal, for they appeared in passages which show Oldham's deep concern for his art in an uneasy and unworthy age—one of Juvenal's own favourite themes.

---

[1] See supra, p. 95.

Pope possessed a copy of Oldham's poems and marked out those works he thought most striking.[1] These, surprisingly, do not include the most influential on the subject of poetry in general and satire in particular: the *Letter from the Country to a Friend in Town*, and *Upon a Printer*. In the second, Oldham had lashed out at a pirate of his work in the same spirit which provoked Pope to write 'A knave's a knave to me in ev'ry state'. But Oldham made no pretence at a moral motive. He readily admits his personal resentment; he is willing to confide that the real inspiration of his satire lies in the need to vent his spleen:

> But I, whom spleen, and manly rage inspire,
> Brook no affront, at each offence take fire:
> Born to chastise the Vices of the Age
> Which pulpits dare not, nor the very Stage:
> Sworn to lash Knaves of all degrees, and spare
> None of the mind, however great they are:
> *Satyr*'s my only province, and delight,
> For whose dear sake alone I've vow'd to write:
> For this I seek occasions, court Abuse,
> To shew my Parts, and signalize my Muse . . . .[2]

This is more Juvenalian than Horatian, yet it is most like Pope.

The narrow line separating talent from genius divides Oldham's lines:

> Born to chastise the Vices of the Age
> Which pulpits dare not, nor the very Stage

from Pope's:

> Yes, I am proud; I must be proud to see
> Men not afraid of God, afraid of me:
> Safe from the Bar, the Pulpit, and the Throne,
> Yet touch'd and sham'd by *Ridicule* alone.

(Second Dialogue of the Epilogue to the *Satires*, ll. 208–11.)

Though we may enjoy Oldham's swaggering candour, there is a clumsiness in his self-advertisement compared with Pope's more subtle and powerful characterization of his role. Here are two pictures of the honest poet—the one, like Juvenal, driven to rage by

---

[1] See H. F. Brooks, 'Bibliography of John Oldham', *Proc. Oxford Bibliographical Society*, Vol. 5, Part I (1936), pp. 28–29.

[2] Oldham, *Some New Pieces* (1681), p. 131.

the crimes of society, yet with a rough pleasure in his self-appointed task; the other, like Horace, aloof from the vices of the age, but supported by an epic poet's pride in his exemplary work, and profoundly aware of the elevated duty of his art. Pope's lines lead on easily to the next:

> O sacred Weapon! left for Truth's defence,
> Sole Dread of Folly, Vice and Insolence!
> Rev'rent I touch thee; but with honest zeal!
> To rowze the Watchmen of the Publick Weal.
>
> (ll. 212–15.)

The honest poet is no longer a figure of irreverent frankness; he is playing a heroic role; he is above a mere indulgence in rage for its own sake, for he is dedicated to truth. Yet essentially the same spirit as Oldham's lies behind Pope's satire—the delight in exercising his peculiar talents, and the need to find a subject on which to spend his passion. Pope's sincerity may be raised to a public and general level, but it is always intensely personal. He devised a style which brought his whole personality into play, so that the verses tingle with the nervous excitement of his own temperament even when they are proclaiming universal sentiments.

There are occasions in Oldham's poems when his devotion to his art reaches an intimacy to which Pope responded. On the whole he is content to assume the role of the anonymous poet, the spokesman for honesty, unconcerned with personal details, but sometimes the stamp of genuine experience appears, as in the description in the *Letter from the Country to a Friend in Town* of his returning confidence in his work and his struggles at composition:

> 'Tis endless, Sir, to tell the many Ways
> Wherein my poor deluded self I please . . .
> When at first search I traverse o're my mind,
> None, but a dark, and empty Void I find:
> Some little Hints, at length like Sparks, break thence,
> And glimm'ring Thoughts, just dawning into Sense:
> Confus'd a while, the mixt Ideas lie,
> With nought, of Mark, to be discover'd by,
> Like Colours, undistinguish'd in the Night,
> Till the dusk-Images, mov'd to the Light,

Teach the discerning Faculty to chuse,
Which it had best adopt, and which refuse . . .
Meanwhile, with inward Joy, I proud am grown,
To see my Work successfully go on;
And prize my self, in a Creating-Power,
That could make something, what was nought before.[1]

This is a familiar account of the working of the creative imagination, but it is made fresh by being described as a personal experience. The intimacy does not go deep, but it moves Oldham to some
exact and delicately illuminating metaphors, and it gives him an
occasion for describing his 'inward joy' in composing. And it is
near to those passages in Pope's later poetry where his devotion to
his work reveals itself in a flash of unexpected poignancy. The old
image of the muse as the mistress had been given a new significance. Like an intrigue, the art of writing involved desire, pursuit,
attainment, with all the accompanying emotions of excitement,
pleasure, satisfaction, and the frequent tedium which an ines-
capable passion imposes. 'This vile and wicked lust of poetry' was
denounced and cherished like an actual infatuation by many of the
better poets of the age, and it gave particular intensity to their observations on the art, as when Pope writes like a lover, fearful of
parting:

This subtle Thief of Life, this paltry Time,
What will it leave me, if it snatch my Rhime?
If ev'ry Wheel of that unweary'd Mill
That turn'd ten thousand Verses, now stands still.
                    (*Imitations of Horace*, Ep. 2. 2, ll. 76–79.)

Oldham's address to his muse is no less sincere and personal, and
the final Horatian lines of this passage from the *Letter from the
Country to a Friend in Town* were imitated by Pope himself:[2]

What was't, I rashly vow'd? shall ever I
Quit my beloved Mistress, Poetry?
Thou sweet beguiler of my lonely hours,
Which thus glide unperceiv'd with silent course:
Thou gentle Spell, which undisturb'd do'st keep

---

[1] *Some New Pieces*, pp. 126–7.
[2] See Pope, *Imitations of Horace*, Satire I, ll. 97–100.

My Breast, and charm intruding care asleep:
They say, thou'rt poor, and unendow'd, what tho?
For thee I this vain, worthless world forego:
Let Wealth and Honor be for Fortunes slaves,
The Alms of Fools, the prize of crafty Knaves:
To me thou art, what ere th'ambitious crave,
And all that greedy Misers want, or have:
In Youth, or Age, in Travel, or at Home,
Here, or in Town, at *London*, or at *Rome*,
Rich, or a Beggar, free, or in the Fleet,
Where ere my fate is, 'tis my fate to write.[1]

Here was a tone, both valuable and important, which Dryden could not command. Dryden's pleasure in composition reveals itself in the pace and energy of his verse, but he allowed himself personal comment only in his letters and occasional criticism. Oldham makes it a part of the texture of his poetry: the old convention of the satirist speaking in his own person is extended to the poet speaking about his most intimate concern—poetry, and, since the tone of the poem (either direct or epistolary satire) is usually personal and lively, the result is informal, fluent, and often even emotional. It suggests the presence of a personality behind the verse. Oldham's attempts at this were much simpler and clumsier than Pope's, but Pope was to be its supreme master, and no one blended again so perfectly magniloquent public exhortation with the quicksilver moods of the individual mind.

Neither of the satires in which Oldham expressed his views on poetry was a true imitation, but the tradition of writing about poetry, either in precept, as in the *Ars Poetica*, or personally and apologetically as in satire, came from the Latin poets. It was as an imitator in the widest sense that Pope admired and copied Oldham. He observed very carefully the way in which imitation had chastened and dignified Oldham's violent style, and how it had deepened his range. The imitation, as Oldham conceived it, allowed as much contemporary reference as the poet chose, so long as the work retained the authority of tradition. In other words, the topical vigour characteristic of contemporary satire was held in

---

[1] *Some New Pieces*, pp. 128–9.

check by continual allusion to another poet's work, of which the general moral reflections were allowed to remain unchanged. The imitator's skill was to relate particular circumstances to the general theme of a work. In the *Imitation of Boileau's 8th Satire*, Oldham, for instance, keeps close to the original outline—an attack on man the reasoning animal (already taken by Boileau from Montaigne)—but he draws his examples from the religious controversies, the new science, and the political issues of his day in England. If animals are wiser than men it is because they do not waste time in dispute:

> Who ever saw *Church* and *Fanatick* Bear,
> Like savage Mankind, one another tear? . . .
> Or when was't heard upon the *Libian* Plains,
> Where the stern Monarch of the Desert reigns,
> That *Whig* and *Tory* Lions in wild jars
> Madly engag'd for choice of Shrieves and May'rs?[1]

Animals do not engage in fruitless speculations, nor like the virtuosi 'teach deep mysteries Of Arts for pumping Air, and smothering Flies'. They know nothing of local tyrannies, like the recent Royal attack on the rights of city boroughs:

> They fear no dreadful *Quo Warranto* Writ,
> To shake their ancient privilege and right . . . .[2]

But Oldham never confined himself to contemporary instances. In the same poem his attack on the respect paid to wealth rouses him to a powerful vein of moral generalization and some savage sarcasm:

> He, *that is rich, is everything, that is,*
> *Without one grain of Wisdom, he is Wise,*
> *And knowing naught, knows all the Sciences:*
> *He's witty, gallant, virtuous, generous, stout,*
> *Well-born, well-bred, well-shap'd, well drest, what not?*
> *Lov'd by the Great, and courted by the Fair,*
> *For none that e're had Riches, found despair* . . .[3]

Johnson could have borne out these commonplaces from his later experience; the life of a professional writer from Oldham's time to

<hr>

[1] *Poems and Translations* (1683), pp. 10–11.
[2] Ibid., p. 11.   [3] Ibid., p. 16.

his was, indeed, peculiarly fitted to demonstrate this truth. But Pope, while he might admire the well-adjusted tone of these lines, could not have imitated them with integrity. He had never been poor enough to justify this; besides, in his role as moral author it must never be suggested that he envied wealth. He turned the same idea a different way, then, with a more subdued irony in his first *Moral Essay*, where he comments on the respect paid to high society:

> 'Tis from high Life high Characters are drawn;
> A Saint in Crape is twice a Saint in Lawn . . .
> Wise, if a Minister; but, if a King,
> More wise, more learn'd, more just, more ev'rything.
>
> (*Moral Essay* I, ll. 87–88, 91–92.)

Almost always in his extensive use of Oldham Pope toned down the vigorous forthright manner he had condemned in his conversations with Spence, but he kept the personal accent. He combined Oldham's shrewd observation and sharp reflection with a more elevated strain of generalized eloquence, and he retained the feeling of the poet's personality intruding into the verse, but transformed it into a more self-conscious and dignified device. Above all, he recognized in Oldham's work a useful new approach to the main problem of the satirist—how to remain independent and yet concerned with the life of his time. Oldham had made the imitation a formal excuse for satire which was free of the stigma of party journalism. It was a most important development. A poet could now mix realistic material with sincere commentary, and use the traditional, truculent, honest tone of the satirist in a work which was neither ephemeral nor partisan. Thus a convention which might seem to restrict the poet in fact increased his range of freedom and independence. While he relied on the support of his original, he was free to build a new structure on these foundations: he could illustrate with topical material and argue traditional truths in his own personal way.

It has often been said that the Augustans enjoyed the skill and ingenuity of giving a contemporary turn to the classics, and that they were writing for an audience who appreciated this exhibition of

wit and light learning. But there was a deeper reason for the popularity of the form, certainly with such a poet as Pope. It had refined
the older convention of the burlesque or travesty, and above all had
shown how satire could be made respectable and independent at
a time when it was in danger of losing moral authority through
its connexion with contemporary issues. And all this had been
achieved without any loss of either vitality or relevance. Yet such
a form could have developed only at a time when a wide variety of
satire was being practised, when the appetite for realism had provoked a complementary need for the restraint of authority and convention, and when circumstances forced the poet to be freshly
aware of his position and integrity. The influence of the ancients,
together with the pressing sense of immediate events and opinions,
found a varied and novel expression in the imitation as Rochester
and Oldham used it. In Pope's hands it became yet more serious and
subtle. Basically satirical, the imitation could also include personal
reflection, elegiac sentiment, informal compliment, and a vivid
commentary on the ways of the world. Augustan poetry, in every
convention, was trying to combine a clear and just picture of life
with the poet's sincere reflections on it.

V

SOME COMMON ATTITUDES
IN RESTORATION POETRY

I. *Town and Country*

SOCIAL poetry seldom seems original, if only because poets of the same group enjoy repeating the same themes in a similar tone. It is at once competitive and communal. The most marked instance of such a group in England is the circle of Court wits at the Restoration, whose poetry displays a characteristic common blend of insolence, wit, harshness, and elegance. The manners and code of a small aristocratic circle which was deliberately scandalous in its thought and behaviour became, under their influence, the fashionable ideal for anyone with pretensions to wit or gentility. Their code is most consistently recognizable in their attitude to love, the favourite pastime of the Court. For the wits love is essentially an appetite, the satisfaction of which more often evokes tedium than tenderness, and the pursuit of which produces the intellectual delights of intrigue, argument, and persuasion, combined with the uneasy pleasures of desire. Descriptions of love's enjoyment in their work are often brutal and obscene. Discussions of its intricacies exhibit a curious interweaving of smooth metaphysical playfulness and hard satiric realism.

An occasional flash of the old traditions of love poetry occurs in their verses, as in Rochester's lines 'An age in her embraces past, Would seem a winter's day', but there is nothing lyrical in the wits' attitude to love itself. Here they are almost entirely sceptical, their irony extending to the poet himself in his role of lover:

> Love a Woman! you're an Ass,
> 'Tis a most insipid Passion;
> To chuse out for your happiness
> The sillest part of God's Creation.[1]

[1] Rochester, *Poems*, op. cit., p. 25.

The object of this absurd, degrading, and irrational impulse inevitably attracts even fiercer criticism. She is abused for her coldness, mocked for her modesty, scorned for her dissipation, or limed like a bird with the impudent dialectic the wits loved to practise—the rhetoric of persuasion. Answering his mistress's complaints that she will not risk love, since men are always faithless, Etherege neatly retorts:

> It were a madness to deny
> To live because we're sure to die.

(*To a Lady, Asking Him How Long He Would Love Her*, ll. 17–18.)[1]

These light exhibitions of intellectual skill are only possible because the mistress is always treated as object and never as subject, and because it is essential to the convention that her coldness or modesty should be taken as a mere disguise which it is the function of the poet to expose. Thus it would seem at first that the witty lyricist is the extreme opposite of the honest satirist: his tone is patently insincere; he is playing an elaborate game of bluff. When Dorimant dismisses Belinda after he has seduced her in Etherege's *Man of Mode*, he whispers 'Everlasting love go along with thee', but neither he, nor she, nor the audience, would dream of supposing that he means what he says. In an earlier scene we have watched him casting off a previous mistress; in a later he proposes marriage to yet a third and is accepted. The phrase is a mere tag from the high-flown style of lovers' compliment, the language of heroic tragedy, that ideal and courtly counterpart to real and courtly cynicism. Yet in spite of this, the Court wit does profess a sort of sceptical honesty, and thus he is not, after all, entirely opposed to the realistic satirist. This, he says, is what love is like. Since the passion is unreasonable and transient, honesty demands that it should be regarded as an appetite and used as such, and politeness requires that it should be pursued with all the wit, polish, and vivacity that can give rational satisfaction.

There are no heroines in the poems of the wits, only beauties, young or ageing, natural or artificial. Sometimes they appear as Arcadian shepherdesses, sometimes as town coquettes, according to

---

[1] Sir George Etherege, *Poems*, ed. J. Thorpe (Princeton, 1963), p. 2.

whether the poem is lyrical or satiric, but they never bear any resemblance to the goddesses of the Petrarchan convention. New standards had gradually taken the place of the old. Women were occasionally allowed to make a suitable retort, as in D'Avenant's song in *The Unfortunate Lovers* (pb. 1643; acted 1638), an early work in which already the familiar figure of the deceived girl is being replaced by the new woman who is well able to take care of herself:

> Love's weather in maids should seldom hold fair:
>   Like April's mine shall quickly alter,
> I'll give him tonight a lock of my hair
>   To whom, next day I'll send a halter.
>
> I cannot abide these malapert males
>   Pirates of love, who know no duty:
> Yet love with a storm can take down their sails
>   And they must strike to adm'ral Beauty.[1]

There is often little sentiment in either type of woman in Restoration poetry. The forsaken girl is more rueful than pathetic as the poet examines her case in cool reflective tones:

> Farwell ungratefull Traytor,
>   Farwell my perjur'd Swain,
> Let never injur'd Creature
>   Believe a Man again.
> The Pleasure of Possessing
> Surpasses all Expressing,
> But 'tis too short a Blessing,
>   And Love too long a Pain.[2]

The spirited mistress talks with a kind of swagger which still sounds hoydenish in spite of its self-conscious rationalism:

> A CURSE upon that faithless Maid,
> Who first her Sex's Liberty betray'd;
> Born free as Man to Love and Range,
> Till nobler Nature did to Custom change,
> Custom, that dull excuse for Fools,
> Who think all Virtue to consist in Rules.[3]

[1] D'Avenant: *Dramatic Works*, ed. J. Maidment and W. Logan, vol. iii (1873), p. 88.
[2] Dryden, Song from *The Spanish Fryar* (1680), ll. 1–8.
[3] Aphra Behn: *Works*, ed. M. Summers, vol. iii (1915), p. 396.

This attitude has been judged in many different ways. It has been condemned as vile, and interpreted as a rationalization of the war of the sexes, and a manifestation of a new spirit of experiment in matters of conduct. None of these opinions explains entirely its attraction or its limitation. One critic has called the song from Dryden's *Spanish Fryar* 'music-hall sentiment',[1] and with justice, but behind this use of trite commonplaces, slickly versified, lies the same assumption that inspired the more serious poetry of the age—that what has been generally experienced and admitted is the proper subject of realistic literature. The poetry of statement, even though the statement is cheapened and vulgarized, is the characteristic of the popular song, and these poems are popular songs for society which appeal by their neat expression of the commonplace and by their stylishness. They are essentially fashionable, and, like all fashionable things, they play upon certain fundamental if not very worthy sentiments—admiration of youth, success, and riches.

To find our admiration, even our envy, of these qualities mirrored clearly in poems or plays is to be drawn into a charmed circle where such desirable attributes seem eternally within reach. If the convention persuades us of a world where they are possible and actual it has succeeded, but at best the conviction can only be a fleeting one and must therefore be sustained by extreme artifice of plot, or of rhetoric. Such works cannot afford to entertain the even more commonplace truth that youth is temporary and the majority of people neither rich nor successful, or, if they do, like *The Rape of the Lock*, they move immediately into a different range of experience and of art whose limits are neither so rigid nor so flattering to the reader. The conventional pose of the Court wits could not exist in the same form in literature for very long. It depended on the kind of freedom and security that wealth, rank, and success alone could give. Cits and men of the town might try to imitate Buckingham, Sedley, and Rochester, but they could scarcely hope to succeed as spectacularly. In its narrow exclusiveness their attitude carried the seeds of its own decadence.

In so far as this attitude was the product of a new society and a new mood, however, it diffused a wide general influence. Poets

[1] L. C. Knights, *Explorations* (1946), p. 149.

could scarcely help being affected by it, and Pope himself drew upon it, especially in his early work. Yet he was careful to use it in a new way in his satires on women and society, taking over its brilliant observations but rejecting or transforming its restricting limitations. But the convention did not need a great poet to expose its weaknesses. The very public who admired it supplemented it with more familiar material. Like Don Pedro, it was too fine for everyday wear. Traditional ballads, popular songs of a different kind, like D'Avenant's 'My Lodging is on the Cold Ground', simple 'natural' love lyrics translated from Latin or French, were as popular as the old-fashioned Elizabethan and Cavalier lyrics still being published in the miscellanies. By the end of the century a change in taste had set in. The collapse of the dramatists before Jeremy Collier's attack on the immorality of the stage suggests that audiences were growing tired of the stylishness as well as the grossness of the comedies they had flocked to see. At the beginning of the eighteenth century the hard and inflexible spirit of the wits was uncongenial even in satire. There remained of the old convention only the verbal polish, the witty game of antithesis in the love lyric, where one could juggle with youth and age, enjoyment and frustration, pursuit and fatigue, and these had been modified by a gentler mood of tolerance. In Prior's lyrics sentiment suffuses the older attitudes and softens them: his women are frail and faithful, vain but tender.

But it was impossible to ignore what the harsher realism of the older attitude had exposed. The follies and affectations of women and the competitive game of love in society remained conventions of satirical literature. Any new account of women's charms or merits must take account of the ironic contempt of the wits. At the end of the Restoration period there were still innumerable pictures of the beauty trying to escape the years, the beauty at her dressing table or with her lovers. Few of them are as witty as the attacks of Dorset or Rochester, but many are almost as abusive as Oldham's *Satyr upon a Woman, Who by her Falshood and Scorn was the Death of my Friend*.[1] The rough lampoons on Charles II's least popular mistresses, the Duchess of Cleveland and the Duchess of Portsmouth,

[1] J. Oldham, *Satyrs upon the Jesuits* (1681), pp. 145–54.

gave contemporary point and impetus to this kind of satire. Besides, the subject was a useful occasion for detailed description, which the passion for verisimilitude in verse encouraged, and the favourite scene of the mysteries of the toilet neatly, if rather obviously, under-lined a popular topic—the difference between the true and the false appearance. In *The Playhouse, A Satyr* by T.G., gent., the anony-mous poet lingers lovingly over his picture of the actress making herself up into what she is not:

> His Royal Consort next consults her Glass,
> And out of twenty *Boxes* culls a *Face*.
> The Whit'ning first her Ghastly Looks besmears,
> All Pale and Wan th'unfinished Form appears;
> *Till* on her Cheeks the blushing Purple glows,
> And a false *Virgin Modesty* bestows;
> Her ruddy Lips the Deep Vermilion dyes;
> Length to her Brows the Pencil's touch supplies,
> And with black bending Arches shades her Eyes.[1]

Pope's Belinda at her toilet is the heiress of a whole race of such dubious charmers, from this playhouse girl to Halifax's Mopsa arranging her face for an evening's triumph,[2] and one critic has already suggested that Swift in his savage treatment of these themes was drawing on a well-established tradition.[3] But Belinda seems to belong to a different world. For she is a heroine, conceived as a compliment, and a figure in a great poem, so that the dimen-sions in which she moves are more subtle than any imagined by the lesser followers of a blatant and forthright convention. What Pope made of that convention is important enough to be explored more fully in the study of his own work, but it cannot be fully realized without some idea of this background. He recognized the realism and the rigid exactness of the Restoration attack on women and love, and he saw the attraction of the witty society from which it grew. But it was too cramped and simplified for his purpose. What

---

[1] *P.O.A.S.*, vol. ii (1716), p. 376.

[2] Halifax, *To the Countess Dowager of* ——, *The Minor Poets*, vol. i (1751), p. 118. See also *infra*, p. 169 and the Appendix, in which this poem and Dorset's *On the Countess of Dorchester* are printed in full.

[3] I. Ehrenpreis, *The Personality of Jonathan Swift* (1958), pp. 43–49.

he took from it he set in a wider context, so that it appears in its proper proportions against a more traditional and a more complex vision.

A kind of restricted honesty and sincerity belongs to this attitude, in its narrowly accurate observation and its open flouting of traditions and customs which were out of sympathy with the new spirit of society. This very flouting could become an affectation when it was based on nothing more than a fashionable rebelliousness, but more far-reaching effects were brought about by the genuine changes that had begun to take place in ways of thinking about society and environment. Fashionable society in the Restoration was, as it has always been since, urban society centred in London. Town life and all it entailed of the experience of political affairs, literary cliques, business, and social pleasure acquired a character of its own which was at once polite and deeply engaged in the issues of the time. It has been a critical commonplace for centuries to recognize that Augustan literature is mainly town literature. The attitude of the wits was uncompromisingly that of town men. The country is rarely mentioned in their poetry. It merely provides a useful antithesis to the town, or a sketchy background for the popular epistolary form—letters from a poet in the town to a friend in the country, or vice versa. In the comedies of the time the country is invariably referred to as a wild hinterland beyond the reach of civilization, where everything is damp, melancholy, barbarous, and old-fashioned. It is peopled by ridiculous country squires, leftovers from the Elizabethan age, bumpkins who can scarcely speak a recognizable language. Satire directed against them is rougher and more confident than the exposures of the folly of fops, which, after all, was only an excessive and unsuccessful parody of ideal fashionable standards, and, as such, a lapse of taste in degree rather than in kind.

This approach was inevitably limited and unhelpful for a serious poet, especially since older attitudes to the country lingered on in literature, complicating the whole issue. Even the wits accepted the prettiness of the pastoral convention, turning it into artificial settings for love songs, and alluding through it to their polite knowledge of the classics. But neither this, nor the thin trickle of topographical poems copied from *Cooper's Hill*[1] are such an immediate reflection of the prevailing mood as was the Horatian ideal of the country as a place of healthy retreat, an ideal setting for the temperate, wholesome, and thoughtful life.

Marvell himself, after the Restoration, ceased to write as he had done about nature. What had disappeared was the old Renaissance world of myth and philosophy which lay behind *The Faerie Queene* or *Comus*, in which nature's extravagant beauty and abundance could represent God's handiwork, innocent and good as it was his creation, marred and depraved by man's fall, and yet still the great glass in which the poet's thoughts, moods, and emotions could find their counterparts. The Nature of the seventeenth-century poets, the divine hieroglyph, was too closely associated with intricate metaphysical and occult speculations to hold further attractions for men who believed with Bacon that the external world should be studied and observed, not mythically or emblematically interpreted. But no age has ever been able to neglect nature in its poetry. It remains always the chief source of imagery, of simple moral ideas and of general emotions.

Restoration poets found other sources of rural poetry than those of Elizabethan or seventeenth-century writers. Satire, so often obsessed by the active life of town or Court, needed a contrasting ideal of retreat. Horace retired from Rome to his Sabine farm; Juvenal shows his Thales, in the third Satire, leaving the capital for the innocence of the country. A purely pastoral picture of happy idleness was too near that paradisal vision which haunted Renaissance minds to be tolerable to a more worldly society, but the tastes and aspirations of the new poets were pleased by the Georgic view of the country as a place of happy and healthful employment, near to the simplicity of primitive life, uncorrupted but industrious. As the period advanced, and with it the habit of imitating Latin poetry, these two views, the Horatian and the Georgic, were more consciously and academically cultivated. The country becomes progressively more ideal and classical. The emotions connected with it become

---

[1] Some of these, like Cotton's *Wonders of the Peak*, were mainly descriptive: others, as their titles suggest, were more ambitious attempts at the descriptive historical vista poem, e.g. Manning's *Greenwich Hill* (*P.O.A.S.*, vol. iv (1707), pp. 410–22).

more pronounced and stylized. Something of the same process can be seen in town poetry. The Restoration poet appears to be in the thick of town life, scarcely pausing for description, but only for brief details and allusions (as in Dryden's prologues and epilogues); but the later Augustans are careful to identify and picture the town, standing back and observing its details with as much pleasure as earlier writers had felt in re-creating the country. Swift's town eclogues and Gay's *Trivia* are the characteristic works of poets who, at the end of a long tradition, can playfully invert the common convention by treating town life in the Georgic style as wittily as others had exposed country boredom in terms of urban satire.

But Restoration poets were freshly aware of country life in its Horatian guise (one which, of course, had already been used, especially by Jonson and his followers), because what they were doing, though in an obvious sense traditional, was yet new. Their vision of rural retreats where country gentlemen led a robust and responsible life was not entirely taken from the classics, nor much dependent on native traditions. It grew out of their town satires, their sense of the defects as well as the attractions of urban life, and the moral assumptions that lay behind these. It related too, much more closely than ever before, to actual political and social circumstances. The countryman they described was not an idealized shepherd, or an honest rustic of the type that was to become so popular later in the eighteenth century. He was the landowner, the gentleman who played his own part in the State. On the one hand he is seen in the tradition of the wits as like Sir Tunbelly Clumsy, the boorish country gentleman; on the other, in serious poetry, he is exemplified by someone like Dryden's 'honoured kinsman' John Dryden of Chesterton in the county of Huntingdon, a Justice of the Peace, a local lord, benevolently ruling his own community, a hunter and a husbandman who represents all the sober virtues of the good life. Dryden was not alone in painting him. His rival Shadwell, in the play *Epsom Wells* (1673), composed a song that celebrates the same sort of existence. Like Dryden, Shadwell recognizes its Horatian colour, but the terse realism of his account is far removed from any artificial ideal. He briefly rejects the commotion of the town:

> Oh, how I abhor
> The tumult and smoak of the Town,
> The Clamours of War,
> The glittering Court, the fraudulent Gown,
> The Suburb debauches,
> The Cheats of the City,
> The rattling of Coaches,
> And the noise of the men they call witty.

In direct contrast comes his account of the virtuous countryman:

> But give me the man from all vanity free,
> With good store of Land,
> And a Country Command,
> Who honest dares be.
> Who Justice dares do, and the Nation will serve,
> And ne'ere from his true Country principles swerve.
>
> Give me the good man that lives on his own grounds,
> And within his own bounds
> Has room for his Hawks and his Hounds.
> Can feast his own Tenants with Fowls and with Fishes,
> And from his own plenty with good store of Dishes,
> And not with damn'd Wine, but with good *English* Ale
> O'er their faithful hearts can prevail,
> And nothing to others does owe.
> But from his own house hears his own Oxen low,
> And his own Sheep bleat,
> While the grateful sound sweet Echoes repeat.
> This, this is the man that is truly called great.[1]

This, too, is the man that is truly called honest. So far we have only seen the forthright poet appearing in that role. Statesmen praised by their protégés sometimes achieved the honour, but never the City money-grubbers, the Court sycophants, the literary time-servers, and the whole race of satirized town-dwellers. Almost every period since the Middle Ages has chosen the country as the setting for its favourite virtues—innocence, joy in life, profusion, and, in later periods, freedom and imaginative sympathy. The Restoration saw it as the home of honesty.

[1] Shadwell: *Works*, ed. M. Summers, vol. ii (1927), pp. 139–40.

What relation to reality did this picture bear, or the contrasting one of the caricatured boobies of comedy? The question can properly be asked of literature which claims such close relationship to life. The answer in this instance justifies the claim. Of no other convention is this so true. Shepherds have seldom been so innocent and love-absorbed as pastoral pretends, and certainly never so talented. It is absurd even to look at pastoral in these terms unless, like Johnson, we want to make pastoral itself look absurd. But the strength of all the best Augustan conventions derives from their peculiar new ties with reality. Country gentlemen in the late seventeenth century were not at all unlike either of these two pictures, and it would be hard to tell how much of characters like Sir Roger de Coverley and Squire Western was drawn from this very convention of depicting the old-fashioned, unpolished, honest country gentleman, and how much from actual observation.

Macaulay has brilliantly epitomized the paradoxical mingling of clownishness and nobility in characters of this kind at the time:

Unlettered as he was and unpolished, he was still in some most important points a gentleman. He was a member of a proud and powerful aristocracy, and was distinguished by many both of the good and of the bad qualities which belong to aristocrats. His family pride was beyond that of a Talbot or a Howard. He knew the genealogies and coats of arms of all his neighbours, and could tell which of them was so unfortunate as to be a great grandson of aldermen. He was a magistrate, and, as such, administered . . . justice, which, in spite of innumerable blunders, and of occasional acts of tyranny, was yet better than no justice at all. He was an officer of the trainbands; and his military dignity, though it might move the mirth of gallants who had served a campaign in Flanders, raised his character in his own eyes and in the eyes of his neighbours. Nor indeed was his soldiership justly a subject of derision. In every county there were elderly gentlemen who had seen service which was no child's play. . . .

Thus the character of the English esquire of the seventeenth century was compounded of two elements which we are not accustomed to find united. His ignorance and uncouthness, his low tastes and gross phrases, would, in our time, be considered as indicating a nature and a breeding thoroughly plebeian. Yet he was essentially a patrician, and had, in large measure, both the virtues and the vices which flourish among men set from their birth in high place, and accustomed to authority, to observance, and to self-respect.[1]

In case we should be tempted to the easy conclusion that the importance of honesty in Augustan literature is simply another instance of the tradesman's morality of the new middle class, we ought to pay particular attention to this aspect of it. Shadwell's honest countryman, like Dryden's honoured kinsman, is one of Macaulay's esquires, even though Shadwell himself was a Whig and a City supporter. He is a master of tenants, a lord of the manor, with his own independence, and independence was a prerequisite of honesty as the Augustan understood the word. The possession of land is one of the most obvious forms of independence, more valuable possibly than the possession of great inherited wealth, since it carries with it immediate duties and responsibilities. The country gentlemen made up an aristocracy of their own—traditional and patrician, yet distinct from that of the peerage:

The Commons were the *communitas communitatum*, originally, a quasi-federation of shires and boroughs; the knights of the shire in the eighteenth century were the consuls of the county republics . . . the distinguishing characteristics of the country gentlemen were as a rule neither political acumen and experience nor Parliamentary eloquence, but an independent character and station in life, and indifference to office.[2]

Honesty could clearly be attributed to the ideal type of this character, and honesty was a virtue not in any obvious sense restricted to one class at a time when the whole pattern of social and political life was more intricate and yet more coherent than any arbitrary divisions would suggest. But if it was not an attribute of any one section of society, it reflected the new concerns of them all. Thomas Carte the historian revealed the most crucial of these concerns in a letter he wrote to Swift, complaining that no valuable history of England had as yet been written, because of neglect of those documents which reflected the most important aspect of the country's development—its civil life.[3] Of this life, honesty was the

---

[1] Lord Macaulay, *History of England*, vol. i (1849), pp. 321–3.

[2] Sir L. Namier, *The Structure of Politics at the Accession of George III*, 2nd ed. (1957), pp. 5–6.

[3] Nichols, *Literary Anecdotes of the Eighteenth Century*, vol. ii (1812), pp. 477–8, note.

pre-eminent virtue. Honour had been the ideal of a chivalric military society; honesty epitomized all that was best in a world where peace and prosperity in a well-ordered state was the common aim.

In literature, however, no convention can reflect simply the background of its own age when other traditions from other periods have contributed to it. The pastoral world with its image of innocence and ease still haunted men's imaginations. Pepys, a true townsman, who had once entertained some ladies by discoursing 'in defence of the city against the country or court'[1] (*Diary*, 14 June 1664), was delighted on his trip to Epsom at the simplicity of the patriarchal shepherd he met there; but his satisfaction at the idea of inheriting his father's country property at Brampton—'Altogether [it] is very pretty; and I bless God that I am like to have such a pretty place to retire to'[2] (*Diary*, 9 October 1667)—belonged to a more realistic and a stronger convention—the Horatian. The country gentleman of the Restoration saw himself through the glass of Horace. He was a Roman figure, *integer vitae, scelerisque purus*, happy with his few paternal acres, his health, and his usefulness. The convention was inevitably challenged and debated, especially in satire, while the argument Pepys had entertained between the respective merits of town and country was continued in poems praising each, or in actual verse dialogues. In these Horace is often cited in support of the country life. Its healthful delights are seen as typical of his ideal of temperance, moderate activity, and intelligent occupations:

> Once how I doated on this Jilting Town,
> Thinking no Heaven was out of *London* known;
> Till I her Beauties artificial found,
> Her Pleasure's but a short and giddy Round;
>
> .   .   .   .   .
>
> Quite surfeited with Joy, I now retreat ⎫
> To the fresh Air, a homely Country Seat; ⎬
> Good Hours, Books, harmless Sports and wholesom Meat. ⎭
> (*The Town Life*, ll. 1–4; 9–11.)[3]

---

[1] S. Pepys *Diary*, ed. H. B. Wheatley, vol. iv (1894), p. 160.
[2] Ibid., vol. vii (1896), p. 140.
[3] *P.O.A.S.*, vol. i (1716), Part I, p. 190.

Sometimes the poet ventures no further into the country than to one of the fashionable spas, which, in their way, were as polite as the town itself. Rochester had satirized Tunbridge Wells, but one of the works in *Poems On Affairs of State*, purporting to be written by Mr. Causton, Merchant, presents it as an ideal blending of social pleasure and healthy country air. It recommends, as suitable holiday reading in this resort, the inevitable Horace:

> Are you dispos'd to read a Poet? then
> Our old Acquaintance *Horace* is the Man,
> He'll please, which way so'er your humour lean.
> (*Tunbridgialia or The Pleasures of Tunbridge*, ll. 236–8.)[1]

Pope himself was ideally fitted by the circumstances in which he lived to make use of both these conventions. He spent half the year at his parents' home at Binfield in Windsor Forest, and the other with his friends in town, so that in his early life he played out the contrasting roles of countryman and townsman. In the first part of his career his poetry moved between the two extremes of solitude and social intercourse, and it bears many of the marks of this literary tradition, which by the time he was writing was so completely established that a poet could use it as he pleased. Like Gay, he could parody the pastoral and make both the form and the country itself seem a little ridiculous, though still charming, in the mingling of rude rustic detail and affected literary sentiment. Or, like Brown and Ward, he might describe visits to barbarous country villages for purely comic effect; or, like the anonymous author of *The Grove: Or, the Rival Muses*,[2] he could contrast the virtues and vices of urban and rural life.

The Grove, first published in 1701, is a curious and interesting poem, which takes the form of a debate between a love-sick poet, Theron, who has retired to the country to heal a broken heart, and his town friend Cycnus, who tries to coax him back to society. Theron begins the debate by a traditional contrast between the corruption of the town and the innocence of the country. Cycnus

---

[1] Ibid., Part II, p. 208.

[2] *P.O.A.S.*, vol. iv (1707), pp. 348–65. H. Macdonald comments that *The Grove* 'appears to have been written by John Froud'; see his *John Dryden, a Bibliography* (1939), p. 300.

paints the delights of the town. Theron replies with a glowing tribute to nature, and Cycnus responds with a vigorous passage in which he describes the low dissipation of country feasts—a Breughel-like picture, far removed from the harmless and idyllic festivities of Herrick's rural poems. He adds to this a description of a country landowner who certainly never appears in the world of benevolent Horatian squires. Miserliness is scarcely a peculiarly rustic vice, but its meanness is emphasized by a setting of sinister desolation and a decaying country mansion. Pope remembered this passage when he described Cotta, his contrast to that bounteous countryman the Man of Ross, in *Moral Essay* III; this passage from *The Grove* had already established the essential details:

> Here in an old thatch'd House by Tempests torn,
> By all but him, and Owls, and Bats forlorn,
> There lives a Wight, run mad for love of Gold,
> (They call him *Colon*) wretched, rich, and old.
> No Spouse, no Off-spring ever grac'd his Bed;
> Too rough to Love, too covetous to Wed:
> No menial Servants round his Table wait,
> No croud of Beggars throng his silent Gate,
> Alas! the Wretch himself scarce dares to eat.
>
> (ll. 269–77.)[1]

Theron retorts with an account of the literary disgraces of the town, jibing at Grub Street hacks like Tom Brown or Ned Ward, and recalling that eternal figure of scorn, Elkanah Settle. Compliments are paid, however, to the patrons of the new age, particularly Dorset (once Lord Buckhurst, of the inner circle of the Restoration wits), and Halifax. The poem concludes with a characteristically ironic trick. Cycnus produces his final ace by telling Theron that his mistress is not, after all, false, and Theron, overjoyed at the news and quickly forgetting the joys of the country, rushes back to town in ecstasy.

Almost all the conventional attitudes we have touched on so far are brought together in *The Grove*: the coldness of the coquette and the falseness of fashionable love; the honesty and innocence of the country and, by contrast, its boorishness; and finally, the

---

[1] *P.O.A.S.*, vol. iv (1707), p. 355.

contemporary state of poetry. A decade later, when Pope began his literary career, they were so well established that their influence was unavoidable, and he drew on them as often as on the greater traditions of English poetry. Pope was not alone in this. We have already mentioned Swift's satiric verses against women, and their debt to the wits' tradition of anti-female insult, but Swift also found it useful to adapt other conventions of this school of satire that suited his deeper feelings as well as his spleen. His poetry is deliberately unprofessional (the poetry he wrote after his early clumsy Pindarics, that is), and his impromptu rhymes, his carefully contrived anti-poetic burlesque, his idiom, spare where so many of the works in the genres he appears to be imitating are elaborate, are informal and casual to an extent which seems to cast doubt on the whole serious art of verse-making. It is this which prevents us from considering him in detail as representative of the main tradition of Augustan poetry, and which, perhaps, has inhibited his most friendly critics from doing more than noting the importance of his verse, and the neglect into which it has fallen. Nevertheless, many of Swift's poems fall into some of the well-defined conventions we have already traced. *A Description of Morning* (1709) and *A Description of A City Shower* (1710), both contributed to the *Tatler*, in their careful enumeration of factual detail mingled with the controlled tone of parody, illustrate that consciousness of traditional form, and the desire to be realistic under the ironic guise of using it, which is best exemplified in the delicate parody of Gay, and which, as we shall see, could only be perfectly achieved after a long-established practice of classical imitation and the vogue for carefully defined genres. Each is a town eclogue, using the careful and affectionately familiar tone of country poetry for the contrary purpose of making real and recognizable that town life and atmosphere which had so often been repudiated as corrupt and uncongenial. But the tone of precise honesty enables Swift to be at once humorous, ironic, and exact about detail, with a concentrated factual realism which conveys by implication a positive pleasure in observing those phenomena which were usually generalized for attack under the common heading of the tumult and noise of the town.

It has perhaps less frequently been noticed that Swift's irony is equally humorous and unsavage in those poems on women which owe much to the Restoration convention, but which do not serve his occasions of anger and disgust at the physical reality in contrast to the poetic ideal. *Cadenus and Vanessa*, characteristically puzzling and oblique in its apparent frankness and its deliberate flouting of the reader's curiosity, shows Swift using the convention to convey his own mixed feelings of embarrassment and gratification at Vanessa's infatuation for him. He succeeds in admitting his own mortification and condemning its sources as trivial and malicious, by putting the strictures he feared others might make into the mouths of the tattlers of the town—those familiar fops and women of fashion who earlier in the poem have called Vanessa mad for being more interested in Montaigne than in the latest millinery or gossip. He is, too, actually aware of their likely response to the situation:

> So tender of the Young and Fair?
> It shew'd a true Paternal Care—
> Five thousand Guineas in her Purse?
> The Doctor might have fancy'd worse.
>
> (ll. 652–5.)[1]

Similarly his answer to Vanessa, his offer of friendship, provokes in her a reply singularly appropriate to his own abhorrence of cant and high-flown protestations in poetry or in love. Vanessa speaks frankly and claims that he has taught her plain speech for plain truth:

> The Nymph in sober Words intreats
> A Truce with all sublime Conceits.
> For why such Raptures, Flights, and Fancies,
> To her, who durst not read Romances;
>
> In lofty Style to make Replies,
> Which he had taught her to despise.
>
> (ll. 792–7.)[2]

The situation is typical of Swift's irony. Each expected objection is met with an equally unexpected response: the love-sick girl

---

[1] *Swift's Poems*, ed. Harold Williams, vol. ii (1958), p. 707.
[2] Ibid., p. 711.

becomes a rational exponent of honesty; the rational Dean an
awkward and disingenuous sophist. The dilemma is left unsolved:

> But what Success *Vanessa* met,
> Is to the World a Secret yet . . .
>
> (ll. 818–19.)[1]

It is not only a love of bafflement but a genuine humorous capacity
for seeing situations and arguments in reverse which makes this
poem characteristic of the great ironist of *Gulliver's Travels*. But it is
important to notice, too, that the convention which could be used
more crudely for surprise effects in a poem like *The Grove: Or, the Rival
Muses* was capable of as subtle and complicated handling as this.

Swift, also, could speak plainly in open and unironic compliment
to a woman, unlike his predecessors in the Restoration tradition.
The obverse of their bitter satire was the idealization of the rhapsodic love poem, or the elaborate Pindaric eulogy. To both of these
Swift was sworn enemy. He shares with Pope a determination to
tell the truth, but, unlike Pope, he wants to show that this can be
done by paring down the elements of the craft, or consciously
laughing at them. His birthday poems to Stella make great play
with the poetic pains he endures every year to produce them for the
occasion, but the whole intention is to insist that true honesty and
simplicity need no complications of device in the style. He uses
metaphor only to emphasize imperfection; Stella's appearance is
'An Angel's Face, a little crack't'; and he praises sparingly, if not
grudgingly, by the standards that he is attacking. Yet when the
true compliment comes it is written with a genuine passion which
derives partly from his disgust at the false standards on which most
women are judged. Those very ideals of youth, beauty, and success
which Pope was to find so inadequate in the tradition of the wits are
openly attacked by Swift:

> Then Cloe, still go on to prate
> Of thirty six, and thirty eight;
> Pursue thy Trade of Scandall picking,
> Thy Hints that Stella is no Chickin,
> Your Innuendo's when you tell us

---

[1] *Swift's Poems*, vol. ii, p. 712.

That Stella loves to talk with Fellows
But let me warn thee to believe
A Truth for which thy Soul should grieve,
That, should you live to see the Day
When Stella's Locks must all be grey
When Age must print a furrow'd Trace
On ev'ry Feature of her Face;
Though you and all your senceless Tribe
Could Art or Time or Nature bribe
To make you look like Beauty's Queen
And hold for ever at fifteen.
No Bloom of Youth can ever blind
The Cracks and Wrinckles of your Mind,
All Men of Sense will pass your Dore
And crowd to Stella's at fourscore.

(ll. 39–58.)[1]

The very rigidity of the convention bred its own refutation; we shall see that Pope, even more subtly than Swift, elaborated an answer in terms of sense and time to the simple unidealistic standards of the Restoration wits of the Court and the town.

Swift has no poems in praise of the country life; his exile to Ireland weighed too heavily on him, and besides, he had no taste for canting conventions that seemed to him, as much as to Johnson, to bear no relation to real experience. Some of his ephemeral poems give a genuine impression of eighteenth-century local life, however, and he chooses for them a deliberately casual metre, as in *The Description of an Irish Feast*, which uses all the conventional attributes of coarse country jollity, but in such a style and idiom that they take on a new vividness:

O there is the Sport,
    We rise with the Light,
In disorderly Sort,
    From snoring all Night.
O how was I trick't,
    My Pipe it was broke,
My Pocket was pick't,
    I lost my new Cloak.   (ll. 13–20.)[2]

---

[1] *Swift's Poems*, vol. ii, p. 735.   [2] Ibid., vol. i, p. 245.

It is well known that Addison persuaded him to elaborate *The Story of Baucis and Philemon* and that 'in a poem of not two hundred lines Mr. *Addison* made him blot out fourscore, add fourscore, and alter fourscore'.[1] Addison saw the work as an accomplished and ironic Ovidian parody, but in Swift's first version the bucolic pair have a rough simplicity which directs the reader's attention to the true humorous point of the poem—the metamorphosis of their humble environment to an ostentatious church and of Philemon himself to a smug parson. Swift is again using the convention for his own humorous purposes of reversal, but in the process he succeeds in striking a note of greater simplicity and realism than any of his contemporaries. Even the good wife's kitchen in Dryden's version of the *Nun's Priest's Tale* is not so vivid as the hovel in which this country pair live and the fare they offer their unrecognized guests:

> And then the hospitable Sire
> Bade Goody Baucis mend the Fire
> Whilst he from out the Chimny took
> A Flitch of Bacon off the Hook,
> And freely from the fattest Side
> Cutt off large Slices to be fry'd;
> Which tosst up in a Pan with Batter,
> And serv'd up in an earthen Platter;
> Quoth Baucis, this is wholsom Fare,
> Eat, Honest Friends, and never spare. . . .
>
> (ll. 55–64.)[2]

This simplicity has all the independence which the role of Parson lacks. Philemon transformed 'Carry'd it to his Equalls high'r, But most obsequious to the Squire'. In the second and more elaborate version the old couple are finally metamorphosed into yews, but the greater sophistication of form does not suit Swift's genius so well as this plain and pointed spareness.

Swift's refusal to present himself as a serious poet should not prevent us from seeing how well he could use the traditions and conventions that were to hand for his own deflating purposes. His use of them reminds us, too, how these very conventions had grown out of a movement towards greater realism and honesty and a

---

[1] Delany, *Observations* (1754), p. 19.   [2] *Swift's Poems*, vol. i, p. 91.

repudiation of the ideals which the hyperboles of panegyric had for so long represented.

II. *Ancients and Moderns*

One of the most serious and far-reaching changes in attitude that took place in the Restoration and early eighteenth century, and which is reflected in various ways in poetry, was the view of truth and reason which gradually emerged from the long battle of the ancients and the moderns. It was not in any sense predominantly a literary quarrel; politics, religion, and thought in general were all affected by it, and its influence in the writing of the time was so complicated and extensive that only certain aspects of it are relevant to our subject or can be treated here. But in order to understand these, some account must be given of the progress of the argument, particularly in its effect on literature.

The battle of the ancients and the moderns directly affected literary satire only at the moment of the attack of the Christ Church wits on Bentley for his proof of the spuriousness of the Phalaris epistles. Once this had happened, however, many of the most important figures in Augustan literature were drawn in. Swift was the cousin of Sir William Temple, whose essay *On Ancient and Modern Learning*, a modest contribution to the general dispute, had been the immediate occasion of this particular skirmish, and Francis Atterbury, who was the real author of Charles Boyle's attack on Bentley, was shortly to become an intimate friend of Swift and Pope and a powerful influence on the latter's satiric career. The role of these men can only be seen and understood in the perspective of an earlier stage of the dispute, which centred on the conflict of Aristotelian philosophy and experimental science. This argument had already spread to those religious and political questions which were the vital subject-matter of Restoration satire. A purely academic dispute might have served as a source of private jokes and references (as indeed this one did), but it could scarcely have left its mark on the tone of literature and thought in general unless it had touched on much broader topics.

It was from Christ Church that the attack on Bentley originally came, and we can follow the course of the debate in the fortunes of that college, for they reflect in little many of its wider concerns. In the Commonwealth the college had been invaded by Presbyterian and Independent divines, who proposed in *A Modell for a Colledge Reformation*[1] that the Dean and Canons should be turned out and the Students set to work on such useful subjects as geography, optics, mechanics, and anatomy. As a result, the college, after the Restoration, kept up a consistent policy of disapproval of modern studies, under the leadership of its formidable Dean, Dr. John Fell.[2]

Christ Church was not alone in its suspicions. Though the Royal Society had to all intents and purposes started at Wadham College, where Boyle had carried out much of his most important work, the University was hostile and suspicious, afraid that Gresham College was setting up as a rival institution and intended to confer its own degrees. Many looked on the experimentalists themselves as upstarts, combining the worst follies of occultism with a new blasphemy—the confident appeal to human reason alone. At the best they were ridiculed as eccentrics. Pepys tells us that even the King, the official founder of the Society, joined in the general jesting: 'Gresham College he mightily laughed at, for spending time only in weighing of ayre, and doing nothing else since they sat' (*Diary*, 1 February 1663–4).[3] At the worst they were attacked as dangerous madmen. Dr. South, in an address to the University in 1669, is said to have sneered at them in a phrase which set the tone for all subsequent ridicule: 'Mirantur nihil, nisi pulices, pediculos et seipsos.'[4] The futility of their speculations was also a *folie de grandeur* of the mind; they were the victims of pride and false reason.

The University's ridicule echoes a serious fear. The King's patronage of the Royal Society did not prevent critics from suspecting it of covert treason through its spirit of innovation.

[1] See R. F. Jones, 'The Attack on Science', in *Pope and His Contemporaries: Essays Presented to George Sherburn* (1949), p. 101.
[2] Wood's *Life and Times*, ed. A. Clark, vol. iii (1894), p. 56. Describing the opening of the Ashmolean Museum, Wood writes of the exhibits, 'many that are delighted with the new philosophy are taken with them, but some, for the old, look upon them as baubles. Ch. Ch. men not there.'
[3] S. Pepys *Diary*, vol. iv (1894), pp. 28–29.
[4] Isaac D'Israeli, *Quarrels of Authors* (1814), vol. ii, p. 21. D'Israeli gives no reference for this phrase of South's and I have been unable to find any direct source for it.

Nonconformists had notoriously encouraged modern studies during the Commonwealth, and this inevitably left its stigma.[1] In the confusion of the times the new learning was indiscriminately associated with atheism, Catholicism, radical democracy, and despotism. Its utilitarianism, its appeal to reason alone, and its optimistic view of progress were a challenge to much that was affirmed by tradition and had been publicly reaffirmed by the Restoration.

In 1684 Christ Church was again involved in a political matter which had its bearing on the dispute when the Dean, at the instigation, it is said, of the King, deprived John Locke of his Studentship. Locke had aroused suspicions while he was up by his interest in modern studies (Wood recalls him as 'a turbulent spirit, clamorous and never contented', who at a meeting of a chemical society he had joined scorned to take notes like the rest);[2] he was also tainted with Whiggism, and escaped to Holland with Shaftesbury, to whom he acted as secretary after the Popish Plot. In Oxford at least the moderns were growing to be looked on as Whig in politics and atheists or dissenters in religion, while the supporters of the old learning were as inevitably associated with tradition, monarchy, the Establishment, and gentility.

This clear-cut distinction was by no means so evident in the larger world outside. There men as cultivated as Evelyn, as indispensable to the Government as Pepys, as well-connected as Boyle, and as celebrated as Wren and Dryden were proud to be members of the Royal Society, while the most popular satire against the virtuosi came from the pen of the Whig dramatist Shadwell, in his comedy of that name. Suspicion takes many forms, and the confusion of attacks on the Royal Society is proof of the distrust with which men looked at the new approach to learning. Henry Stubbe, for instance, accused the Society of plotting to restore popery to England, and in *Campanella Revived, or an Enquiry into the History of the Royal Society* (1670) he declared it to be founded on the principles of Campanella, who had advocated uniformity of religion and politics to leave men free for scientific and philosophical speculation. Such a danger was very real to the men of the Restoration when memo-

---

[1] See M. K. Starkman, *Swift's Satire on Learning* (Princeton, 1950), p. 10.
[2] Wood's *Life and Times*, vol. i (1891), p. 472.

ries of the Protectorate were so fresh and fears of Catholic France so strong. There was in any case a common tendency to associate Catholicism with Dissent as both extremist and dangerous to constituted authority.

It may seem strange that this complicated situation was resolved by ridicule and compromise rather than by open war, but the dispute between the old and the new learning took the same course as the religious and political quarrels of the day. The latter terminated not in civil war but in the Revolution Settlement, and the former spent itself in journalistic skirmishings in which neither side emerged victorious until the eighteenth century brought a truce. For one thing, it was impossible to distinguish clearly enough between the affiliations of the various combatants to make an absolutely safe concerted attack on all fronts. Dean Sprat, for instance, the historian of the Royal Society, was an eminent churchman, later to become Bishop of Rochester. He had turned his coat at the Restoration, but his violent opponent Stubbe could scarcely criticize him on this score, since he himself had been a protégé of Sir Henry Vane's, and could only excuse his apparent support for the Commonwealth by pleading loyalty to his patron rather than political conviction. Too many men on each side were tarred with the same brush for one to accuse the other confidently, and it was natural that, in time, the safer device of ridicule and satire should replace the double-edged weapon of political blame.

The English fear of absolute authority did not give rise to any alternative despotism, but rather to that spirit of general tolerance and compromise of which Locke's works were the reasoned expression and the moderate Revolution Settlement the first practical example. In literature, the individual scepticism of the satirists reflects the same tendency, and it was this spirit that allowed the ancients the freedom to attack, but gave the moderns the same liberty to pursue their own ends. The principle of honesty, 'giving to every man his due', to some extent operates here. The realism of the satirists perhaps owed something to the habit of close observation which the new philosophy required, but even more to that spirit of scepticism it was said to encourage. The new tone of poetry was that of writers free to speak for themselves, but, lacking the detachment of the experimentalist, they found themselves often out of sympathy with the aims of the weighers of air and the dissecters of animals. It was not yet clear how the experimenters were contributing to the immediate business of living, and though intellectual curiosity might be pleased by their activities, common sense and moral instinct condemned them as frivolous or inhuman. For the most part, to Restoration and Augustan writers, they are figures of fun. Though Dryden, with his lively curiosity, admired any advance in knowledge, Rochester, combining gentlemanly indifference with a destructive pessimism, saw the operations of the 'new' reason as, in their own way, as futile as Aristotelianism. In his *Satyr Against Mankind* he distinguishes, like Boileau, between right and wrong reason, and the scientific intelligence which operates on a purely intellectual level is contrasted with the self-preserving instinct that tells a man how to live and how to enjoy life:

> My Reason is my *Friend*, yours is a *Cheat*,
> Hunger call's out, my Reason bids me eat;
> Perversely yours, your Appetite does mock,
> This asks for Food, that answers what's a Clock?
>
> (ll. 106–9.)[1]

To this extent, then, the new poetry drew strength from some of the same attitudes of mind as the new philosophy, but there was no similarity in their aims.

The controversy over the Phalaris letters was the last appearance of Christ Church in this long battle, and it was also the point at which polite literary society became actively engaged. So far the disputes between Rapin and Fontenelle in France on the nature of pastoral had been the only important literary branch of the ancients and moderns argument; Rapin's *Dissertatio de Carmine Pastorali* (1659) having been translated by Creech in 1684, and Fontenelle's *Discours sur la nature de l'églogue* appearing in 1688.[2] In 1690 Sir William Temple's essay *On Ancient and Modern Learning* epitomized in much more general and wide-ranging terms the larger implications of the debate. In it Temple made a connexion between the new

---

[1] Rochester, op. cit., p. 121.
[2] For details of this literary dispute see J. E. Congleton, *Theories of Pastoral Poetry in England, 1684–1798* (1952).

movement and the recent troubles in a tone of implied moral criticism which extended the literary argument to philosophic and ethical issues. As Temple saw it, when men lost their faith in the wisdom of tried experience they lost their sense of proportion with it, and, in his *Essay on Poetry*, Temple observes that the society of his day is suffering from this disruption:

There are no where so many Disputers upon Religion, so many Reasoners upon Government, so many Refiners in Politicks, so many Curious Inquisitives, so many Porers upon Books, nor Plodders after Wealth. And yet no where more Abandoned Libertines, more refined Luxurists, Extravagant Debauches, Conceited Gallants, more Dabblers in Poetry as well as Politicks, in Philosophy, and in Chemistry.[1]

This elegant jeremiad has a familiar ring, with its age-old complaint against irresponsibility, the love of novelty, and human folly. But it was particularly directed against the new spirit of experiment he attacks in the essay *On Ancient and Modern Learning*, the restless, inquiring, sceptical attitude from which much contemporary literature also derived. Serious writers had already shown themselves aware of the problem of mingling this new attitude with a respect for the ancients, for traditional forms and ideas in literature, but Temple, making out his case for the superiority of the classics, implies that the task is wellnigh impossible because of the fundamental folly of the modern mind. Imitation of the ancients and satire against the present are all that appear to be left to the poet who accepts this attitude.

Temple's approach, however, helped to provide a starting-point for new, conservative literary principles, and an impetus for specifically moral satire, of the kind that is curiously lacking in Restoration verse. It is remarkable that in the 1690s, and for a short time until the appearance of Addison, Swift, and Pope, poetry was largely concerned with imitation, and even more with translation from the ancients, as if the robust vitality of previous satire had now begun to look dangerous and characteristic of the triviality of a 'modern' approach. Since the Revolution more circumspect poets turned

---

[1] Sir W. Temple, *Essay on Poetry*, ed. J. E. Spingarn (1909), p. 76.

their attention away from political life, and the effect of the European dispute on the merits of the ancients and the moderns had been to convince them that if they could not match the greatest poets of the past, at least they must show recognition of their superiority by copying them. There was very little in the work of the next two decades, except the popular satires and anonymous broadsides, to maintain the Restoration standards of 'honest' poetry, though, as we shall see, a notion of sincerity, closely related to honesty, began to show itself gradually in the work of the new respectable amateurs.

Temple was not so much open to attack on the grounds of his complaint against the moderns, as on a simple error of fact in his praise of the ancients. He took the Phalaris epistles, which he gave as an example of classical superiority, to be genuine. Here, unfortunately, his reliance on tradition led him astray. Macaulay in his essay on Temple makes great play with the fact that he could not even read Greek, but had he been able to he would certainly never have discovered what only Bentley's scholarly methods could arrive at—proof of the spuriousness of the letters. Bentley's proof came to be associated almost accidentally with Temple's essay. A moderate and well-reasoned answer to that essay had come from William Wotton, chaplain to the Earl of Nottingham and a Fellow of the Royal Society, in 1694, in his *Reflections Upon Ancient and Modern Learning*. In the meantime Charles Boyle of Christ Church had begun an edition of the Phalaris epistles on the request of Dean Aldrich, Fell's successor after the flight of Massey, Roman Catholic Dean under James II, and in the process Boyle came across Bentley, then King's Librarian. Boyle accused Bentley of having behaved obstructively to the amanuensis who was collating the manuscripts for him, and the hot-tempered scholar was goaded into a reply which took the form of a complete proof of the spuriousness of the epistles under sixteen different headings. This proof was appended to the 1697 edition of Wotton's *Reflections*, although Bentley made it clear to Wotton that he was not personally concerned in the dispute between the ancients and the moderns, and was only anxious to make good use of both branches of learning. In the circumstances, however, it was impossible for him to avoid being drawn into the whole debate. His temerity aroused a violent response from Christ Church; an obscure pedant had taken issue with a favoured and noble pupil, which in itself seemed to be evidence of the proud assertiveness of the upstart modernists. That Bentley was a classical scholar whose whole life was devoted to the literature of the past mattered little. He was an authority upon the ancients, but not on tradition, and his method of approaching his material, like the scientists', struck at the roots of the old way of learning. He came to it with complete impartiality, concerned only with fact and reason, and unmoved by the glow of traditional veneration surrounding it.

The reply from Christ Church came in the form of a pamphlet, *Dr. Bentley's Dissertations on the Epistles of Phalaris examin'd* (1698), which was attributed to Boyle, but was, in fact, largely the work of his more accomplished tutor, Atterbury. Boyle's early letters to Atterbury show him to have been attracted by the new philosophy —at least the new moral philosophy. On 15 November 1690 he wrote an account of his studies to his tutor, saying: 'I have just made an end of Locke: I was all along extremely pleased with him. I think there is a great deal of very good sense in him; and I believe a great part of it is his own: besides, his language is sound, proper, and pure; and his instances so familiar, that anyone may understand him.'[1] Here, then, we find a young man, from the same college, not ten years after Locke had been deprived of his Studentship, telling his sympathetic tutor, without a qualm, how convincing a philosopher he finds him. His enthusiasm for Descartes was even greater; he produced an entirely proper, unoriginal but up-to-the-minute appreciation of this modern philosopher for his tutor:

Descartes has much outdone his predecessors; and besides, throughout his Principles, there is thought and connexion; for, if I am not mistaken, he seldom says anything that may not be deduced from something that went before: he loves to give an account of all particulars that he can tolerably bring in; and we are only sorry that he has given an account of no more, for now we can only say that he has laid a good foundation for a very substantial building. In short, I take him to be a very great man, a sound naturalist, and a good

[1] F. Atterbury, *Epistolary Correspondence*, ed. J. Nichols, vol. ii (1783), p. 2.

mathematician; what he says is not only generally new, and his own, but more intelligible and more satisfactory, than all that stuff the silly world had so long been contented with. And it is indeed to me an argument of his merit, that he has been able, among the most sensible men, to make so great a progress through the innumerable companies of Aristotelians, that with their sympathies and antipathies had blocked up the way for so many ages together. These are most of the reflections I have made upon Descartes at present. . . .[1]

The wits who replied to Bentley were, then, by no means Aristotelians. Atterbury himself, that argumentative divine, who later became Bishop of Rochester and was exiled for his Jacobite plotting in 1722, was a man most characteristic of the new age. His interests were not in the dispute between the ancients and the moderns at all. Like most other educated men he had wholly accepted the new. But his sympathy did not extend to the scientific method as a whole, particularly when it touched on literature, or the *status quo* in society. A learned man, he was impatient of pedants, and looked forward himself to taking an active place in the world. While he was still a Student of Christ Church his ambitions were directed to a wider future, and when his father was alarmed at the idea of his leaving the academic life and severing his fortunate connexion with Boyle, Atterbury wrote to him:

—My pupil, I never had a thought of parting with, till I left Oxford. I wish I could part with him to-morrow on that score; for I am perfectly wearied with this nauseous circle of small affairs, that can now neither divert nor instruct me. I was made, I am sure, for another scene, and another sort of conversation; though it has been my hard luck to be pinned down to this. I have thought and thought again, Sir, and for some years: now I have never been able to think otherwise, than that I am losing time every minute I stay here. The only benefit I ever propose to myself by the place is studying; and that I am not able to compass. Mr. Boyle takes up half my time, and I grudge it him not; for he is a fine gentleman; and while I am with him I will do what I can to make him a man: college and university business take up a great deal more; and I am forced to be useful to the Dean in a thousand particulars; so that I have very little time.[2]

---

[1] Atterbury, op. cit., vol. ii, pp. 8–9.
[2] Ibid., vol. i (1783), pp. 9–10.

This letter makes it very clear why Atterbury was such a congenial friend to Pope, Bolingbroke, and Swift. His impatience with the pettiness of academic life and his confidence that the greater world is the best place for a man to act in were typical of the attitude poets and writers had generally adopted since Dryden. Even the neat distinction Atterbury makes between the 'fine gentleman', his pupil, and the 'man' he will make of him if he can is a remarkable instance of how instinctively he shared the new attitude towards true worth and merit. He respects Boyle's position, but he is more concerned with the 'honest' task of fitting him to play a reasonable part in active life.

Boyle was clearly nervous of Atterbury's contribution to his pamphlet, for his tutor wrote angrily to him in 1698 after Boyle had sent him back the manuscript of the pamphlet, complaining that the young man had always been unwilling to take his advice, and that 'In laying the design of the book, in writing above half of it, in reviewing a good part of the rest, in transcribing the whole, and attending the press, half a year of my life went away'.[1] The work, however, was an immediate success, though it made no attempt at a reasoned answer to Bentley's proofs. It was an attack on the scholar himself and all that he stood for, scurrilous and witty, which set the tone for all subsequent contributions to the battle. William King's *Dialogues of the Dead*, for instance, followed this line in 1699, ridiculing the futility of the scientific method. King was one of the first to make an explicit connexion between the new scholarly criticism in literature and the plodding exactitude of the experimenter.

From Shadwell to King one of the favourite devices for ridiculing the virtuosi had been to parody their more detailed and accurate accounts of collections or experiments, a method that could be joined to the favourite literary device of the catalogue. Parodies of Royal Society reports play the game of juxtaposing incongruous items, which is one of the sources of 'the art of sinking' in satire. Against this background, Pope's enumeration in Book IV of *The Dunciad*—'A Nest, a Toad, a Fungus, or a Flow'r' (l. 400)—needs no extra satirical pointing. The catalogue itself would recall

<hr />

[1] Atterbury, op. cit., vol. ii, pp. 21–22.

innumerable other examples of insignificant objects described in earlier satires to prove the futility of the virtuoso's studies.[1]

The frequent use of such catalogues in satire added a new contempt to the objects mentioned in them—shells, insects, specimens of every kind—a scornful emphasis which gave greater point to Pope's love of degrading insect imagery. In the hands of a satirist sympathetic to the new learning, like Marvell, a miscroscopic image could be used with no hint of contempt for the method involved:

> With *Hook* then, through the *miscroscope*, take aim
> Where, like the new *Controller*, all men laugh
> To see a tall Lowse brandish the white Staff.
>
> (*Last Instructions*, ll. 16–18.)

Hook is Marvell's accessory here. His illustration of a louse crawling on a human hair, as magnified under the lens, provides the poet with a grotesque satirical image for Clifford with his white staff of office. But when Pope was writing it was practically impossible to use such imagery without reflecting back scorn on the scientist, and he was well aware of this. Thus he presses home his double attack by pointing the analogy between the critic and the scientist, each blindly peering at the minutiae of his subject:

> The critic Eye, that microscope of Wit,
> Sees hairs and pores, examines bit by bit:
> How parts relate to parts, or they to whole,
> The body's harmony, the beaming soul,
> Are things which Kuster, Burman, Wasse shall see,
> When Man's whole form is obvious to a *Flea*.
>
> (*The Dunciad*, Bk. IV, ll. 233–8.)

Even when science and criticism were not the objects of Pope's attacks, he found the precision which satires on science had given to this degrading imagery useful for expressing his own contempt. Other satirists had been fascinated by the analogy of their victims with 'insects such as these, from filth begun'. Pope followed them in his early imitations of Dorset's lyric on the Countess of

---

[1] Sutherland (*The Dunciad*, Twickenham ed., vol. v (1943), p. 381), refers to *The Virtuoso's Will*, *Tatler*, No. 216, 26 Aug. 1710.

Dorchester, where he exchanged the image of the rotting veal in Dorset's last stanza for one of 'insects fair'—'First Grubs obscene, then wriggling Worms, / Then painted Butterflies' (*Phryne*, ll. 23–24). He returned to these images in his picture of Sporus, 'This painted Child of Dirt that stinks and stings' (*Epistle to Arbuthnot*, l. 310), and Lady Mary—'So morning Insects that in muck begun, / Shine, buzz and fly-blow in the setting sun' (*Moral Essay* II, ll. 27–28). The peculiar accuracy proper to a subject of scientific scrutiny, as well as a more traditional disgust, attaches itself to these minims of nature and helps to give Pope's satire its concentrated point and sharpness.

If the final phase of the battle between the old and the new ways of thought had merely influenced poetry by providing a fresh range of satirical imagery and reference, it would be relatively unimportant to our study. But it had effected more than this. The lively scepticism which, as we have seen, both scientist and 'honest' poet in the Restoration shared to some extent seems by the beginning of the eighteenth century to have died down, giving way on the one hand to the detachment of men of great scientific achievement like Locke or Newton, and on the other to a deeply ingrained distrust of experiment for its own sake and a cautious pessimism, intense in Swift, cultivated and melancholy in Pope. The political settlement, the social prosperity, the general tolerance of the new age gave rise superficially to a prevailing optimism, but every student of the period has noticed the gloomy conservatism of so many of the Augustans—Swift and Johnson in particular. Pope, by nature more sanguine and enthusiastic than either of these, yet reflects the general caution, the mood of reserve and resignation which distinguished the ancient faction from the modern. He accepted Temple's moral conservatism as a form of wisdom—one that seems at first sight to have little in common with the spirit that helped to inspire the ideal of honesty in Restoration verse. Indeed, this ideal had changed inevitably with changing circumstances—but the change was one of emphasis rather than of nature. Honesty remained the independent integrity of a man who has come to terms with the world as he sees and knows it. Some of the trends in poetry which had reflected this were already established conventions by the time the changing emphasis became apparent—detailed realism, for instance, and a flexible mode of address. But with the new atmosphere of acquiescence in the *status quo* which made itself felt in the 1690s, and the new concern for politeness and correctness which we shall examine more closely in the next section, honesty was no longer a question of taking up arms in the struggle of the moment, or of arguing a case in language appropriate to the audience. Coming to terms with the world as he saw it was now not simply a matter of the poet's knowing which side he was on in temporary disputes, for the world itself had changed and had begun to seem more stable and confirmed. Honesty, giving to every man his due while retaining one's individual integrity, had begun to involve the poet's view of human nature as a whole, and his general moral standpoint. The battle between the ancients and the moderns, in science, philosophy, and literature, had been waged from this moral standpoint, and it was scarcely possible to write satire without, in some degree, reflecting its issues.

In Pope's poetry this attitude was closely bound up with one of the most important subjects of the dispute—right and wrong reason. The sin of wrong reason—reason divorced from the wisdom of the past or of personal experience of the present—was pride. And pride is the perfect object of serious satire, at once appalling and ludicrous. Whereas the paradox of the past had been that pride, the root of the deadly sins, was also the great heroic virtue and lay behind so much of what belonged to honour, it had no proper place in this new civil society where independence and integrity could flourish among the retired and the obscure, and an honest man, not a hero, was the noblest work of God. Honesty is not a virtue easily associated with pride, though it may be supported by that proper self-esteem which the Augustans saw as a form of reasonable self-love. Since honesty involves knowing oneself and one's limitations as well as recognizing one's true capacities, nothing is more dishonest than to overestimate the power of pure reason or the importance of the physical world, as the experimental scientist may, or to overvalue one's own work, as the bad poet or hack writer often does, or to assume complete jurisdiction over the tastes and opinions of others, like the critic. This was the attitude Pope learned from friends like Swift and Atterbury, who had played leading roles in the battle of the ancients and the moderns, and from Bolingbroke, whose Epicurean scepticism looked back to Rochester in its recognition of the power of instinct and self-love and the limitations of pure reason.

Swift, in his *Battle of the Books* and *The Tale of a Tub*, had attacked equally Aristotelianism and modernism, ridiculing the speculative philosopher and the virtuoso, the man of letters to whom nothing exists after the ancients, and the modern who knows that he must be the best writer because he is the last. Either extreme fell into the lunacy of pride, by refusing to take into account the facts which can only be learned from an experienced view of both past and present. Pope, who had learned from the art of imitation how to join a classical and a modern inspiration, drew from the moralists his habit of setting individual follies and sins in a context of general and traditional ideals of conduct. But this was not all that the issue of the ancients and the moderns forced on the attention of poets. It had its effect, too, on the prevailing interest in truth as a proper subject for poetry. Was truth simply a matter of impartial observation and careful investigation of fact, as the experimental scientists seemed to suggest? The Restoration wits had seemed to imply this in stripping off the appearances and trappings of the Petrarchan ideal of love; the satirists in exposing vice and folly in poems of such detailed verisimilitude; even the party poets in their efforts to persuade their readers that they were dealing in hard facts. But might not truth also involve ideas and convictions, not susceptible to immediate observation or analysis, but handed down from the past and accepted by men with veneration and respect? This was Temple's attitude, in supporting the ancients against the moderns, and no poet, unless he was prepared entirely to reject the past, could afford utterly to deny it. Even the Restoration writers, modernists though they appeared in spirit, had not broken completely with tradition. Dryden, indeed, had tried to combine both attitudes. His love of modern realism and of the ancients, his pleasure in tracing historically the growth of arts and civilization to their present zenith, and above all, his search for a style at once natural and universal, pointed to his acceptance of both these faces of truth. Pope recognized this comprehensiveness in Dryden and took it to be one of the marks of his greatness. But his own emphasis was on the side of the traditional, the general, and the conservative, more consciously than Dryden's had ever been.

The poets of the early eighteenth century were inevitably affected by the judgements and assumptions that had been made on both sides of this long argument. They never seem quite so open-minded as Dryden, nor, strangely enough, so good-humouredly detached, even though none of them was more closely involved in contemporary affairs than he had been. But Dryden's partisanship was occasional and topical, whereas a more impalpable sense of general commitment pervades their work. They were not primarily supporting a party or a cause, though they might be associated with one. Their real concern, whether they were satirizing learning or fashionable life, was to defend and preserve a whole way of thought and living which they believed to be the best, and which seemed threatened by some of the dangerous tendencies of modernism. These tendencies had emerged in Dryden's lifetime, but they had only become clearly recognizable since his death in the course of that prolonged debate between the old and the new. Pope and his friends were deliberately re-examining their whole philosophy, looking back to the past to justify it, and beginning to state their premises and display a consistent moral and social attitude in their poetry to demonstrate it. Honesty had forced them into this re-assessment. Other conservative attitudes in literature itself encouraged them in this, and none was more important to Pope than the extraordinary little renaissance of academic classicism which took place at the very end of the seventeenth century, and in which he himself was reared.

III. *Classicism and Correctness*

The earliest letter Pope wrote to Wycherley, when he was a boy of sixteen, contained a very proper tribute from the young poet to Dryden: 'I think with you, that whatever lesser Wits have risen since his Death, are but like Stars appearing when the Sun is set, that twinkle only in his absence, and with the Rays they have borrowed from him.'[1] These lesser wits were, however, the very men who gave Pope his first introduction to the literary world. Wycherley himself was not one of them. He had outlived a popularity which belonged to the more unruly age of literary fashion, the coterie of the Restoration wits, but he was in touch with the new arbiters of taste. It was he who showed the manuscript of Pope's *Pastorals* to William Walsh, and Walsh, in the eyes of his contemporaries, was one of the most luminous of that galaxy of little stars which had risen at Dryden's setting. When Pope later added to the manuscript the names of the men through whose hands it had passed before publication, they included Walsh, Congreve, and Garth, all of them members of the circle of protégés and friends who surrounded Dryden in his last years and who, after his death, believed that they were carrying on the tradition of his work.

Through the 1690s and the first decade of the eighteenth century, literary taste was dominated by this group. They took their tone and general principles from Dryden's later work. Formal odes, imitations, and translations of the ancients were their stock-in-trade, and they seldom attempted satire. This minor classical revival was produced as much by changing circumstances as by arbitrary fashion. Fastidious academic exercises in translation became the respectable pastime of men who were either independent or professionally occupied in other ways. Garth (the only real satirist among them) was a successful doctor, Walsh a Whig Member of Parliament, and Congreve, as Johnson records, disgusted Voltaire by preferring to be regarded as a gentleman rather than as a writer.[2]

Men like these were scarcely to be tempted into the dangerous quicksands of serious political satire. The political climate of the country had changed since the Revolution, and moderates of both parties, relieved that civil war had been avoided, were more concerned with techniques of government than with fundamental divisions of principle. Dryden had been forced to give up political satire with the expulsion of James II, but many of his followers, men like Garth, Congreve, and Walsh, were themselves supporters of the

---

[1] *Correspondence of Pope*, ed. G. Sherburn, vol. i (1956), p. 2.

[2] Johnson, 'Life of Congreve', *Lives*, vol. ii, p. 226. Congreve's independence was secured by a series of sinecures he received from the patronage of Charles Montague, Earl of Halifax, and others, which kept him comfortably till his death.

Revolution and more inclined to praise than to criticize. Moreover, poets had begun to find other and more profitable ways of advancement than journalism. The writers of the Restoration had had little to lose by their attacks. The most they could aspire to was a pension, a laureateship, or the position of City Poet. But new careers were open to the talents of their successors, and the next generation was to see Prior an ambassador and Addison Secretary of State.

The poetry of the time reflects this situation. Such sentiments as these from *The Country Parson's Advice to those little Scriblers, who pretend to write better Sense than Great Secretaries: Or, Mr. Stephen's Triumph Over the Pillory* (1706) were common:

> *Libels*, that raise the trembling *Poet's* fears,
> And set Mankind together by the Ears.
> These to avoid, in dull Translation Trade,
> *Bowyer*, and *Savage*, and *Oldmixon* read;
> Or deal in News, and write whate'er you will,
> But mind you *Scrible* on the *right Side* still.
>
> (ll. 19–24.)[1]

Prior had sneered at Dryden's enforced caution, describing how he 'brought the venome of a Spiteful *Satyr*, To the safe innocence of a *dull Translator*' (*Satyr on the Modern Translators*, ll. 51–52), but Prior himself is an interesting example of the poet who learned to steer a skilful course in this delicate situation. He began his literary career by satirizing the satirists. This was conventional enough, but the particular attitude behind his early work, the *Satyr on the Modern Translators* and *A Satyr on the Poets, in Imitation of the Seventh Satyr of Juvenal*, does not reflect much credit on him. He seems to find the poverty of hacks and the disgrace that fell on Dryden a fitting reward for their temerity in launching out at all into political attack. More than this, he takes a positive pleasure in describing it. It is hard to explain his vicious dislike of Dryden, already apparent in the famous *Hind and the Panther Transvers'd*, in which he collaborated with Charles Montague and which was said to have reduced Dryden to tears by its gratuitous insults. Perhaps we can infer from it a mingled fear of and distaste for the old insecure position of the professional, which he describes in a passage of his *Essay on Learning*,

[1] *P.O.A.S.*, vol. iv (1707), p. 63.

where the mingled irony and worldly prudence is markedly different from Cowley's wounded complaints or Dryden's experienced bitterness. Prior even allows himself a touch of self-congratulation at having avoided the path which proved so treacherous for his predecessors:

But I had two Accidents in Youth which hindred me from being quite possest with the Muse: I was bred in a Colledge where prose was more in fashion than Verse, and as soon as I had taken my First Degree was sent the Kings Secretary to the Hague, there I had enough to do in studying French and Dutch and altering my Terentian and Virgilian Style into that of Articles Conventions and Memorials, So that Poetry which by the bent of my Mind might have become the business of my Life, was by the happyness of my Education only the Amusement of it, and in this too, having the Prospect of some little Fortune to be made, and Friendship to be cultivated with the great Men, I did not launch much out into Satyr; which however agreable for the present to the Writers or Incouragers of it does in time do neither of them good, considering the uncertainty of Fortune, and the various change of Ministry, where every Man as he resents may punish in his turn of Greatness;[1]

In such a situation there was every opportunity for the cultivated amateur or the academic dabbler to devote his attention to the manners of his art rather than to its substance. Prior himself was sufficiently a poet of the tradition to demand realism of tone and subject-matter even for 'the amusement of his life'. His witty, relaxed account of life at The Hague as an ambassador belongs entirely to the Horatian tradition of Rochester, though with a new polish which suggests an altogether lighter approach to the art. The lines *Written in the Year 1696* are society verse of an airier sort than any of the epistles of the Court wits:

> While with Labour Assiduous due pleasure I mix
> And in one day attone for the Busyness of Six
> In a little Dutch Chaise on a Saturday Night
> On my left hand my Horace and   on my right
> No Memoire to compose and no Post-boy to move
> That on Sunday may hinder the softness of Love:

[1] Matthew Prior, *Literary Works*, ed. H. B. Wright and M. K. Spears, vol. i (1959), p. 583.

> For her, neither Visits nor Parties of Tea
> Nor the long winded Cant of a dull Refugée
> This Night and the next shal be Hers shal be Mine
> To good or ill Fortune the Third we resign:
> Thus Scorning the World and superior to Fate
> I drive on my Car in processional State.
>
> (ll. 1–12.)[1]

These lines are in the tradition of Dryden's *Epistle to Sir George Etherege*—an equally lighthearted ambassador to the Dutch—but their realism is of a different sort. Stout Dutch wives have been exchanged for the genteel and anonymous nymph; there is no mention of the heavy merriment and carousing Dryden pities Etherege for having to endure. Instead the tedious duties of the week are lightly recounted to contrast with the elegant amours of the weekend, and the whole tone is polished, delicate, polite, and without a touch of the rough realism of the earlier convention. This is play poetry, discreetly naturalistic, and its predominant quality, charm, is not so easily found in the work of the Restoration wits.

The same difference distinguishes Prior's love lyrics from earlier ones. Most of his are epigrammatic and depend on a witty turn in the last stanza; they repeat too the old stock situations in the mythological guise that disgusted Johnson. At their best they show delicacy and point, but the overtones of serious witty argument which Rochester, Sedley, and Etherege succeeded in catching, and their consistently satirical tone, have both gone. In place of the former we have the natural monologue of *A Better Answer*; in place of the latter a more intimate mood where sentiment and a feeling for personality mingle in the women he addresses and in his attitude to them. Prior's lyrics are more tender, and this is the effect of his tone of privacy, intimacy, and personal feeling. The verses *Written in the Year 1696* are politer than the epistles of the wits, and the lyrics are prettier than theirs; and as the first lacks the more obviously honest qualities of the Restoration realists, so the second avoid the tough candour of their invitations to love. But though he relinquished the harshness of satire, Prior did not turn his back on the new ideals of social poetry. When he talks of himself or his mistresses in verse the

[1] Prior, op. cit., p. 158.

effect is one for which honesty is far too public a term, and politeness too frigid. Sincerity, in spite of his ironic lightness, is Prior's
prevailing tone. The lover in *A Better Answer*, who courts others in
verse but loves Chloe in prose, is recognizably an 'honest' character;
he equates sincerity with plainness.

Thus while Prior refused to meddle with politics in verse, and
chose to write *Alma*, his light treatise on that popular topic the
folly of speculative reasoning, as a burlesque epistolary exercise in
octosyllabics, he retained enough of the old tradition to turn it to
his own less serious purposes. In doing so he introduced, in a modest
way, fresh possibilities of tone and mood. His lyrics are more
domestic than courtly, but he dresses them up with deliberate and
parodied elegance in mythological costume; he is enough of a wit
to make his sympathy and his sincerity stylish.

But the less contentious verse to which most poets of the end of
the seventeenth century turned was translation and imitation. Few
of them had the poise or dexterity of Prior in adapting the classics to
lightly sociable uses. Most of them, in fact, believed that they were
doing justice to Dryden's memory by remaining copyists, for his
reputation at his death in 1700 was as a master of technique and
translation rather than as a satirist. The envious hatred which had
found a new vent against him in his later years of disgrace still
flared out in works like *A Description of Dryden's Funeral*,[1] in which
the author[2] jeeringly describes the lamentations of Dryden's
friends at his death:

> But stay my Muse, the Learned G——th appears,
> He sighing comes, and is half drown'd in Tears:
> The famous G——th, whom Learned Poets call
> Knight of the Order of the Urinal.
>
> (ll. 127–30.)

---

[1] *P.O.A.S.*, vol. ii (1716), p. 229.

[2] 'Malone says this piece was probably by Tom Brown'; see *Dryden Bibliography*,
p. 295. Pope may have known this poem and remembered it in *The Dunciad*, judging
by the following lines from it:

> A troop of Stationers at first appear'd,
> And Jacob T . . . . n, Captain of the Guard;
> Jacob, the Muses Midwife, who well knows
> To ease a lab'ring Muse of Pangs and Throes;
> He oft has kept the Infant Poet warm,
> Or lick'd th'unwieldy Monster into Form.

Garth, as these lines suggest, was better known as the author of *The Dispensary*, and as Dryden's admirer, than as a respectable writer of academic verses. In 1717 in the Preface to his collection of translations of Ovid's *Metamorphoses* Garth was still reminding his readers of the indecent obscurity of Dryden's tomb in the Abbey:

> The only Talents in Esteem at present are those of *Exchange-Alley*; one Tally is worth a Grove of Bays; . . . *Mr. Dryden* is still a sad, and shameful Instance of this Truth: The Man, that cou'd make Kings immortal, and raise triumphant Arches to Heroes, now wants a poor square Foot of Stone, to show where the Ashes of one of the greatest Poets that ever was upon Earth, are deposited.[1]

Most of his praise for Dryden in this Preface is inevitably reserved for his power as a translator, though Garth admits that 'as an Inventor he was rich', but his real intention is to present Dryden as the great pupil of the ancients.

The cult of translation had originated in France, but Roscommon in his *Essay on Translated Verse* (1684) claimed that the English, 'in gen'rous emulation of this art', had beaten the French at their own game. There is a strong vein of honest chauvinism in the lines with which he supports this view:

> *Vain* are our *Neighbours Hopes* and *Vain* their *Cares*,
> The *Fault* is more their *Languages* then theirs.
> 'Tis courtly, florid, and abounds in words,
> Of softer sound than ours perhaps affords;
> But who did ever in *French Authors* see
> The Comprehensive *English Energy*?
> The weighty *Bullion* of *One Sterling Line*,
> Drawn to *French Wire*, would thro' whole *Pages* shine.
> I speak my *Private* but *Impartial sense*,
> With *Freedom*, and (I hope) without *offence*:
> For I'le Recant, when *France* can shew me *Wit*
> As strong as *Ours*, and as *succinctly Writ*.[2]

National pride played a part in establishing the vogue for translation, but a more secret sympathy with the spirit of Latin poetry,

---

[1] *Ovid's Metamorphoses, Translated by the most Eminent Hands* (1717), p. xx.

[2] Roscommon, *Essay on Translated Verse* (1684), ed. J. E. Spingarn, *Critical Essays of the Seventeenth Century* (1908), vol. ii, p. 298.

which was very strong in Dryden, stirred a response in his followers. In the ancients they found a code of natural morality, a clear rational attitude to life, and a cultivated tradition of worldly poetry. The public religion of the Romans, with its machinery of gods and fabulous creatures, was no more a stumbling block to them than it had been to an earlier age. Medieval poets had moralized Ovid allegorically, and the Elizabethans found in him an animate world of nature ideally pictured in the myths and mysteries of the *Metamorphoses* and the *Fasti*. The Augustans more often preferred to think of him as the witty and sometimes tender observer of the intricate ways of love, but when forced to consider the problems of the myths they drew their own congenial conclusions. Garth, after a perfunctory attempt to explain them scientifically, turns with relief to his own brand of worldly wisdom. Ovid has surely never found a more practical interpreter. Among the trite lessons in everyday prudence to be learned from the *Metamorphoses* is, for instance, that of Phaeton, which, Garth explains, teaches us that 'he who would climb to the Seat of *Jupiter*, generally meets with his Bolt by the way'.[1]

Under such scrutiny the gods and goddesses themselves dwindled to abstractions, and it soon became clear that, without any living world of myth to inhabit, the creatures of mythology could only be used like statues to fill a niche or dignify a garden. In poetry their proper place was in panegyric or formal description, and even here they quickly became the standby of minor poets with nothing to express but empty adulation or ambition of grandeur. But Prior's facetious ingenuity in handling them in his lyrics had shown how, even now, they might be exploited by a witty poet to offset everyday reality, and by Gay in particular this device was extended successfully. The episode of Patty in Book I of *Trivia* is an ingenious parody of a Georgic digression, explaining the origin of pattens through an engaging burlesque mixture of artifice and realism. Patty, the blue-eyed maid of the Lincolnshire fens, only succumbs to Vulcan's advances when a cold in the head reduces her to submissive gratitude for his god-like invention of the thick-soled mule. Johnson complained that an honest blacksmith could have done as much for her, but an honest blacksmith would

---

[1] *Ovid's Metamorphoses*, p. xvii.

immediately have transformed the tone of the poem from irony to sentimental realism. To Gay the pleasure of it was in finding a new way of making honest rustic reality more absurdly recognizable while at the same time wittily parodying the earnestness of the cult of imitation.

But what pleased Dryden's followers most in the ancients was their interpretation of life and conduct. They were both natural and universal—an infallible guide for anyone who hoped to write well about the way men feel and act. William Walsh, in a well-known passage from the Preface to his *Letters and Poems* of 1692, contrasted this naturalness with the artificiality of the moderns in love poetry:

> Those who are conversant with the Writings of the Ancients, will observe a great difference between what they and the Moderns have publish'd upon this Subject. The occasions upon which the Poems of the former are written, are such as happen to every Man almost that is in Love; and the Thoughts such, as are natural for every Man in love to think. The Moderns on the other hand, have sought out for Occasions that none meet with but themselves; and fill their Verses with Thoughts that are surprising and glittering, but not tender, passionate or natural to a Man in love. . . .
>
> I am satisfied that *Catullus, Tibullus, Propertius* and *Ovid* were in Love with their Mistresses while they upbraid them, quarrel with them, threaten them and forswear them; but I confess I cannot believe *Petrarch* in Love with his, when he writes Conceits upon her Name, her Gloves, and the Place of her Birth. I Know it is natural for a Lover, in Transports of Jealousie, to treat his Mistress with all the Violence imaginable; but I cannot think it natural for a Man, who is much in Love, to amuse himself with such Trifles as the other.[1]

If conduct is the criterion for what is natural and therefore good in a love poem, Walsh is right. But his standard is one of almost unliterary realism. Here is the belief in the pre-eminence of subject-matter carried to new lengths; a love poem is an expression of love, and to be judged as such, not on its merits as a poem. It follows that naturalness, or truth to common experience, and sincerity are its most important qualities. Walsh was not alone in holding this view. John Oldmixon, in the Preface to his translations of Anacreon, refers

---

[1] W. Walsh, *Letters and Poems* (1692), A3r—A4r.

approvingly to Walsh's comments, and instantly proceeds to make his own claim to sincerity: 'You will find nothing in this little Volume, but what was the Real Sentiments of my Heart at the time I writ it.'[1] An unlikely boast for a book largely composed of imitations, but Oldmixon knew very well what kind of advertisement would be most persuasive. We find, then, that already at the turn of the century honesty was being extended to include 'the real sentiments of the heart', integrity of private as well as public feelings, at least in love poetry. Prior's verses lightly suggested it; Walsh claimed to have discovered it in the ancients.

If the sentiments of the Roman poets seemed as natural in the modern world as when they were first written, it must be assumed that they were felt sincerely. Such at least was the reasoning of the Augustans. The word 'sincere' was beginning to carry as much emotional weight as the word 'honest', and in Pope's poetry particularly both qualities combine in his treatment of private and public themes to form a consistent attitude to life and letters. Strange as it may at first seem, there is no paradox in the fact that Pope discovered this attitude partly through his apprenticeship to the ancients. The men who encouraged him in his youth, writers like Garth and Walsh, had already declared that the best place to find that simplicity and truth to nature on which sincerity depends was in the literature of Rome.

Translation of the classics, therefore, in which the labour of versifying adds nothing to transform or obscure the original ideas, seemed to the Augustans an admirable discipline and a genuine literary activity. 'Invention labours less but Judgement more' than in original composition, but the subject-matter was proved by its survival through the centuries to be 'nature', and there were always opportunities for exercising imagination in the choice of language by the translator, and for a sort of creative sympathy in his understanding of the original. Roscommon had compared this relationship between the translator and his author to friendship:

> United by this *Sympathetick Bond*,
> You grow *Familiar, Intimate,* and *Fond*;

---

[1] J. Oldmixon, *Poems on Several Occasions* (1696), A6r.

>   Your *thoughts*, your *Words*, your *Stiles*, your *Souls* agree,
>   No longer his *Interpreter*, but *He*.[1]

This social relationship, like that between the poet and his reader, carried with it certain strong and responsible obligations of sympathy, accuracy, and intelligibility. Pope, echoing the opinion of Roscommon and Buckingham with regard to imitation and the ancients, was yet nearer to Dryden, who had liked to trace poetic genealogies and remark how the soul of one poet could be transfused into another. A family relationship bound together the poets of the past and the present:

> For to say truth, whatever is very good sense must have been common sense in all times; and what we call Learning, is but the knowledge of the sense of our predecessors. Therefore they who say our thoughts are not our own because they resemble the Ancients, may as well say our faces are not our own, because they are like our Fathers: And indeed it is very unreasonable, that people should expect us to be Scholars, and yet be angry to find us so.[2]

Pope preferred imitation to translation because of this sense of continuity, and he found it inevitable that a poet should draw on all the resources of tradition in his own work. He was not, however, influenced by the standards of pallid good taste and academic accuracy which haunted so many of his contemporaries. William Benson, Milton's champion, and Joseph Trapp, the first Professor of Poetry in Oxford, both translators of Virgil, attacked Dryden's licence in his version of Virgil. The game of finding fault with Dryden's Virgil was indeed played by anyone with literary pretensions, and it is pleasant to find Pope, very early in his career, receiving the pedantic criticisms of his friend Cromwell on Dryden's *Aeneis* with cool indifference: 'As to your Letter of Critical Remarks on *Dryden's* VIRGIL, I can only say, most of what you observe are true enough, but of no great Consequence (in my Opinion at least).'[3] Pope's own earliest printed poems, the *Pastorals*, were themselves imitations, progressively revised and altered on the advice of his many supervisors. Walsh was delighted by them; Sir William

---

[1] Roscommon, op. cit., p. 300.
[2] Pope, *Poems*, op. cit., The Preface of 1717, p. xxvii.
[3] Sherburn, op. cit., vol. i, p. 124.

Trumbull, a man of learning as well as a statesman, was so impressed by them and by Pope's translation of the Sarpedon episode that he tried to encourage the young man to turn from imitation to translation: 'to . . . proceed in translating that incomparable Poet [Homer], to make him speak good *English*, to dress his admirable characters in your proper, significant, and expressive conceptions, and to make his work as useful and instructive to this degenerate age, as he was to our friend *Horace*'.[1] Granville 'the polite', who also saw the *Pastorals* at an early stage, was himself, in Antony Wood's phrase, 'a dabbler in another's Helicon', and had begun as a poet by imitating Waller. Halifax,[2] to whom they were shown, was a translator too, and, according to Pope himself, foolishly vain of his classical accomplishments. To all of these men it seemed proper and laudable that a young poet should begin as an imitator, and they quickly responded to the grace with which Pope captured the spirit of those whose ambition was to restore to modern poetry the elegance and simplicity of the ancients.

As an imitator Pope mingled Virgil and Ovid in the love complaints of the *Pastorals*, but he had not forgotten that the principle of imitation as Dryden had understood it extended beyond the ancients. He adapted Spenser's refrain from the *Epithalamium* for the third pastoral, and introduced conceits of the kind familiar from seventeenth-century love lyrics:

> O were I made by some transforming Pow'r,
> The Captive Bird that sings within thy Bow'r!
>
> *(Summer*, ll. 45–46.)

In 1705 Sir William Trumbull was writing to Pope to return the copy of Milton's *Minor Poems* that the young man had lent him, and it was from them that many of the descriptive passages of the *Pastorals* derived. Pope copied *Comus*, ll. 290–1,

> While lab'ring Oxen, spent with Toil and Heat,
> In their loose Traces from the Field retreat;
>
> *(Autumn*, ll. 61–62.)

---

[1] Sherburn, op. cit., vol. i, pp. 45–46.

[2] Charles Montague, Earl of Halifax, whose first literary effort in English was his collaboration with Prior, *The Hind and the Panther Transvers'd*, liked to think of himself as the Maecenas of the age.

and in the next line glances back at *L'Allegro*, l. 81:

> While curling Smokes from Village-Tops are seen,
> And the fleet Shades glide o'er the dusky Green
>
> (*Autumn*, ll. 63–64.)

The smoking chimneys originated for Milton, as for Pope, in Virgil (*Eclogue* I, l. 82), 'et iam summa procul villarum culmina fumant', and the strength of the classical tradition is so strong from *L'Allegro* to *Lycidas* that Pope was both safe and correct in choosing to vary his pastoral landscape with Miltonic touches.

Deference for a popular mode and a genuine sense of continuity in literature so thoroughly inspired Pope's use of imitation that he remained in this sense an imitator all his life. Parnell in his ode *To Mr. Pope* calls on Horace, Ovid, Callimachus, Virgil, and Homer to join him in praise of the poet who had matched them in such works as the *Essay On Criticism, Windsor Forest, The Rape of the Lock, The Temple of Fame*, and the translations of the *Iliad* and *Odyssey*. Pope had made good use of the rather tepid classical revival in which he was bred. It is easy to forget that he did not begin his poetic career as a satirist, but that his early literary background was that of the gentlemen writers who, in the interests of politeness and safety, had relinquished the rougher form. He established his reputation as a correct imitator, a writer of academic verses, and even in the *Essay On Criticism* he flattered the taste of his contemporaries by setting himself up in the school of Horace and Roscommon as an arbiter of sound literary values. All this was necessary before he could discover his own peculiar bent for satire, but his apprenticeship enabled him, when he felt secure enough, to return to those poets who, in his early youth, had been generally condemned as too rough, too insolent, and too much concerned with topicalities to be seriously considered as sources. Pope never liked to admit his debt to them too openly, but Oldham and Rochester, as much as Dryden, in fact provided him with the ideas, forms, and modes of expression which helped to mould his moral satires. The tone of responsibility, of honest and serious judgement, and of personal sincerity which he assumed in his later works depended, however, on an already established literary tradition which grew out of the work of the

imitators and classicists of the 1690s. Before he could have recourse
to the material of the Restoration, Pope needed to secure himself
with his contemporaries as correct, classical, and independent. The
little interlude of popular translation and imitation had provided
a breathing space in the Augustan tradition of honest poetry which
allowed certain new emphases to enter into the common tone of
realism and argument. When Pope had shown what he could make
of this, and had secured for himself a central position in the poetry
of his own time, he was free to display, obliquely and indirectly, his
kinship with the earlier and more vital Restoration satirists.

The writers of that period, and the conventions they had originated, indicated the direction Augustan poetry might take. In them
Pope found a wide range of topics and styles, some of which we have
already discussed—social, philosophical, and political issues, varying modes of address, monologue, public statement, immediate
declamation as in prologues and epilogues spoken from the stage,
historical survey, epistolary intimacy. The work of the Restoration
poets had also displayed a prevailing temper which suited one aspect of Pope's genius, his flexible versatility. But it presented him,
at the same time, with certain problems of technique and adaptation.
One of the most vital of these problems was how to include in the
new forms those traditional attitudes which, for all its vigour, topical satire had tended to neglect—particularly the emotions of enthusiasm and grief, which the older forms of the panegyric and the
elegy had embodied and which now, with the discredit of the
former, were losing ground. To Pope the problem was as much
personal as poetic. He had found some opportunity to express
feeling in lyrical and descriptive verse based on imitation, and he
was therefore less content with an idea of satire which laid its
greatest stress on wit and contemporary point and tended deliberately to neglect the reflective or the enthusiastic. By nature he
was a man of sensibility and quick feelings, and, unlike Dryden, he
was impelled to make satire involve much more than fine raillery or
Juvenalian rage. The justification of Pope's moral satire lay in the
wide range of experience it covered—praise set against blame, the
present seen against the perspective of the past, personal sincerity
co-operating with public concern.

Panegyric was gradually becoming discredited, but the notion of honesty which had grown up, partly as a satiric convention, was the source of a new kind of compliment. A moderate and attainable standard of the just man had been sketched out in terms of other conventions: in the Horatian epistle praising the innocent and industrious usefulness, the independence, of country life and the dignity of the squire; in epistles to professional men and in verse treatises that recommended candour, shrewdness, and tolerance to the critic, and sincerity, simplicity, and intelligibility to the poet. In all of these instances the cult of imitation had reinforced a natural tendency in the temper of the time. Poets, to some extent, had found themselves choosing 'natural' love lyrics from the past, intimate epistles, sociable verse treatises that avoided the engagement of contemporary issues while yet underlining the common interest in sincerity, communication, and a kind of general naturalism as opposed to the immediate realism of purely local and temporary subjects. Pope was bred up to these ideas, and, like all true poets, he loved to celebrate. His satire is mingled with praise for general virtues accepted in all ages and circumscribed by no particular degree or position. The Honest Muse which he invoked, giving to every man his due, looks for exemplary subjects as well as for objects of scorn. If the cult of imitation had taught him how to relate his gifts to those of the past, it had also led him to look for virtues which were recognized in all generations—to accept the wisdom of the ancients in contrast to the more local and prejudiced assessment of the moderns, particularly of those immediate predecessors who had openly proclaimed their allegiance to party and to temporary causes. Inflated compliment in the old style had been so patently abused for these ephemeral ends that it had begun to look like the counterpart of that irresponsible abuse of which so much Restoration satire had consisted. But against the background of a fervent, traditional, yet realistic delight in modest virtue, the qualities celebrated by a Horace and a Pope, satiric rage might yet seem more than an exhibition of skill as in Oldham, or an element in 'the spite and mischief of the fray'; it might be shown as sober and justified moral comment on the nature of man in general and on his particular actions.

One further reason for the effect of completeness Pope aimed at and achieved in his moral satire is the elegiac strain that runs through it, reminding the reader of the brevity of life and the record of human history. He had found this strain in Dryden, not in set elegies like *Eleonora*, but running like a thread through all his work, a deep response to the Latin sense of transience. Pope's own training as an imitator confirmed his love of this elegiac mood, and he combined it with a feeling for the past encouraged by the habit of reflection. The topical satirists had too often turned their backs on the past, but an imitator and a traditionalist like Pope could not follow them in this. Whereas the simple contrast of past and present had helped earlier satirists to point their indignation, he shows a subtler feeling for the shifting emphasis in life between activity and stillness, society and retreat, the pervading sense of the immediate present and of the passing of time. This elegiac strain, strong in both Pope and Johnson, again justifies the honest observations of the moral satirist, and often touches a note of pathos or even of tragedy which Restoration poetry had too often lacked. Imitation of the ancients had strengthened this vein in Pope's work, and his training as an imitator had not only secured him a respectable position in the literary society of his time; it had helped him to discover more than one direction in which his peculiar talents, as well as the traditions of the school from which he derived, could develop.

VI

POPE

I

'IT is vanity which makes the rake at twenty, the worldly man at forty, and the retired man at sixty.—We are apt to think that best in general, for which we find ourselves best fitted in particular.'[1] Pope made this remark to Spence when he himself had been living a life of semi-retirement for many years, not so much by choice as by necessity. His health prevented him from travelling or sharing the gayer pursuits of his friends, and his religion debarred him from any position in public life. He was born to books by inclination, but he was born to retirement perforce, in strong contrast to predecessors and contemporaries like Dryden, Addison, Prior, and Swift. The literary tradition he inherited was one in which the poet was an active member of society, and Pope could not but be aware of the peculiarity of his position. Vanity was not the original cause of his retirement, and though he was vain, this was seldom the source of his most cherished attitudes and convictions.

From the start Pope took on the colouring of his associates. He was affectionate and sympathetic, and he possessed that imitative faculty which so often goes with literary genius; all his life he was remarkably susceptible to the influences of his environment and his friends. As a young man he wrote to Henry Cromwell in the style of the fashionable rake, rallying him on his intrigues and hinting at adventures of his own. There is no evidence that Pope ever led a dissipated life beyond Cibber's malicious and unproved story, refuted by Cheselden the surgeon, who told Spence that Pope 'had been gay, but left that way of life upon his acquaintance with Mrs. B'.[2] But he had enough of a young man's vanity to want to be thought 'the gayest valetudinaire, most thinking rake alive'. In the same year that he was bantering with Cromwell, however, he was defending himself to Caryll against the criticisms of pious Catholics who had

<hr>

[1] Spence, *Anecdotes*, ed. S. W. Singer (1820), p. 203.   [2] Ibid., p. 309.

been offended by some lines in the *Essay on Criticism*.[1] The role of honest moralist was as important to him at this early stage as that of the young man about town. Neither was insincere. They helped him to feel that he was not different from other men, and that he was at one with the literary tradition to which he was bred.

Johnson noticed how soon Pope acquired the 'cant of an author'[2] in his early letters to Wycherley. The same instinct was at work here. His precociousness, his friendship with literary men, and his instinct for self-protection all led him to assume these conventional defensive poses, in order to see himself as an already established member of literary society. Pope needed this sense of community, and he was lucky to find it so early in the group of admiring patrons and poets who gave him a foretaste of the security of success. Yet, though he needed reassurance, he was never in doubt about his poetic powers. At twenty he claimed that he kept pictures of Dryden, Milton, and Shakespeare 'in my chamber, round about me, that the constant remembrance of 'em may keep me always humble'.[3] He must have been as often kept proud by the company he chose.

The many roles Pope assumed in his poems and letters—witty gallant, Horatian critic, moralist, philosopher, lover, and friend—were signs of imaginative sympathies often at variance with his actual experience. He easily acquired the conventional attitudes of the day, and just as easily modified them under the influence of his companions. He was equally sincere in protesting liberal Catholicism to Caryll, misanthropy to Swift, and stoicism to Bolingbroke, for in each case the strain was touched off by respect and affection for the friend. Pope's political ideas, in so far as he professed any, were the result of these friendships. Of his general opinions, a conservative Catholic like Edward Blount could say 'Mr. Pope is a whig, and would be a Protestant, if his mother were dead',[4] yet in a few years he had become closely associated with the Tory party. It was hard to predict on purely rational grounds which attitude Pope would adopt. He clung to the outward title of his faith despite the efforts of friends like Atterbury and Swift to convert him. After his

---

[1] Sherburn, op. cit., vol. i, pp. 126–9. The lines in the *Essay on Criticism* are 687–97.
[2] Johnson, *Lives*, ed. G. B. Hill, 'Life of Pope', vol. iii (1905), p. 91.
[3] Sherburn, op. cit., vol. i, p. 120, 25 June 1711. [4] Spence, *Anecdotes*, p. 327.

mother's death he remained a Catholic; perhaps he recognized the advantage of being forcibly precluded from public life for which neither his health nor his temper fitted him.

The extent to which Pope's views were liberal was due as much to the feeling of the age as to his private opinions. Fundamental differences had been forgotten for a while, and a moderate Whig and a moderate Tory would have agreed with the poet in his assertion:

> For Forms of Government let fools contest;
> Whate'er is best administer'd is best:
>
> (*Essay on Man*, Ep. III, ll. 303–4.)

Swift himself had turned Tory on religious rather than political grounds, when he quarrelled with the Whigs over their attitude to the clergy. The views he put forward in *The Sentiments of a Church of England Man* (1708) were very near to Pope's: '. . . few states are ruined by any Defect in their Institution, but generally by the Corruption of Manners; against which, the best Institution is no long Security, and without which a very ill one may subsist and flourish'.[1] In this new Toryism, forms of government were no longer disputed. It was a moral and conservative attitude, in which old dogmatic ideas, like the Divine Right of Kings, had been quietly relinquished in favour of concepts of sound government and a maintenance of the *status quo* in the balance of power in the State. The writers of the new age were moralists who were concerned not with speculation and theory but with men's conduct in society and administration.

This moral bias lies behind Pope's serious attitudes. He related everything to the wisdom of experience and the rules of good conduct—rules so self-evident that he could eventually reduce them to the simple assertion 'there needs but thinking right and meaning well'. But the first is not so easy, and the second recalls an ominous aphorism about good intentions. It is not a statement that will bear intellectual scrutiny. Yet this was Pope's sincere conviction, for morality was to him 'a sensation of the heart' rather than a matter of right reason. It belonged to that region of instinct and emotion from which poetry itself springs.

[1] Swift, 'Sentiments of a Church of England Man', in *Bickerstaff Papers*, ed. H. Davis (1940), p. 14.

From his youth Pope was conscious of certain popular moral and literary conventions which he could adapt for himself, and he instinctively turned to them for reassurance. His enforced solitude, for instance, was easier to bear in the light of the poetic ideal of retreat. Writing to Steele in 1712, Pope admitted this, wryly conceding that for him it was making the best of the inevitable: 'Thus Sir you see I would flatter my self into a good opinion of my own way of living. *Plutarch* just now told me, that 'tis in human life as in a game at tables, where a man may wish for the highest cast, but if his chance be otherwise, he is e'en to play it as well as he can and to make the best of it.'[1] But Plutarch's authority made all the difference. When he sat alone at Binfield or at Twickenham, he could recall without flattery that this was the way of life both ancients and moderns had recognized as the wisest and best. Indeed Pope became a living example of the justness of the convention. When Bolingbroke returned from exile to seclusion, he thanked Pope for having taught him the value of retirement by his own example: 'In the mean time let me refer you to our friend POPE. He says I made a philosopher of him: I am sure he has contributed very much, and I thank him for it, to the making an hermit of me.'[2] The author of the *Fitzosborne Letters*, William Melmoth, cited Pope as the modern proof of the truism that the retired life was the source of poetry, in a verse epistle on the conventional subject *Of Active and Retired Life* (1735):

> Were high ambition still the power confess'd
> That rul'd with equal sway in every breast,
> Say where the glories of the sacred nine?
> Where Homer's verse sublime, or, Milton, thine?
> Nor thou, sweet bard! who 'turn'd the tuneful art,
> 'From sounds to things, from fancy to the heart',
> Thy lays instructive to the world hadst giv'n,
> Nor greatly justified the laws of heav'n.[3]

The literary commonplace of withdrawing from the world 'to view the storm ashore' was luckily apposite to Pope's own condition.

There is a poignancy, however, in Pope's confession to Steele,

---

[1] Sherburn, op. cit., vol. i, p. 147 (18 June 1712).
[2] Bolingbroke, *Letters on the Study and Use of History* (1752), vol. ii, p. 224.
[3] Contained in Dodsley's *Collection* (1763), vol. i, p. 203.

which was exchanged for greater assurance when he wrote in the
Essay on Man,

> Honour and shame from no Condition rise;
> Act well your part, there all the honour lies.
>
> (Ep. IV, ll. 193–4.)

His life was a hard discipline in training himself to act well his own
part, and from the start he was forced to see what sacrifices and
assumptions it would involve. Pope intended to make the poet's
part as noble as the philosopher's, and as active and absorbing as
the statesman's. 'The life of a wit is a warfare upon earth', he wrote,
echoing the complaints of Cowley, Dryden, and Prior with a new
conscious pride. But it was a warfare he created for himself. He deliberately turned his literary life into a campaign, so that he would
not be restricted to living vicariously through his friends' concerns.
He was determined to have his own sphere of action. Like Bolingbroke, Pope believed that we taste the pleasures of retirement
better for having been in the world. Everything seemed to conspire
to prevent him from enjoying a real participation, but he set out
to create it for himself, not always with dignity or success, but with
the ardent sincerity he felt for anything concerned with his art.

   Pope appropriated to himself all those views on poetry and society
which Oldham, Rochester, and Dryden had adopted from classical
authors and from tradition. He made them peculiarly his own. In
his early poems there is a sway of sympathy between the life of
action and the life of retreat which recalls his peculiar position and
the literary tradition to which he belonged. There is much stylized
feeling in the *Pastorals* and *Windsor Forest,* and they are, in one sense,
poems of retirement, the work of a young man letting his imagination play over old forms and conventions and bringing them to life
with touches of observation and sentiment inspired by his solitary
reading. The *Essay on Criticism* is very different. Compact with sense
and evidently the product of a coterie tradition of wit, it parades
before the reader the poise and sophistication of a young poet boast-
ing of his literary milieu. Literature is not its only subject. It presents literature as a part of social and moral life, and suggests that
the poet is in close touch with a wider world. Pope had caught all
the overtones of the current popular topics: the Ancients against

the Moderns (ll. 394 ff.), the attack on Dullness (ll. 388–94), the contempt for hired flattery (ll. 408–23), and the concern for purity and propriety of expression which runs throughout the whole poem. Even more ambitiously, he related these subjects to a wider range of ideas, calling on the moral satirists, Oldham, Rochester, and Boileau, as well as the verse critics, Roscommon, Buckingham, and Walsh, to emphasize the general principles of honesty and truth that lie behind literature. His character of the ideal man of letters (ll. 631–42) is made up from materials already provided by the Restoration critics and satirists, but he presents it with a new fervour. For Pope responded to the standards of honesty, candour, and sincerity as warmly as Dryden had responded to the older ideals of heroism and magnanimity. The *Essay on Criticism* foreshadows clearly the lines along which his moral satire was to develop.

Most striking of all in this early poem, however, is its sheer brilliance. Like *The Rape of the Lock* it is a work of imagination and a labour of love—the love of the craft of verse itself. Pope seems to have caught Dryden's exuberance in that wide range of images drawn from optics, art, architecture, physiology, metaphysics, and observation of ordinary life which gives the poem its air of having as much to do with life as with letters. Though he could not quite match Dryden's command of such a wide field, Pope copied from him too the survey or prospect of literary history, the catalogue of poets and critics of the past, with its suggestion of the heroic style telescoped to the limits of an epistolary poem. His own reading and the many subjects he had discussed with Wycherley and Walsh went to the making of *The Essay on Criticism*. It is a deeply allusive and imitative poem.

> Where-e'er you find *the cooling Western Breeze*,
> In the next Line, it *whispers thro' the Trees*.
>
> (ll. 350–1.)

had been anticipated by Boileau, and Pope might have remembered as he wrote the lines Oldmixon's translation of Boileau's *Second Satire*:

> To praise a *Phillis* for a *thousand Charms*;
> The next verse shews the *Poet in her Arms*;
> When *Chloris* is inform'd *how much he Loves*,
> The Rhime informs you *that she cruel proves*.[1]

[1] John Oldmixon, *Poems on Several Occasions* (1696), 'The Second Satire of Boileau, English'd', p. 80.

The *Essay on Criticism* was the product of Pope's new literary and
social life. Its brilliance reflects the optimism of a young poet who
has just found his place in the world of letters.

If we may believe Pope, *The Temple of Fame* was composed in 1711,
a year earlier than the *Essay on Criticism*, though it was not published
till 1715. In this work the most striking quality is the description,
particularly Pope's picture of the same kind of prospect of literary
history as he had introduced into the *Essay on Criticism*. Chaucer
provided him with a framework, but the whole poem is more like
one of the formally posed historical paintings which were the eighteenth century's idea of the heroic in art. The style itself suggests
that heroic elevation was in Pope's mind when he wrote it. Critics
have sometimes recalled Pope's love of painting to account for his
touches of vivid and sensitive detail, but we should remember that
painting did not mean to Pope the representation of minute particulars. Instead, he would have learned from Jervas the principles
of the grand style, how to imitate the broad conceptions of Raphael,
how to set figures according to the rules of *contra-posto*, and all the
rules of the art as Du Fresnoy had described them in his verse
treatise. *The Temple of Fame*, from this point of view, has as much
right to be called a history poem as a composition by Thornhill has
to be called a history painting. Yet, highly coloured and pictorial as
it is, it suggests some of the interests of Pope's maturity in an elementary form. He was to learn other ways of setting his sentiments
in an historical context, but *The Temple of Fame* is evidence of his
concern to do this even before he 'stoop'd to Truth, and moraliz'd
his song'.

Though the historical aspect of the poem was as yet only a part
of the picture gallery of Pope's imagination, the conclusion, a conventional meditation on Fame, moved him more nearly, and he deliberately turned it into a personal confession of his moral faith:

> Nor Fame I slight, nor for her Favours call;
> She comes unlook'd for, if she comes at all:
> But if the Purchase costs so dear a Price,
> As soothing Folly, or exalting Vice:
> Oh! if the Muse must flatter lawless Sway,
> And follow still where Fortune leads the way;

Or if no Basis bear my rising Name,
But the fall'n Ruins of Another's Fame:
Then teach me, Heaven! to scorn the guilty Bays;
Drive from my Breast that wretched Lust of Praise;
Unblemish'd let me live, or die unknown,
Oh grant an honest Fame, or grant me none!

(ll. 513–24.)

Pope neither lived unblemished nor died unknown, though he never hesitated to make these moral professions in his poetry. But he improved on the solemn ingenuousness of this declaration, and his later poems exhibit a subtle blending of moral assertion, autobiography, and irony, in which his life and his art are inextricably bound together. The professional argumentative poet had always needed to make certain large claims for himself, but the arrival of a poet like Pope, to whom his art was as much a *raison d'être* as a profession, was all that was wanted to turn the conventional attitude into a personal conviction. Invoking the Honest Muse was, for Pope, not merely a way of looking at literature or at life; it was a way of looking at himself. As early as 1711 he was aware of this personal need for moral justification, and the clumsy sincerity of the conclusion of *The Temple of Fame* betrays the intensity with which he felt it.

Pope's readers were accustomed to this attitude, and were less struck by it than by the technical skill which was shown in all his early poems, and particularly in *The Essay on Criticism*. His friends were impressed with the idea that he was destined for something even more serious, and Cromwell urged him to turn to drama:

Oh happy Favourite of the Muses! how *per-noctare*, all night long with them? but alas! you do but toy, but skirmish with them, and decline a close Engagement. Leave Elegy and Translation to the inferior Class, on whom the Muses only glance now and then like our Winter-Sun, and then leave 'em in the dark. Think on the Dignity of Tragedy, which is of the greater Poetry, as *Dennis* says, and foil him at his other weapon, as you have done in Criticism. Every one wonders that a Genius like yours will not support the sinking *Drama*;[1]

Pope's reply to this letter was a facetious account of his amorous feelings, a suggestion, perhaps, that the poetry of sentiment rather

[1] Sherburn, op. cit., vol. i, p. 136 (7 Dec. 1711).

than 'the greater poetry' was his *métier* at the moment. In his next work he left the serious moral tone and the survey of history that he had touched on in the *Essay on Criticism* and *The Temple of Fame*. He did not return to them for many years, until the later Epistles and the *Essay on Man*. The masterpiece of this early period, *The Rape of the Lock*, is a completely different kind of work—a poem about love, a lyrical satire, in which the fashionable wit of a lively convention mingles with the more romantic ideas that had grown up in the privacy of Pope's imagination.

II

If the genius of Pope's later poetry is friendship, that of his earlier work is love. He had a warm imaginative sympathy with passions life inevitably frustrated in 'the little Alexander the women laugh at'; he liked nothing better than to hint at personal experiences behind his most formal love poems. At the end of the *Elegy to the Memory of an Unfortunate Lady* he singles out the figure of the poet and makes him into a lover, and by this he transforms the work into a personal lament:

> Ev'n he, whose soul now melts in mournful lays,
> Shall shortly want the gen'rous tear he pays;
> Then from his closing eyes thy form shall part,
> And the last pang shall tear thee from his heart,
> Life's idle business at one gasp be o'er,
> The Muse forgot, and thou belov'd no more!
>
> (ll. 77–82.)

This is very different from Dryden's elegiac mood. The last verses of *To the Memory of Mr. Oldham* say nothing about the sentiments of private friendship, and the love of Antony and Cleopatra adds little to the general emotion of the lines from the last scene of *All for Love*:

> Think we have had a clear and glorious day
> And Heaven did kindly to delay the storm
> Just till our close of evening.
>
> (v. i, ll. 389–91.)

Dryden makes little appeal to personal emotion. He gives to

common griefs their common value. Pope gives them their individual intensity.

A whole group of poems deals with themes of love and transience, sometimes with lyric overtones, as in the *Elegy* and *Eloisa to Abelard*, sometimes satirically, as in *The Rape of the Lock*, and often in epistolary poems like those *To Miss Blount with the Works of Voiture*, *To Miss Blount on her leaving the Town after the Coronation*, or, later, *Moral Essay* II, *To a Lady, of the Characters of Women*. All these were composed before 1717 except the last, which is a mosaic, made up of fragments of characters and reflections written earlier.

The *Elegy* and *Eloisa to Abelard* are poems of sentiment in the heightened rhetorical style. The *Elegy* is full of heroic feeling:

> Is there no bright reversion in the sky,
> For those who greatly think, or bravely die?
>
> (ll. 9–10.)

and *Eloisa to Abelard* is written in 'the language of the heart', which Pope here interprets as a mingling of the heroic tragic vein with Crashaw's luxurious style and his own lyric manner. The setting is theatrical and picturesque, yet truth to nature is the key to the poem. Its success was such that Mrs. Thrale tells us it was a favourite with 'all the kept mistresses of the town', which she takes as a tribute to its 'Nature and Passion'.[1] It is Pope's modern version of the heroic epistle, the letter of a deserted woman to her lover, originated by Ovid; but his version is also an original. In the first place the poem is based on the real letters of an historical person, a fact which recommended it to Johnson, who observed approvingly of the poem, 'the heart naturally loves truth'. In the second place, everything is done to make 'the well sung woes' as personally moving as possible. 'The Epistle of Eloise grows warm, and begins to have some Breathings of the Heart in it, which may make posterity think I was in love', Pope wrote to Martha Blount (perhaps in 1716), and he added: 'I can scarce find it in my heart to leave out the conclusion I once intended for it.'[2] The conclusion as it stands, where Eloisa addresses herself to some future bard who may find

---

[1] *Thraliana*, ed. K. C. Balderston, 2nd ed. (1951), vol. i, p. 536.
[2] Sherburn, op. cit., vol. i, p. 338 (Mar. 1716?).

himself in her plight, turns the last lines of the poem into a personal confession. With the help of Pope's letters, posterity has assumed that when he wrote it he was indeed in love, with Lady Mary Wortley Montagu, who was travelling in eastern Europe when the poem was composed. Once again Pope had related a literary convention to the circumstances of his own life.

The other poems of the group are a different kind of hybrid. In them personal tenderness is infused into the moral and social tone of the *Essay on Criticism*. The idea of a moral love poem is scarcely attractive, and it is chilling to read how Pope, remarking to Spence that no poem was worth writing unless it contained a moral, maintained that even in love verses 'it may be flung in by the way'. But he was too good an artist to fling anything in by the way, as these poems show. They are not 'moral' in any obvious sense, for they possess a kind of gaiety that turns quickly to wit or tenderness, and they display all that responsiveness to the world of appearance which is one of Pope's most attractive poetic qualities. Only the epistle *To Miss Blount with the Works of Voiture* (the least successful of them) has something of the heaviness we associate with didactic poetry. In the others satire, compliment, reflection and description form a shifting pattern through which the shadows of older conventions of the Restoration wits momentarily emerge. The essay *Of the Characters of Women* and the epistle *To Miss Blount on her leaving the Town* belong to two traditions we have already discussed in Restoration verse—the attack on women, and the town satire against the country, although, as always with Pope, they are developments, not simple imitations.

The epistle comparing the town to the country is the form of *To Miss Blount on her leaving the Town after the Coronation*. Many of the conventional attitudes are there, with a hint, even, of a definite Restoration source. The country is not an idyllic retreat, but a sad and solitary prospect for a society beauty at the end of the season. Harriet, in *The Man of Mode*, had lamented her return

To a great rambling lone house, that looks as it were not inhabited, the family's so small: there you'll find my Mother, an old lame Aunt, and my self, Sir, perch'd up on Chairs at a distance in a large parlour; sitting moping like three or four Melancholy Birds in a spacious vollary. . . . Pity me, who am going to that sad place. Methinks I hear the hateful noise of Rooks already—kaw, kaw, kaw—[1]

A similar fate awaits Pope's Zephalinda. The little comedy of rustic life, where the heroine trifles 'o'er cold coffee with the spoon' and submits to the booby squire who 'makes love with nods, and knees beneath a table', is introduced by a catalogue of the same brief details as appear in Etherege's play:

> She went, to plain-work, and to purling brooks,
> Old-fashion'd halls, dull aunts, and croaking rooks . . .
>
> (ll. 11–12.)

We do not know whether Pope was thinking of Etherege, for the picture had become so conventional that he used it casually in his private letters, teasing Martha Blount in the same terms when her sister was still in town, and she at home: 'Let your faithless Sister triumph in her ill-gotten Treasures; let her put on New Gowns to be the Gaze of Fools, and Pageant of a Birth-night! While you with all your innocence enjoy a Shadey Grove without any leaves on, & dwell with a virtuous Aunt in a Country Paradise.'[2]

Again Pope transformed convention in this epistle and complicated it. The country house and its household are exact and real. Behind them lies the solid benevolent tradition of Horatian rusticity. The grove where Zephalinda dreams of town triumphs is romantically vague, a poetic vision of a rural retreat. Pope delights in both aspects. There is a touch of irony in that he is weary with what she is dreaming of. 'Vext to be still in town', the poet conjures up from the materials of conventional witty disparagement an innocently dull yet delectable picture of country life. Society and retirement play equal parts in the poem: country life is gently mocked but described with loving care, while town society is at once despised and desired—the poet's burden and the dream of an idle girl on a summer evening.

The Rape of the Lock shows the same balance between the romantic and the moral mood. A deliberate ambiguity surrounds the heroine, the setting, and the situation itself. As material for a comedy of the sexes in typical Restoration style, the original incident of the theft

---

[1] Etherege, *The Man of Mode or Sir Fopling Flutter* (1676), V. ii.
[2] Sherburn, op. cit., vol. i, p. 375 (Nov. 1716).

of Arabella Fermor's hair was ideal. Indeed the setting and the characters in this poem belong to the world of Restoration comedy. But Pope added another dimension which, while it is not displayed openly until the close, is implicit in every ironic detail. In *The Rape of the Lock* there is as much criticism of the vanity and insincerity of the fashionable game of love as sympathy with its voluptuous atmosphere of sentiment; as much censure of the world of fashion as delight in its elegance. Pope does not scruple to show Belinda as vain, foolish, and affected, but she is still the romantic heroine, painted with a lover's admiration:

> If to her share some Female Errors fall,
> Look on her Face, and you'll forget 'em all.
>   (Canto II, ll. 17–18.)

Yet Belinda can be both chided and advised, and this removes her from her sisters of Restoration comedy and satire. Clarissa, with a return to the old idea of transience and a sound moral doctrine based on that, reminds her of matters more serious than the blow to her vanity:

> Oh! if to dance all Night, and dress all Day,
> Charm'd the Small-pox, or chas'd old Age away;
> Who would not scorn what Huswife's Cares produce,
> Or who would learn one earthly Thing of Use? . . .
> Beauties in vain their pretty Eyes may roll;
> Charms strike the Sight, but Merit wins the Soul.
>   (Canto V, ll. 19–22, 33–34.)

Clarissa is written off as a prude by the fops and the ladies, and any Restoration wit would have agreed with them. There is no room for 'good humour' or 'merit' in their world. Age is no matter for reflection to them, but a misfortune only to be endured by being mocked at. The Restoration poet comments on his mistress:

> All her arts can ne'er retrieve her,
> Poor Aurelia's growing old.[1]

Once in a while he may offer fidelity, but he is more likely to move on to the next love while his own youth lasts. Age is the demon that haunts his world. Congreve himself could scarcely offer advice to Millamant, or allow his audience to reflect that the great differ-

---

[1] *New Academy of Compliments*, 1671. 'When Aurelia first I Courted', ll. 7–8.

ence between her and Lady Wishfort, that comic parody of Millamant's charming affectation, is that the one is young and the other
old. But Pope was on Clarissa's side. He concludes the satire with
a variation on the traditional elegiac theme of transience, and
though he turns it to a love compliment, it is a gently relentless
counterpart to Clarissa's warning. He promises Belinda immortality
in his verse, but like all poetic immortality, it is bought at the price
of death and the triumph of time over her beauty:

> For, after all the Murders of your Eye,
> When, after Millions slain, your self shall die;
> When those fair Suns shall sett, as sett they must,
> And all those Tresses shall be laid in Dust;
> *This Lock* the Muse shall consecrate to Fame,
> And mid'st the Stars inscribe *Belinda's* name!
>
> (Canto V, ll. 145–50.)

This conclusion makes the satire as elegantly serious a work as
any lyric of Marvell's. Indeed *The Rape of the Lock* is a lyric satire,
a poem of love and admiration and regret, as well as a witty display
of mock-heroic ingenuity. The hard clear world of Restoration
comedy is reflected in it as in a convex mirror, exact and beautiful,
but contained within another dimension that makes its small perfection look both comic and sad.

This is a long way from the Restoration attack on woman, and
yet it is on that convention that these poems of Pope's are based. He
had already practised it in the character studies of Sylvia, Phryne,
and Artemisia, and he had remembered Halifax's *On the Countess
Dowager of* ——, where the characteristic picture of an ageing
beauty is combined with a moral comment on her absurdity:

> Nature did ne'er so equally divide
> A Female Heart, 'twixt Piety and Pride:
> Her Waiting-maids prevent the Peep of Day,
> And, all in Order, on her Toilet lay
> Pray'r-books, Patch-Boxes, Sermon-notes and Paint,
> At once t'improve the Sinner and the Saint.[1]

The heart divided between Piety and Pride was the source of

---

[1] See Appendix for this poem of Halifax's in full, and for Dorset's poem on the
Countess of Dorchester, on which Pope's *Phryne* and *Artemisia* were based.

Pope's early sketch of Sylvia, who became Narcissa in *Of the Characters of Women*, and the disarray of Mopsa's dressing-table was echoed in Belinda's toilet with its confusion of 'Puffs, Powders, Patches, Bibles, Billet-doux'. He remembered too Rochester's brilliant study of the affected country lady in *Artemisia in the Town to Chloe in the Country*, and had modelled Sir Plume on the portrait of the witless fop in *Tunbridge Wells*. Rochester had powerfully conveyed the gestures and the inane conversation of his beau:

> He puzzled bites his Nails, both to display
> The Sparkling Ring, and think what next to say,
> And thus breaks out afresh: Madam, I gad,
> Your luck, last Night, at Cards was mighty bad
> At Cribbidge Fifty nine, and the next Show,
> To make your Game, and yet to want those Two;
> G—— D-me, Madam, I'm the Son of a Whore,
> If in my Life, I saw the like before.[1]

> (*Tunbridge Wells*, ll. 107–14.)

But Pope compresses his dialogue, description, and gesture to even narrower limits, without losing 'the harmony of the numbers' which he criticized Rochester for neglecting. Yet in spite of its superiority, the famous portrait of Sir Plume in *The Rape of the Lock* belongs clearly in this tradition and is only one example of how much Pope owed to Rochester.

Pope not only polished the tradition, however; he changed its whole tone. Addison and Prior had softened the attitude of the satirists towards women, the one in his essays, the other in his lyrics. Pope went further. There is as much savagery in *Moral Essay* II, *Of the Characters of Women*, as in many of the anonymous satires of the old convention; the character studies of Narcissa, Atossa, and Chloe, though restrained even in comparison with his own earlier practice pieces, are more effectively lethal in their precision and ruthless accuracy. Yet these parts are not the sum of the whole poem. Its setting has some of the aesthetic and lyrical elements of his poems of sentiment. The work begins as in a gallery where the pictures, all differing in pose and all alike in features, represent woman in her various moods. As the figures step down from the

---

[1] Rochester, op. cit., p. 90.

canvasses and proceed to act their proper parts, glimpses of the real world intrude like pictures, providing a series of dramatic interludes that vary the discourse—Papillia's park, Chloe's room, where 'she, while her Lover pants upon her breast, can mark the figures on an Indian chest'. The framework of the poem is discourse—a reflective monologue, in which the author plays an important role, and the actions of the characters are linked by a commentary which prepares us for the moment when they are dismissed and the poet himself steps forward. Rochester had made a rough attempt at this device in *Timon* and in *Tunbridge Wells*, but though he achieves an effect of immediacy by it, he falls short of the intimate sincerity which arises from Pope's skilful use of rhetoric and realism.

When Pope speaks in his own person at the conclusion of *Moral Essay* II, he does so to relate everything he has written to the wider concerns of feeling and morality of which he himself appears as guardian in all his poems. He turns first to a prospect of the life of the women we have seen in momentary activity—a brief history of their common experience:

> At last, to follies Youth could scarce defend,
> It grows their Age's prudence to pretend;
> Asham'd to own they gave delight before,
> Reduc'd to feign it, when they give no more:
> As Hags hold Sabbaths, less for joy than spight,
> So these their merry, miserable Night;
> Still round and round the Ghosts of Beauty glide,
> And haunt the places where their Honour dy'd.
>
> (ll. 235–42.)

In the course of the poem, the characters have progressed from portraits to living people, and finally to phantoms in this last image where fancy lingers retrospectively over what has been censured, giving the satire for a moment the kind of lyrical resolution which concludes *The Rape of the Lock*. The epilogue to this epistolary comedy repeats the moral of the earlier poem and of *To Miss Blount with the Works of Voiture*:

> Ah Friend! to dazzle let the Vain design,
> To raise the Thought and touch the Heart, be thine!
>
> (ll. 249–50.)

and the conclusion is again a love compliment through which Pope insinuates ideas of tenderness and friendship which counterpoint the severity of his satire. Thus the realism of the Restoration tradition is reproduced in a new setting, and a broader one which takes into account time and virtue.

The idea of time in this second Moral Essay is associated with the retrospective survey which Pope had already used in *The Temple of Fame* and the *Essay on Criticism*. But here the survey extends only over the span of a human lifetime, and the effect is intimate rather than grand. It is still an historical perspective, however, a general background against which the particular instance can be measured. Youth and age, the past and the future are the poles between which Pope's satire turns. They inform the witty observations with ironic inevitability and sober sadness:

> See how the World its Veterans rewards!
> A Youth of frolics, an old Age of Cards,
> Fair to no purpose, artful to no end,
> Young without Lovers, old without a Friend,
> A Fop their Passion, but their Prize a Sot,
> Alive, ridiculous, and dead, forgot!
>
> (ll. 243–8.)

Pope had already learned how to create for himself in his poetry a role in which he might represent the tried values of tradition and at the same time reveal his personal feelings and individual sensibility. He had made himself a correct imitator, but he had not turned his back on more recent conventions. Having mastered the academic and the polite, he took over the honest realism of the Restoration style and combined both with his own peculiar bent in order to acquire a new tone of sincerity. In this style, at once flexible and clear, he could be both detached and involved; it was the perfect medium for what he chose to do when 'he stoop'd to truth and moraliz'd his song' as circumstances changed in his personal life and in the State. The impulse which persuaded him to turn 'from sounds to things, from fancy to the heart' was as characteristic of the new Augustan approach to poetry as it was of his own genius. Already in his early work he had discovered a style and an attitude appropriate to it.

III

In September 1712 the Tories began to negotiate the Treaty of
Utrecht, and the occasion gave poets of both parties a chance to
celebrate the end of war. At the suggestion of Granville, Lord
Lansdowne, who was then Secretary at War, Pope took out his
topographical poem *Windsor Forest* and tagged on to it an enthusiastic
compliment to the Queen and a glowing picture of the prospects of
trade. His letter to Lansdowne, who had accepted the dedication,
was nervously fulsome: 'I thank you for having given my poem of
Windsor Forest its greatest ornament, that of bearing your name in
the front of it.'[1] He even asked Lansdowne to correct and polish
his verses. Pope's whole tone at this point suggests uncertainty. He
was beginning to make new acquaintances in Swift's set and was
growing tired of the 'little Senate' round Addison, with whom he
was uneasily associated. There were poetic rivals in Addison's
camp, though minor ones. Thomas Tickell was the immediate
cause of the breach between Pope and Addison, when the latter
sponsored Tickell's translation of Homer (indeed, some suspected
he had written it himself); and he had appeared already as a com-
petitor in 1712 with his poem *On the Prospect of Peace*. Pope wrote
anxiously to his friend Caryll, asking him if he preferred Tickell's
lines on trade to his own: 'And lastly, the description of the several
parts of the world in regard to our trade: which has interfered with
some lines of my own in the poem called Windsor Forrest, tho'
written before I saw his; I transcribe both and desire your sincere
judgment whether I ought not to strike out mine, either as they
seem too like his, or as they are inferior.'[2] Caryll satisfied him, and
the lines were left in. But Tickell was a competent poet, and such
a favourite of Addison's as to cause Pope some uneasiness. It must
have been galling to one of his temperament to be confronted in
so many occasional poems by Addison's protégé. Even his Prologue
to *Cato*, of which he complained that the audience on the first night
clapped him into a Whig, was matched by Tickell's *To Mr. Addison
on his Tragedy of Cato*.

Pope did not wish to be associated exclusively with one political

---

[1] Sherburn, op. cit., vol. i, p. 172 (10 Jan. 1712/13).
[2] Ibid., p. 157.

party. His earlier friends, Walsh, Garth, and Congreve, had been Whigs; his most intimate later friends were to be Tories, though he never lost his contacts with the other party. There was less rivalry, however, in the Tory circle. Men like Bolingbroke, Harley, and Swift were supreme in their own fields, and their appreciation naturally seemed more rewarding than the professional scrutiny of Addison and his followers. Like Addison, Pope could bear no brother near the throne, not so much from simple envy as from a protective fear for that one talent which had to serve him in the place of the variety of gifts possessed by more ordinary men. But it is fruitless to try to apportion the blame in the quarrel between him and Addison. Perhaps no one has described the truth of the situation with more understanding than Isaac D'Israeli:

Tempers of watchful delicacy gather up in silence and darkness motives so shadowy in their origin, and of such minute growth, that, never breaking out into any open act, they escape all other eyes but those of the parties themselves. These causes of enmity are too subtle to bear the touch; they cannot be inquired after, nor can they be described; and it may be said, that the minds of such men have rather quarrelled, than they themselves: they utter no complaints, but they avoid each other.[1]

Pope's new friends were a different sort of men. Swift was at the height of his public importance in 1712, and by the end of the year the Scriblerus Club had been formed, of which he, Pope, Arbuthnot, and Gay were the principal members. Swift was the leading spirit, and through him the others came into contact with Harley, Bolingbroke, and Atterbury, who influenced Pope's outlook on life more decidedly than even his literary friends. The club, with its quasi-philosophical colouring, kept him in touch with the learned traditions of humanist satire in Rabelais and Erasmus, and the more recent issues of the battle of the ancients and the moderns, while meetings with Harley and Bolingbroke gave Pope the precious feeling of taking a full part in the world of affairs.

Both these new aspects of his life affected his poetry. Pope was now concerned primarily with the translation of Homer, which took him ten years in all. During this decade the only new poems of

[1] Isaac D'Israeli, *Quarrels of Authors*, vol. i (1814), pp. 240-1.

any substance he composed were *Eloisa to Abelard* (1717), *To Mr. Addison* (1720), and *To Oxford* (1721). His edition of Buckingham's works[1] and of Shakespeare appeared in this period, but most of his energies were concentrated on the translation, which not only acquired for him prestige he was never to lose, but also gave him financial independence, dispelling that bogy of insecurity which had haunted so many of his predecessors. The 1728 *Dunciad*, however, and in particular the Variorum *Dunciad* which followed it the next year, was the fruit of the new society into which he had moved by 1713.

The Variorum notes and additions to the *Dunciad* put the poem in the category of the satires against learning which grew out of the ancients and moderns dispute. But it is something more than this. *The Dunciad* returns to the mock-heroic form for a purpose so different from that of *The Rape of the Lock* that the two works scarcely seem to belong to the same kind. In the early poem Pope's imagination was full of romantic and lyric themes, his memory was haunted by the world of Restoration comedy even more than by the epic. In *The Dunciad* he was more deeply concerned with his own idea of the noble and heroic, the true epic values, but seen in ironic reverse. The counterpart of the prevailing chaos in the world of dunces is a moral order which Pope fully realized and expressed only in his later satires. This order took shape in his imagination under the pervasive influence of his new friends, in particular Swift and Bolingbroke.

The first three books of the 1729 *Dunciad* belong to the tradition of literary satire, and references to Butler, Oldham, Dryden, to private Scriblerus jokes and such vendettas as that of the wits against Bentley, are as much part of the fun as references to the epic. For there is fun in *The Dunciad* as there is in *MacFlecknoe*. It was written to rid Pope of literary gnats and nuisances, and also to show off his skill in handling a complex form and in bringing together an almost inconceivable variety of allusions to the whole range of the satire of the past half-century. For this reason we should not search too earnestly for its particular moral. If there is any, it is not personal, but one that was implicit in Pope's models. His predecessors had associated good poetry with honesty and sound principles,

---

[1] John Sheffield, Duke of Buckingham, author of the *Essay on Poetry*.

while, by a simple contemporary matter of fact, bad poetry was connected with pamphleteering and all the shady business of trading in wit.

Though a recent critic[1] has pointed out that there is a serious action in *The Dunciad*—the removal of the Empire of Dullness from the City to St. James's, once the centre of courtly wit—there is no deeply felt political or economic criticism behind this. Pope was obliged to associate Grub Street and the City in order to make good his allusions to that ready-made mythology of City hacks— Ogilby, Settle, and Blackmore—already immortalized by Dryden. In Dryden's days the City had certain precise social and political associations which were already changing slightly in the eighteenth century. But the religious associations of Puritanism and the Good Old Cause attached themselves less to the merchants of the later period, and so the traditional attack on hypocrisy, or puritanical distrust of pleasure and of the arts, had ceased to have the same significance in relation to the City in the eighteenth century. The great merchants who helped to found the Bank of England were not the coarse fanatics Dryden had depicted (it is questionable that they ever were), but men whose power and wealth made their children eligible matches for the aristocracy, and who were fostering a culture of their own—not the homely spectacles of Smithfield, but the literature of *The Spectator* and the novel. Pope's animosity against the City, in so far as it existed in reality as opposed to literary convention, was due to the influence of Bolingbroke, who had publicly stated his disapproval of the creation of a moneyed interest by the Whigs to balance the landed interest.[2] Here again there is a rather different social and political emphasis. The Property Qualification Act of 1710 (usually called Bolingbroke's Act) had established that county members must have landed property worth £600 a year, and borough members £300, and the preamble states that the purpose

---

[1] A. L. Williams, *Pope's Dunciad* (1955).

[2] In *Of the Use and Study of History*, vol. i, p. 46, Bolingbroke accuses the Whigs of having undermined the stability of the country by the following means: 'The notion of attaching men to the new government, by tempting them to embark their fortunes on the same bottom . . . the notion of creating a new, that is a monied interest, in opposition to the landed interest or as a balance to it, and of acquiring influence in the city of London at least by the establishment of great corporations. . . .'

of the Act was 'to preserve the Constitution and freedom of Parliament'. The arguments used by its supporters would have appealed particularly to Pope: that men of property could be independent because they had no need to accept bribes, and that landed men, by the security and responsibility of their possessions, were more likely to be independent than merely moneyed men. This question of independence and freedom from corruption had already begun to play an important part in the literary development of the figure of the country gentleman, the honest Horatian hero. Pope carries it to further lengths; his real attack on the City is the same as his attack on the Court or society—an attack on money values and corruption. It is only as part of a traditional literary convention that he turns to the coarse familiar abuse in which Dryden expressed his scorn for those 'godly' hypocrites the mercantile class. Pope's own friendship with men like the Bethels, the one brother a City merchant, the other a Whig landed gentleman, and both descended from Dryden's Shimei, would have prevented him from making any glib personal association between the City and bad taste. He preferred to retain the older satirical tradition of attack on money itself as the root of all evil, and proclaims himself as anxious to 'bare the mean heart that lurks beneath a star' as to expose Sir Balaam, the *nouveau riche*, whose simple values are destroyed by prosperity. Pope's City background in *The Dunciad* was, then, part of a well-established literary convention, and to look for a wider or more contemporary significance in it can be misleading. The moral of the poem was evident to readers familiar with the Restoration poets. If 'Nature's chief masterpiece is writing well', then Nature's chief monstrosity is writing badly. This is the real justification of Pope's attack.

Once this is accepted, we can enjoy the humour and imaginative range of *The Dunciad*. Pope is here challenging Dryden in the art of being ingeniously funny. His echoes of Dryden are many: the absurdity of the Lord Mayor's procession takes us back to *Mac-Flecknoe*, the braying of Blackmore to the Prologue to *The Pilgrim*, the style of the satire to the attacks on Og and Doeg:

> Know, Settle, cloy'd with custard and with praise,
> Is gather'd to the Dull of antient days,

> Safe, where no critic damns, no duns molest,
> Where Gildon, Banks, and high-born Howard rest.
>
> (Bk. I, ll. 247–250.)

The poem is graver than *MacFlecknoe* because of the difficulty of sustaining humour at such length, and because of the effect of re-capitulating in a personal context all the overtones of a long satiric tradition. Oldham's influence is almost as strong as Dryden's. His *Satyr* in which Spenser's ghost laments the condition of poetry is often echoed, and Pope caught its note of vigorous condemnation:

> So many now and bad the Scribblers be
> 'Tis Scandal to be of the Company . . .

These lines of Oldham's could be the motto for the poem, for they reveal the source of Pope's anger—the professional's disgust at see-ing his trade debased by hacks. Even the sneers at poverty which De Quincey hated in the poem are a protest against the dishonest poverty that comes from a man's trying to do something for which he is not fitted, and then selling his misapplied talents. The opinion of Johnson, another great professional, is worth recalling on this point:

> In this design there was petulance and malignity enough; but I cannot think it very criminal. An author places himself uncalled be-fore the tribunal of criticism, and solicits fame at the hazard of dis-grace. Dulness or deformity are not culpable in themselves, but may be very justly reproached when they pretend to the honour of wit, or the influence of beauty. If bad writers were to pass without repre-hension what should restrain them?[1]

The Variorum *Dunciad* belongs to the same world as *The Essay on Criticism*. It adds little to the satiric tradition, but it marks the cul-mination of that school of satire which a new literary situation had created, and in which literary standards were related widely to moral and social principles. Pope was not content for long to neglect these principles, or to keep them out of his satire. The fourth book of *The Dunciad*, his last poem, draws on other resources than the conventions of literary warfare. He prepared himself for it by a whole

---

[1] Johnson, *Lives*, 'Life of Pope', p. 241.

series of satires in which style and subject-matter were both modified by his personal experiences and by the influences of the world
in which he lived.

Pope's life after 1717 still swung between the extremes of solitude
and society, but he was gradually establishing a middle way between them. On the death of his father in 1717 he made preparations
to leave Chiswick, where the Popes had moved after selling their
house at Binfield, and in 1719 he bought his villa at Twickenham
and settled there with his mother. He was now ideally situated,
close enough to London to be within easy reach of friends, and yet
still in the country, where he could cultivate more retired pursuits.
There is a passage in his translation of Horace's sixth Satire of
the second Book, which, though it was not published till 1738,
described the kind of life Pope now led with his friends at Twickenham:

> O charming Noons! and Nights divine!
> Or when I sup, or when I dine,
> My Friends above, my Folks below,
> Chatting and laughing all-a-row. . . .
> Each willing to be pleas'd, and please,
> And even the very Dogs at ease!
>
> (ll. 133–6, 139–40.)

Horace's account of the conversation could be translated almost
literally in order to illustrate the topics they discussed:

> Which is the happier or the wiser,
> A man of Merit, or a Miser?
> Whether we ought to chuse our Friends,
> For their own Worth, or our own Ends?
> What good, or better, we may call,
> And what, the very best of all?
>
> (ll. 147–52.)

The answers to such questions are hardly open to dispute, and they
imply an attitude based on emotional convictions—the kind of
feelings that are always uppermost in Pope's moral poetry, however
rational it may seem.

Of course, the picture was an ideal one. Life in the society of

Bolingbroke and Harley was not without those embarrassments that Swift and Pope saw so clearly in the relationships of other men of power with their dependents. Pope was saved from them by his financial and professional independence. Swift was sometimes forced into a more dubious position. An uncomfortable glimpse of Swift, the sturdy advocate of independent honesty, forced to compromise with his principles, occurs in the *Journal to Stella* when he describes his introduction of Parnell to Bolingbroke. Parnell was Swift's protégé, and he too was engaged on a poem on the Peace, which, when it finally appeared, contained the inevitable compliments to the Ministry. He had also inserted several compliments to St. John in person in his *Essay on the Different Styles of Poetry*, which were almost certainly made at Swift's suggestion, for Swift writes in the *Journal*: 'I gave Ld Bolinbroke a Poem of Parnels, I made Parnel insert some Complimts in it to His Ldship; He is extreamly pleasd with it & read some parts of it to day to Ld Treasr who liked it as much; . . .'[1] Though later he remarked 'I value myself upon making the Ministry desire to be acquainted with Parnel; & not Parnel with the Ministry', the service was not performed without some cost to the integrity of both poets. For it was accepted by Pope and his circle that friendship had taken the place of patronage. Pope's compliment to Lansdowne is his only panegyric, and Swift, though he advised others to make the sacrifice, kept his own hands clean. Yet neither of them was immune from the feeling that there was some prestige in friendship with the great. Johnson, who scorned the touch of vulgarity in this attitude, disliked Pope's habit of claiming superior virtue for his noble friends, but Pope was forced to convince himself of the merit of these men before he introduced them into his poems, and his private attitude seems to have been a similar blend of gratification and hero-worship.

Especially in the case of Bolingbroke, Pope was dazzled more by personality than by position. He was disarmed by those courtly habits, that parade of easy negligence and light learning, which characterized Bolingbroke, and this same attraction helped to blind him to Bolingbroke's imperfections as a statesman or philosopher. Both Pope and Swift, for all their apparent scepticism, were easy

[1] Swift, *Journal to Stella*, ed. H. Williams, vol. ii (1948), p. 586.

victims of charm. Swift, who prided himself on his clear-sightedness, wrote of Bolingbroke in 1711:

I think Mr. St. John the greatest young man I ever knew; wit, capacity, beauty, quickness of apprehension, good learning, and an excellent taste; the best orator in the house of commons, admirable conversation, good nature, and good manners; generous, and a despiser of money. His only fault is talking to his friends in way of complaint of too great a load of business, which looks a little like affectation; and he endeavours too much to mix the fine gentleman, and man of pleasure, with the man of business.[1]

Such a combination of qualities would appeal to Pope's romantic sensibilities, and his infatuation with Bolingbroke was lifelong. Bolingbroke's disgrace, exile, and return to retirement appealed even more strongly to Pope, for he came back to England as that favourite figure—the statesman out of place, whom the poet could love and compliment without suspicion of self-interest. His affection for Bolingbroke after his return is one of the most significant factors in his career. Together they discussed the value of retirement, and while Pope innocently gave the dress of poetry to the other's deistic ideas (which Swift more shrewdly recognized for what they were), Bolingbroke set the poet's imagination working in new ways. In particular, one of his main interests, his idea of history, influenced profoundly Pope's attitude towards human nature and conduct.

IV

Bolingbroke studied history, wrote it, and, in a sense, made it. To Pope he must have seemed a living instance of his own theory of 'philosophy teaching by examples'. His approach was to colour all Pope's poetry from the *Essay on Man* to the last book of *The Dunciad*, from the flexible discursive style of the epistolary satires to the tableaux and set pieces of the mock-heroic. During these years Pope's imagination was preoccupied by the way in which the epic ideals of nobility and integrity could be interpreted in the society of his day. The *Essay on Man* itself was not originally intended to stand on its own. It was meant to introduce an ambitious scheme on an epic

[1] Swift, *Journal to Stella*, vol. ii, p. 401.

scale—a treatise on what constitutes virtue in human thought and conduct. Johnson, in his *Life of Pope*, quotes Pope's letter to Swift describing his scheme of a poem to follow the *Essay on Man*, in four epistles: '1. Of the Extent and Limits of Human Reason and Science. 2. A View of the useful and therefore attainable, . . . Arts. 3. Of the Nature, Ends, Application, and Use of different Capacities. 4. Of the Use of *Learning*, of the *Science*, of the *World*, and of *Wit*. It will conclude with a satire against the Misapplication of all these, exemplified by Pictures, Characters, and Examples'.[1] When Pope thought of writing an epic, he turned naturally again to ethical themes of the type which he told Spence would have been included in his projected *Brutus*. But moral attitudes were so much bound up for him with contemporary life, his own and his friends', and with satire, that he naturally expressed them either by personal assertion, or through illustrations and examples in the style of the didactic satirist rather than of the epic poet. The *Essay on Man*, the *Moral Essays*, the *Imitations of Horace*, and the greater *Dunciad* were all made out of subjects and ideas originally intended for the great single poem which was never written.

None of these poems except *The Dunciad* has any clear external form, but all of them possess an inner coherance and unity which is partly due to the way Pope perfected his discursive style, and partly to the implicit moral assumptions that lie behind it. These assumptions are worth comparing with the historical approach Pope learned from Bolingbroke and which was rapidly gaining ground in the early eighteenth century as a mode of thinking.

History as an exemplary discipline had always been held in respect. From the Renaissance onwards two strains of thought regarding history as a branch of literature are to be found, sometimes mingling and sometimes conflicting in critical theory. From the classical rhetoricians the critics took their idea of history as a noble and elevated art. Quintilian, contrasting it with oratory, says that 'it has a certain affinity to poetry, and may be regarded as a kind of prose poem . . . designed to record events for the benefit of posterity, and to win glory for its author'.[2] Traditionally, tragic plots

---

[1] Johnson, *Lives*, 'Life of Pope', p. 183.
[2] Quintilian, op. cit. x. l. 31: 'Est enim proxima poetis et quodammodo carmen

were historical rather than fictional, and the epic itself was sometimes referred to as historical poetry. But, on the other hand, the
superiority of the higher branches of poetry to simple factual history
had long been maintained on the ground which Aristotle used in
defending poetry against Plato: that poetry is 'something more
philosophic and of graver import than history, since its statements
are of the nature rather of universals, whereas those of history are
singulars'.[1]

A full statement of the Renaissance attitude to history, in which
these strains are united, is given by Puttenham in the *Arte of
English Poesie*, Book I, chapters 19 and 20. Chapter 19 opens with
a lofty account of the value of past example in poetry:

> There is nothing in man of all the potential parts of his mind
> (reason and will except) more noble or more necessary to the active
> life than memory: because it maketh most to a sound judgement and
> perfect worldly wisedome, examining and comparing the times past
> with the present, and by them both considering the time to come. . . .
> Right so no kind of argument in all the Oratorie craft, doth better
> perswade and more universally satisfie then example, which is but the
> representation of old memories, and like successes happened in times
> past. For these regards the Poesie historicall is of all other next the
> divine the most honorable and worthy, as well for the common bene-
> fit as for the special comfort every man receiveth by it.[2]

Such exemplary historical poetry, however, need not always be
a record of actual events, 'considering that many times it is seene a
fained matter or altogether fabulous . . . works to no lesse good conclusions for example then the most true and veritable . . .'. Puttenham concludes that histories are of three sorts, 'wholly true and
wholly false and a third holding part of either . . .', and he makes no
distinction of merit between them. To him the word 'historical'
means scarcely more than 'exemplary', and the only condition he
lays down for this exemplary material is that it must be drawn from

solutum, et scribitur ad narrandum non ad probandum, totumque opus non ad
actum rei pugnam que praesentem, sed ad memoriam posteritatis et ingenii famam
componitur.'
   [1] Aristotle, *Poetics* (trans. Bywater), section 9.
   [2] Puttenham, *Arte of English Poesie*, ed. G. D. Willcock and A. Walker (1936),
p. 39.

the lives of 'great and excellent persons', and never from those of the obscure or simple.

At the beginning of the eighteenth century the same views of the nature of history were current, but they had acquired a new slant, not unlike that which had changed the attitude towards panegyric. The poet of Pope's age still thought it good to praise; a noble or virtuous man is an example both to his own age and to posterity. But his compliment is no longer a hyperbolic image of glory: it purports to be a frank and manly appraisal of the real qualities of his subject. Similarly, the Augustans felt that history, to be fully exemplary, must be authentic. The violent changes of rule and the conflicting political theories in the seventeenth century led to a desire for stability and rational continuity, and the eighteenth-century appeal to history was an appeal to carefully selected precedent rather than to ancient authority. The historians and politicians of the period liked to draw analogies between historical situations and the events of their own age, to demonstrate the folly or wisdom of a particular course of action; but the historical parallel must be exact, reasonable, and well authenticated to be genuinely persuasive. This new precision combined with the old love of a traditional moral pattern. If it could not accord greater dignity to history than history already possessed, it could and did endow it with a peculiar immediacy and relevance.

In the seventeenth century, Raleigh's *History of the World* (1614) belongs to the old dispensation, whereas, at the end of the era, Clarendon's *History of the Rebellion* marks the opening of a new period of historical study. Clarendon in his work deliberately intends to justify a political position by 'a full and clear narration of the grounds, circumstances and artifices of this rebellion', and to present to posterity the truth, as he saw it. His history falls under Bacon's heading of the kind of history which represents an action,[1] but with this difference, that the action is one in which the author himself has participated. Clarendon lived through the events he describes, and in the wisdom of retirement (that favourite Augus-

---

[1] Bacon, *Advancement of Learning*, Bk. 2. 2. 5. 'History, which may be called just and perfect history, is of three kinds, according to the object which it proproundeth, or pretendeth to represent: for it either representeth a time, or a person, or an action.'

tan standpoint) he could now reflect on what he had experienced. A new line of historians stems from Clarendon, among them Temple, Burnet, and Swift, all of whom were concerned to leave accounts of their own times. They used history, with its traditional authority and dignity, much as the imitators had used their classical models: to establish and justify their own and their party's attitude.

When Pope was writing, history had become a popular form of literature. Traditional views were respectfully echoed by a hack like Oldmixon (who had himself written a Whiggish account of the recent events in politics), in terms which combined veneration with a new precision: 'History is designed to instruct Mankind by Example, to shew what Men were by what they did, and from particular Instances to form general Lessons in all the various Stations of Life.'[1] He insists that great talent is necessary for selecting 'what is worth relating', but he falls back on the Renaissance view of the exemplary when he adds 'and for making proper Reflections upon Events for the Instruction of the Reader'. On the other hand, Rapin, in his *Les Réflections sur l'histoire*, following Bacon,[2] had maintained that it was not the historian's duty to philosophize upon his material: he observes briefly, 'Disons la verité sans commentaires, si nous avons de force d'esprit pour cela'.

This was the approach of Rapin-Thoyras, whose influential *History of England* was the first to be based on the civil and domestic documents in the care of the Historiographer Royal, at this time the notorious Rymer, third in the distinguished succession from Dryden and Shadwell. Thomas Carte, to whose letter to Swift we have already referred, claimed that the Frenchman failed to understand the inadequacy of Rymer's *Foedera*, and had missed his chance of writing a complete record:

It hath long been subject of complaint in England, that no history hath yet been wrote of it upon authentic and proper materials: and even those who had taken notice of the military actions of our ancestors have yet left the civil history of the kingdom (the most

[1] Oldmixon, *Essay on Criticism (as it regards Design, Thought, and Expression in Prose and Verse)* (1728).

[2] Bacon, op. cit. 2. 12. 'For it is the true office of history to represent events themselves together with the counsels, and to leave the observations and conclusions thereupon to the liberty and faculty of every man's judgement.'

instructive of any) untouched, for want of a proper knowledge of the antiquities, usages, laws and constitution of this nation.[1]

Carte, needless to say, proposed to remedy the deficiency. Despite minor differences, Rapin, Rapin-Thoyras, and Carte shared a view of historiography which impinged on eighteenth-century literary taste. Carte was the scholar who scrutinized his material, and so he censures Rapin-Thoyras for trusting Burnet without assessing his reliability. But although Rapin-Thoyras did not have a developed sense of evidence, his history is based on documents in the modern way. The Augustan poets would have approved the desire for authentic and detailed record, but they would have rejected any assumption that the historian records with complete detachment. In maintaining this, Carte and Rapin-Thoyras would seem to them too like those critics (Rymer was one) whose blind adherence to rule and fact hindered them from a full understanding of their subject. Even more dangerous, they resembled the mole-like scholar such as Bentley, who might prove the facts of a Temple wrong, but who, burrowing blindly after details, was unable to interpret them in the light of experience. Johnson was typically Augustan in his belittling of this kind of history: a bare recording of fact seemed to him to require little talent.

Yet there were other traits in the attitude of both these historians that would have appealed to the Augustans. Carte demanded authenticity; he looked for truth and emphasized the historian's duty of discriminating between fact and hearsay. The new realism, with its insistence on authenticated truth, and the traditional love of example and exhortation were closely mingled in the writing of history. Carte's belief that civil history was by far the most useful branch reflected the admiration of his age for civil virtues as opposed to old chivalric attributes, for honesty before glory. The military exploits of the past, the valour from which, as Temple said, the original idea of nobility derived, were no longer significant for the Augustans. They looked for instruction from the constitutional development of the realm, civil order, and the distribution of power. Spence records how Pope's projected epic on Brutus would have

[1] Nichols, *Literary Anecdotes of the Eighteenth Century*, vol. ii (1812), p. 478, footnote.

contained much material on civil and ecclesiastical polity,[1] and some of this is included in the *Moral Essays* and the *Imitations of Horace*. From this area of human activity arose the new importance of the ideal of honesty, and in some ways the poetry of the Honest Muse is as much the result of the Revolution of 1689 and the events that led up to it as is the English Constitution. Pope himself remarked to Spence that there was not much value in the study of ancient history, since 'we have had a new set of motives and principles all over Europe since the Pyrenean Treaty'.[2] The date of that treaty, 1660, also conveniently marks a new set of motives and principles in literature. It was from Bolingbroke, 'who knows more of Europe, than perhaps all Europe put together at present', that Pope had taken this sentiment.

Bolingbroke, from whom Pope had caught the infection of history, was eclectic in his ideas, but he was also personally active in the events of his time and anxious to justify his own position. Pope considered him the best writer of the age, and his test of good writing was, according to Spence, 'to know thoroughly what one writes about and not to be affected', and 'to write naturally, and from one's own knowledge'.[3] In finding these qualities in Bolingbroke's prose, Pope would have recognized in them something of the same spirit which informed the style of poetry he himself was devising. Bolingbroke's *Letters on the Study and Use of History* display that tricky balance between the general and the particular which had become as much the art of history as of poetry. The peculiar way in which he explains the attractions of history was bound to appeal to a poet committed to the idea that literature should deal with common and recognizable experience. For Bolingbroke related the love of history to the passion of self-love and the desire of recording our own concerns:

> The love of history seems inseparable from human nature, because it seems inseparable from self-love. The same principle in this instance carries us forward and backward, to future and to past ages. We imagine that the things, which affect us, must affect posterity: this sentiment runs through mankind, from CAESAR down to the parish clerk in POPE's miscellany. We are fond of preserving, as far as it is

---

[1] Spence, *Anecdotes*, p. 288.   [2] Ibid., p. 315.   [3] Ibid., p. 291.

in our frail power, the memory of our own adventures, of those of our own time, and of those that preceded it.[1]

A natural instinct for commemoration is as typical of the poet as of the historian, and Pope was keenly aware of his duty to preserve virtuous examples for the future. In his epistle *To Robert, Earl of Oxford* the Muse escorts Harley to retirement and singles him out as an example of nobility, and the Man of Ross, for all his obscurity, is celebrated by the Honest Muse. In satire, Pope claims to record the adventures of his own times for posterity:

> In this impartial Glass, my Muse intends
> Fair to expose myself, my Foes, my Friends;
> Publish the present Age ...
>
>   (*Imitations of Horace, Sat.* 2. 1, ll. 57–59.)

Such poetry is a document of fact, like history itself. In publishing the present age, Pope preserves it.

But just as poetry is more than a bare account of what is passing, history is more than a mere record. Bolingbroke continues:

The child hearkens with delight to the tales of his nurse, he learns to read, and he devours with eagerness fabulous legends and novels. In riper years he applies himself to history, or to that which he takes for history, to authorized romance: and even in age, the desire, of knowing what has happened to other men, yields to the desire alone, of relating what has happened to ourselves. Thus history, true or false, speaks to our passions always.[2]

If history had been compared to poetry originally because of its elevated sweep and its exemplary subject-matter, it had never before been associated so closely with the instinctive emotion of self-love, which dominated Bolingbroke's philosophy as a principle of action. And such an association inevitably brings history nearer to the idea of poetry as something which comes home to the business and bosom of every man. History's appeal to the passions is of the same kind as Johnson mentioned when he observed, of the choice of an 'historical' subject in *Eloisa to Abelard*, 'the heart naturally loves truth'.

The famous definition of history which Bolingbroke casually

---

[1] Bolingbroke, op. cit., vol. i, pp. 11–12.   [2] Ibid., p. 13.

claims to have found 'somewhere or other in Dionysius Halicarn., I think', that 'history is philosophy teaching by examples', could be taken as a partial definition of Pope's intention in his moral satires. And example itself, according to Bolingbroke, moves the passions: '. . . example appeals not to our understanding alone, but to our passions likewise. Example asswages these, or animates them; sets passion on the side of judgment, and makes the whole man of a piece . . .'[1] Oldham's satirical use of example for arousing the emotions of the reader had already illustrated the truth of this principle in poetry, but Bolingbroke's theory gave Pope a further answer to remonstrances against his use of named examples of vice in his works. For in the second Dialogue of the Epilogue to the *Satires* he excuses the naming of bad examples by claiming that he raises esteem for virtue by naming the good as well. He proceeds to a long encomium on those instances of true nobility he has found:

> God knows, I praise a Courtier where I can.
> When I confess, there *is* who feels for Fame,
> And melts to Goodness, need I SCARBROW name? . . .
> Oft in the clear, still Mirrour of Retreat,
> I study'd SHREWSBURY, the wise and great:
> CARLETON's calm Sense, and STANHOPE's noble Flame,
> Compar'd, and knew their gen'rous End the same:
> How pleasing ATTERBURY's softer hour!
> How shin'd the Soul, unconquer'd in the Tow'r!
> (ll. 63–65, 78–83.)

This list of worthies suggests a pantheon of heroes like those statues of their ancestors which, according to Bolingbroke, the Romans put in their vestibules: 'so that whenever they went in or out, these venerable bustoes met their eyes, and recalled the glorious actions of the dead, to fire the living, to excite them to imitate and even to emulate their great forefathers'.[2] Such a particular use of example gave the poet an opportunity of praising in a new and realistic way. Merely to name individuals in such a context—in contrast to the foolish and vicious—raises them to eminence without any resort to ceremonial or hyperbole. Since the Restoration the need for a new way of writing complimentary verse had been

---

[1] Bolingbroke, op. cit., vol. i, p. 17.   [2] Ibid., p. 19.

growing as a protest against the debasement of panegyric. It was strengthened by the concern for exactitude as a sign of truth in the subject-matter of poetry. A poet wishing to celebrate a contemporary event now found himself faced with the difficulty of having to combine enthusiasm with accuracy. Thomas Tickell, for instance, in his poem on George I, *The Royal Progress*, claims that he has rejected the hireling poet's trick of dressing up his hero in fictions:

> When Brunswick first appear'd, each honest heart,
> Intent on verse, disdain'd the rules of art;
> For him the Songsters, in unmeasur'd odes,
> Debas'd Alcides, and dethron'd the gods . . .
> Exploded fancies! that in vain deceive,
> While the mind nauseates what she can't believe.
> My muse th'expected hero shall pursue
> From clime to clime, and keep him still in view:
> His shining march describe in faithful lays,
> Content to paint him, not presume to praise;
> Their charms, if charms they have, the truth supplies,
> And from the theme unlabour'd beauties rise.[1]

The quality of the verse is a sad comment on the pious hope. Who would not exchange it for one of Dryden's outrageous fancies? But it was a point of poetic faith for many of Pope's contemporaries to hold that 'honest hearts intent on verse' as opposed to mere 'songsters' were bound by a strict and literal interpretation of truth, since 'the mind nauseates what she can't believe'. Sincerity and authenticity in praise distinguished the true poet from the hired hack. Perhaps it was the desire to preserve this distinction as much as vanity which induced Pope in the second Dialogue, after his catalogue of great names, to insist that these men were his friends and not his patrons:

> Names, which I long have lov'd, nor lov'd in vain,
> Rank'd with their Friends, not number'd with their Train;
>   (ll. 90–91.)

Poets were anxious to preserve the dignity of their art and to observe the new regard for truth. Johnson's notorious literalism is,

---

[1] Tickell, *The Royal Progress*, in *The Minor Poets*, vol. ii (1749), pp. 176–7.

after all, only the most forceful and well-known expression of a
common attitude to the style and subject-matter of 'honest' poetry.
It was an attitude close to the changing ideas on history. Whereas
to Puttenham history itself could be fabulous as long as it was for an
overriding exemplary purpose, to the Augustan poetry must share
the impartial veracity of history—and for this same exemplary
reason.

Pope's later poetry has much in common with the historical
method Bolingbroke describes. He cites the names of the great—
more often of the present than the past in his satire; he uses the di-
gressive historical retrospect to show how the present can be
judged by the past, as in the long passage on the vanity of human
ambition in the fourth epistle of the *Essay on Man*, which opens with
the examples of Bacon and Cromwell, 'damn'd to everlasting fame'.
The subject-matter, man himself, appeals perennially to our self-
love, and the examples, on Bolingbroke's principle, have the effect
of a catharsis, arousing and assuaging our passions, particularly in
the *Moral Essays*, where, for instance, Wharton evokes our pity,
Timon our contempt, Buckingham our reflective grief, The Man of
Ross our admiration, and Sir Balaam our mirth. Seen from this point
of view, didactic poetry should have an emotional vivacity which
is, in fact, much nearer to the actual effect of Pope's moral satire
than the common idea of his cool reasoning and wit would suggest.

The shape of Pope's epistles, of which there will be more to say,
consists of fluctuating movements from the past to the present, from
the general to the particular, and to some extent this pattern is
illuminated by what Bolingbroke has to say of the shape that history
gives to circumstances:

Thus again as to events that stand recorded in history: we see them
all, we see them as they followed one another, or as they produced one
another, causes or effects, immediate or remote. We are cast back, as
it were, into former ages: we live with the men who lived before us,
and we inhabit countries that we never saw. Place is enlarged, and
time prolonged, in this manner. . . . The events we are witnesses of,
in the course of the longest life, appear to us very often original, un-
prepared, single and unrelative, if I may use such an expression for
want of a better in English; in French I would say *isolez*. . . . Experience

is doubly effective; we are born too late to see the beginning, and we die too soon to see the end of many things. History supplies both these defects.[1]

Traditionally it was poetry not history which seemed to have this pervading design, this logical connexion of cause and effect which Aristotle demanded of the single great action of tragedy or epic. But written history at its best cannot fail to fall into a pattern. Experience extending over time begins to take a recognizable shape: the simplest novel, purporting to follow the life and adventures of a single character, has already the rudimentary outline of a plot in its sequence of events. In poetry, more sophisticated effects had already been achieved with the element of time, as in the relation between narrative, digression into the past, and prophetic vision of the future in the epic. Pope was conscious of all these effects, but the confusion of contemporary episodes, contemporary society, and contemporary characters which he needed to reveal rather than to suppress in his satire, acquired a less formal shape which was inspired by an historical pattern at once realistic and exemplary. History as a moral discipline, showing man in his particular and general nature, recording the passage of time and revealing the causes and effects of action, was close to the eighteenth-century idea of literature, not only in theme but in pattern, as it is seen in such different forms as the didactic satire and the novel of the period.

In Pope's moral epistles this historical influence transmitted through Bolingbroke may well have helped to create a form in which the three prevailing modes of Augustan poetry—satire, panegyric, and elegy—though still distinguished from each other, are brought together in a new and subtle way. Worldly poetry of the gravest sort was Pope's final achievement, and he perfected for it a style which reflected ideally the general and personal nature of his inspiration. Essentially, like everything Pope wrote, the later satires are personal poetry. But their context is the generalization of history which gives to the sentiments their proper setting in the sequence of human life, arousing in the poet perplexed sensations of

---

[1] Bolingbroke, op. cit., vol. i, pp. 40–42.

uncertainty and assurance, and a final reliance on the wisdom of common experience and the judgement of the past.

V

Before Pope 'Stoop'd to truth and moraliz'd his song' in his later satires, he had learned how to rework some of the themes of his earlier poems—the elegiac mood, the moral sensibility which responded to virtue, and the personal tenderness of friendship—into a new sort of poem, a kind of historical and moral panegyric. As examples of this the two epistles *To Mr. Addison Occasioned by his Dialogue on Medals* and *To Robert, Earl of Oxford and Earl Mortimer* are important landmarks in his development as a poet.

To Mr. Addison opens with a survey of Roman history in the style of *The Temple of Fame*, and, if the poem was written in 1711, as Pope claimed,[1] this confirms its closeness to the early work and the familiar tradition of a picturesque account of historical material. But the exclamatory opening and the highly romantic description of the ruins of Rome are soon exchanged for compression of a kind only possible in a poet whose understanding both of the idea of history and of the elegiac mood had deepened and widened. The subject—a medal, commemorating in its small compass some great event—was the perfect image for Pope's paradoxical device of putting much into little and changing one kind of vastness and confusion into order and harmony:

> Convinc'd, she now contracts her vast design,
> And all her Triumphs shrink into a Coin:
> A narrow orb each crouded conquest keeps,
> Beneath her Palm here sad Judæa weeps. . . .
> The Medal, faithful to its charge of fame,
> Thro' climes and ages bears each form and name:
> In one short view subjected to your eye
> Gods, Emp'rors, Heroes, Sages, Beauties, lie.
>
> (ll. 23–26, 31–34.)

Much of the power of Augustan elegiac poetry depends on such large contrasts: triumphs shrunk to a coin, history contracted to

---

[1] See G. Tillotson, *The Rape of the Lock and Other Poems* (2nd ed. 1954), p. 236.

the span of the printed page or the painted canvas. But the *Epistle to Oxford* is a more illuminating example of how Pope was beginning to see one of his favourite themes in the context of history and of public life, and how this affected his whole manner of complimentary address.

This epistle was written at Swift's suggestion, and intended not for a panegyric on Harley, but for an elegy on Parnell, in imitation of Dryden's lines *To the Memory of Mr. Oldham*:

> Such were the Notes, thy once-lov'd Poet sung,
> 'Till Death untimely stop'd his tuneful Tongue.

Soon, however, the interest shifts to Harley himself, portrayed as the centre of a group of friends whose concern with morality and poetry is more important than Harley's own part in public affairs. With Parnell, Harley 'forgot the Statesman',

> For *Swift* and him, despis'd the Farce of State,
> The sober Follies of the Wise and Great;
>
> (ll. 9–10.)

These 'sober follies' were to be the topics of Pope's later satires, but here they are touched on only to be forgotten in the climax of the epistle, a compliment which attributes to Harley those virtues that are the foundation of Pope's vision of heroism and moral order:

> And sure if ought below the Seats Divine
> Can touch Immortals, 'tis a Soul like thine:
> A Soul supreme, in each hard Instance try'd,
> Above all Pain, all Passion, and all Pride,
> The Rage of Pow'r, the Blast of publick Breath,
> The Lust of Lucre, and the Dread of Death.
>
> (ll. 21–26.)

Stoic virtues, which might seem too austere and impassive in themselves, acquire an immense power of conviction when they are set against the particular weaknesses Pope enumerates. 'The rage of power', 'the blast of public breath', 'the lust of lucre', were all to be illustrated in the moral satires, while the dread of death, 'the black fear of death which saddens all', as Pope later describes it, is the spectre haunting this poetry, as it haunts the world of action. By raising Harley above it, Pope endows him with an immortality of fame as substantial in its own way as any of the apotheoses of the earlier panegyrists.

In Pope's original conclusion to the poem, Fame and the Muse both celebrated Harley's greatness, but in his revision that function is reserved for the Muse alone:

> Ev'n now she shades thy Evening Walk with Bays,
> (No Hireling she, no Prostitute to Praise)
> Ev'n now, observant of the parting Ray,
> Eyes the calm Sun–set of thy Various Day,
> Thro' Fortune's Cloud One truly Great can see,
> Nor fears to tell, that MORTIMER is He.
>
> (ll. 35–40.)

The Muse shares the purpose of history—reflecting and distinguishing, giving praise to the truly great and blame to the vicious. Pope had already determined the lines that his future poetry was to take when he wrote this: chastened panegyric for the good, and indignant exposure of the bad. It was reserved for him in the *Moral Essays* and the *Imitations of Horace* to discover a form and a style where the two kinds could come together, unified by the prevailing mood of reflection, and never detached from the vital connecting thread of the poet's own personality. Already, in the *Epistle to Oxford*, the emotional power of this kind of poetry was fully displayed. It can best be judged by Harley's own reaction when Pope sent him a copy of the work. His letter is a genuine and poignant expression of the emotion this poetry can evoke. To feel the power of such epistles, one has only to put oneself in the place of the recipient.

Sir—[wrote Harley],

I received your Packet by the Carrier, which could not but give me great Pleasure, to see you preserve an Old Friend in Memory: for it must needs be very agreeable to be Remembred by those we highly Value. But then, how much Shame did it cause me! When I read your fine Verses inclos'd, my Mind reproach'd me how far short I came of what your great Friendship & delicate Pen would partially describe me. You ask my Consent to Publish it; to what Streights doth This reduce me! I look back, indeed, to those Evenings I have usefully &

pleasantly spent with Mr. Pope, Mr. Parnel, Dean Swift, the Doctor, &c. I should be glad the World knew you admitted me to your Friendship: and, since your Affection is too hard for your Judgement, I am contented to let the World see, how well Mr. Pope can write upon a barren Subject. I return you an exact Copy of the Verses, that I may keep the Original, as a Testimony of the Only Error you have been guilty of.[1]

The most interesting problem confronting Pope in his later work was stylistic. How was he to devise a method of bringing together the three prevailing modes of satire, panegyric, and elegy without reverting to the traditional forms of the two last, or losing, in the greater detachment he demanded of the first, the sense of immediacy and the excitement of revealing his own personal feelings and tastes? The *Essay on Man*, imperfect poem as it is, was Pope's first sustained attempt to solve this problem. It involved him in difficulties which were not entirely surmounted at the first try. The epistle, or essay in verse, was an obvious form for him to choose, but when the intention is to 'expatiate free o'er all this scene of man', the scope of an epistle seems restricted. Satire, with its neat ironic tricks and paradoxes, and its manner of implying more than is actually stated, can cover a wide area at comparatively short length, but direct statement has no such advantages. Pope intended to make a complete and unironic declaration of his beliefs in this work. The progress of the argument ought to give a structure to the *Essay on Man*, but in fact it is no more than a carefully articulated skeleton, and the life of the poem has little to do with it. Pope instinctively looked for some other way of unifying the work.

In the first epistle it is the old image of the chain of being, with all its opportunities for detailed illustration, that is the unifying centre of the poem. But when Pope returned to it in the third epistle, he merely recapitulated its main theme of order without reviving it as a central image. Already he was turning from his earlier pictorial method of organizing the work to a style more flexible and discursive, which he perfected in the fourth epistle. The subject of this last epistle—human conduct and the search for happiness—enabled him to turn to a different style, neither static, pictorial,

---

[1] Sherburn, op. cit., vol. ii, p. 91.

nor purely argumentative, but one which could be at once ironic
and sincere.

After the first ninety lines of this epistle—a dissertation on
happiness—Pope turns from argument to reveal through commentary and illustration an individual point of view. As the topics
merge into each other, the poet's mood changes, and his style with
it. These variations are worked out in a comprehensive but flexible
scheme. It is essential to think of this poetry as discourse, and to
imagine it as spoken rather than as read by the eye. Often the strict
logical division of the paragraphs on the page appears to contradict
the rhythmic, emotional flow of the poetry. For example, the debate
on Virtue (ll. 149–65) concludes not with a resolution, but with
a rhetorical question:

> Who ask and reason thus, will scarce conceive
> God gives enough, while he has more to give:
> Immense that pow'r, immense were the demand;
> Say, at what part of nature will they stand?
>
> (ll. 163–6.)

and the answer to the whole passage appears at the beginning of the
next paragraph, written in an entirely different key, but inextricably linked with what precedes it:

> What nothing earthly gives, or can destroy,
> The soul's calm sun-shine, and the heart-felt joy,
> Is Virtue's prize. . . .
>
> (ll. 167–9.)

The power of the lines is lost if they are read in isolation, since the
poem is not limited to one tone or style of address. It flows on with
the same eddying movement as the poet's thoughts and moods.

Brilliant observations, aphorisms, and simple assertions all find
their proper place within this general movement. Alone they are
little more than trite clichés, but as part of a pattern of self-expression, of a style impressed with the force of an individual mind
in its formal and intimate responses, they acquire power and authenticity which is unexpected. The most famous of them all—
'Know then this truth, enough for Man to know; Virtue alone is
Happiness below'—is only fully effective if it is read in conjunction

with the great and eloquent passage which precedes it. The simplicity of true happiness stands in relief against the tragic elaboration of its 'false scale':

> There, in the rich, the honour'd, fam'd and great,
> See the false scale of Happiness complete!
> In hearts of Kings, or arms of Queens who lay,
> How happy! those to ruin, these betray.
> Mark by what wretched steps their glory grows,
> From dirt and sea-weed as proud Venice rose;
> In each how guilt and greatness equal ran,
> And all that rais'd the Hero, sunk the Man.
> Now Europe's laurels on their brows behold,
> But stain'd with blood, or ill exchanged for gold,
> Then see them broke with toils, or sunk in ease,
> Or infamous for plunder'd provinces.
> Oh wealth ill-fated! which no act of fame
> E'er taught to shine, or sanctify'd from shame!
> What greater bliss attends their close of life?
> Some greedy minion, or imperious wife,
> The trophy'd arches, story'd halls invade,
> And haunt their slumbers in the pompous shade.
> Alas! not dazzled by their noon-tide ray,
> Compute the morn and evening to their day;
> The whole amount of that enormous fame,
> A Tale, that blends their glory with their shame!
>
> Know then this truth (enough for Man to know)
> 'Virtue alone is Happiness below'.
>   (Epistle IV, ll. 287–310.)

This inner unity and principle of growth, which keeps the poem
moving as the poet's mind moves, gives shape to the fourth epistle
of the *Essay*. This may not seem original at first; it reads so easily
and naturally that it is hard to see how any discursive poet would
write otherwise. That they do becomes clear, however, when Pope
is compared with almost any of his contemporaries. Savage and
Young, for instance, both of them ironic, didactic, and indignant,
are unbelievably monotonous in spite of their skill. Their verses are
often interrupted by neat antitheses or brilliant flashes of wit, but

they have only one kind of unity—the simple direct passage from
one couplet to the next. Narrative may demand this plain sequence,
but the whole success of discourse depends on avoiding it. To take
some lines of Pope (not even his best), and contrast them with the
best of Savage, is to see what extraordinary syntactical agility, what
mastery of transition distinguishes Pope from the simple, hammering
emphasis of the minor poet:

> Stuck o'er with titles and hung round with strings,
> That thou may'st be by kings, or whores of kings.
> Boast the pure blood of an illustrious race,
> In quiet flow, from Lucrece to Lucrece;
> But by your father's worth if yours you rate,
> Count me those only who were good and great. . . .
> What can ennoble sots, or slaves, or cowards?
> Alas, not all the blood of all the HOWARDS.
>
> (Epistle IV, ll. 205–10, 215–16.)

> Blest be the *Bastard's* birth! through wond'rous ways,
> He shines eccentric, like a Comet's blaze.
> No sickly fruit of faint compliance He;
> He! Stampt in Nature's mint of extasy!
> He lives to build, not boast, a gen'rous race:
> No tenth transmitter of a foolish face.
> His daring hope, no sire's example bounds;
> His first-born lights no prejudice confounds.
> He, kindling from within, requires no flame;
> He glories in a *Bastard's* glowing name.
>
> (Savage, *The Bastard*, ll. 3–12.)

Savage's individual lines here are more striking than Pope's. They
have all the direct vigour of Oldham, but the whole passage lacks
any but the simplest design. We feel, and rightly, that he cannot
sustain this kind of thing for very long. In spite of their vitality, his
verses possess only a sort of vertical coherence: one follows the next
to amplify a simple idea.

The same is true of Young, a more competent versifier than
Savage, whose *Universal Passion* preceded the *Moral Essays* by at least
four years, and who, according to Swift, was suspected in Dublin of
being the author of the *Essay on Man*. Yet these lines, for instance,

although concentrated and witty, are marred by Savage's simple repetition:

> How guilty These? yet not less guilty They,
> Who reap false glory by a smoother way;
> Who wrap destruction up in gentler words,
> And bows, and smiles, more fatal than their swords.
> Who stifle Nature, and subsist on Art,
> Who coin the Face, and petrify the Heart;
> All real kindness for the show discard,
> As marble polish'd, and, as marble hard.[1]

This passage differs from Pope's on the false scale of happiness in its style of address. Syntax, and particularly the varied use of tenses, is the secret of Pope's success in the lines from the fourth epistle of the *Essay on Man*. As he is exhorting his readers, the prevailing mood is imperative, governed by the verbs mark, see, behold; but within this framework all the dependent verbs shift their tenses between past and present—'Mark by what wretched steps their glory *grows*', 'In each how guilt and greatness equal *ran*', 'What greater bliss *attends* their close of life?' The effect is of alternating vistas and close views, successively reflective and animated, and always moving. Though Young anticipated many of Pope's satirical attitudes in his *Universal Passion*, the greater poet's superiority shows itself most clearly in the intricate pattern of his discourse.

Such was the style which Pope first perfected in the fourth epistle of the *Essay on Man*. Unlike that of *The Dunciad* it is not narrative, nor is it objective even in its irony. All the substance and exactitude required by Augustan standards are present, but it is shot through with the poet's moods, from the most evanescent and personal to the gravest. The *Moral Essays* maintain an even tone of serious irony, while the *Imitations of Horace* with their openly personal manner and their dazzling variety of mood exploit the style to the limits of versatility. In all these poems familiar attitudes and themes of Pope's earlier poetry recur, but modified and transformed by the new pattern of the style. Pope never lost the art of letting praise and blame exist side by side in the ambivalence of his wit, but the *Moral Essays* show him developing this technique more ambitiously.

[1] [Edward Young], *The Universal Passion, Satire The Last* (1726), p. 4, ll. 69–76.

When he explained to Swift his intention of writing an epistle in four parts, as a satire against misapplied talents, he said it would be 'exemplified by Pictures, Characters and Examples', and in his third *Moral Essay*, a satire against the abuse of riches, he used this very method, as with Cotta the miser, a highly conventional picture whose antecedents we have looked at in *The Grove: Or, the Rival Muses*. The Man of Ross, the type of the favourite Horatian figure of benevolence, is also an instance of the new style of panegyric; the death of Villiers—*quantum mutatus ab illo*—the traditional satiric example of tragic contrast, is presented in a detailed picture, while the concluding fable of Sir Balaam, the moneyed cit, is a comic character study. Each of these figures belongs recognizably to the satiric tradition in which Pope was working. The originality of his genius is shown in the way in which he presents them and fits them to the argument of the whole poem.

The central point of this satire is the complimentary account of James Kyrle, the Man of Ross, for which Pope deliberately invoked the Honest Muse, and about which, on grounds of even stricter literal honesty, he was firmly corrected by Johnson. But far more than an accurate account of Kyrle's benevolence was involved in the passage, as we have remarked at the opening of this book. In the mingled style both true and false standards are indicated, while the smooth and lucid propriety of the language suggests the simplicity of the hero's Horatian virtue:

> Who hung with woods yon mountain's sultry brow?
> From the dry rock who bade the waters flow?
> Not to the skies in useless columns tost,
> Or in proud falls magnificently lost,
> But clear and artless, pouring thro' the plain
> Health to the sick, and solace to the swain.
>
> (ll. 253–8.)

Kyrle plants trees and, like Moses, strikes water from the barren rock. In the short space of a couplet Pope thus relates his benevolence to the bounty of nature and the solemn associations of religion. The artlessness of the waterway stands for his honest integrity, as the wasteful splendour of fountains and waterfalls represents the ostentation of wealth. The limpid style crystallizes in its individual devices that larger pattern of praise and blame set against each other which is the essential design of the whole poem. For this eulogy is only the prelude to an attack on proud display which leads to the elegiac set-piece of Villiers's death. The various examples produce an impression of shifting moods that counterpoint Pope's consistent moral attitude, while grandeur and invective, reflective sympathy and contempt, succeed each other until, at last, in the vulgar little tragicomedy of Sir Balaam, with its familiar humour, Pope achieves such detachment that he can afford to conclude the work without any comment whatsoever.

There are, however, some examples of awkward and stiff transitions in the *Moral Essays* which Pope was able to avoid in the more intimately colloquial vein of the *Imitations*, where, following Horace, he could justify every change of topic and mood by the prevailing device of monologue. Here he is neither simply exclamatory nor didactic, and he dazzles and persuades by the warmth and brilliance of a poetic personality which has at last fully come into its own. Many of his favourite devices recur in these poems. His irony plays over the familiar topic of retirement, for instance, in the opening lines of the first epistle of the first Book of Horace:

> St. John, whose love indulg'd my labours past
> Matures my present, and shall bound my last!
> Why will you break the Sabbath of my days?
> Now sick alike of Envy and of Praise.
> Publick too long, ah let me hide my Age!
> See modest Cibber now has left the Stage:
> Our Gen'rals now, retir'd to their Estates,
> Hang their old Trophies o'er the Garden gates,
> In Life's cool evening satiate of applause,
> Nor fond of bleeding, ev'n in BRUNSWICK's cause.
>
> (ll. 1–10.)

All his old concern with the public and private worlds is expressed in this short passage, and Pope flings in a recollection of his own personal wars as well as his country's. A dangerously innocent quietness broods over the passage, over the familiar figure of the re-tired soldier and the rustic carelessness of old trophies hung on garden gates. But 'modest Cibber' exposes the ironic deception at once, and what we are implicitly shown is not rural peace but the self-importance and theatrical pomp of wrought-iron gateways surmounted by plumes and coats of arms. The true beauty of retirement flashes across the mind for a moment in the line 'In Life's cool evening satiate of applause'—one of those lyric verses that light up the satires like quick shafts of winter sunshine—but this too fades into the smooth ambiguity of the last lines.

It is tempting to illustrate further the immense diversity of Pope's style in these later poems, but he himself would have felt that the style could not ultimately be considered apart from the subject-matter. Nevertheless, from this brief survey we can see how the Restoration poets' interest in presentation and address—the epistolary style of Rochester, the personal utterance of Oldham, and Dryden's many variations of tone and manner in his prologues and epilogues—reaches its climax in Pope's brilliant handling of discourse. But he shared with these the main intention of direct communication, of speaking as a man to men. Wit, figurative devices, concealed metaphors, and open personifications were all to him a matter of expression, and he had written in the *Essay on Criticism* that

> true *Expression*, like th'unchanging *Sun*, ⎫
> *Clears*, and *improves* whate'er it shines upon, ⎬
> It *gilds* all Objects, but it *alters* none. ⎭
>
> (ll. 315–17.)

This is the crux of Pope's poetical style. This clarifying, embellishing function is far removed from the romantic idea of composition, where the acts of conceiving and of writing come so close as to be practically indistinguishable, and where the material of everyday perception is re-created by the power of the word. It is different, again, from the Renaissance notion of the function of the poet, the inventor who can create almost a new nature. To transform his material would have seemed to Pope in some sense a betrayal of honesty. Every skill of technique, every experiment in style was directed towards 'things'—to the heart rather than the fancy, and their function was to fortify the subject and persuade the reader to a proper response. The Horatian epistle is a perfect medium for this difficult art. Speaking sometimes alone, sometimes with an

interlocutor, Pope announces his topic and discourses on it, and as
he does so he introduces between the subject and the style an intermediary in the person of the poet himself, at once spectator and
participator, victim and aggressor. His predecessors had made a
rough beginning in their public professions as satirists, but none
of them had created such a full effect of personality. Pope extended
Horace's method of plain speaking into a mode of confession which
forces us to believe that he felt the *ethos* of his moral satires as warmly
as he had felt the *pathos* of his early works.

This very warmth has sometimes been questioned, however, for
the amount of autobiography in the *Imitations* inevitably raises the
whole problem of sincerity, which exists as soon as the claim of
truth is extended from the subject-matter to the poet and his personal feelings. Critics of his own age recognized this difficulty in
Pope's poetry, and Johnson expressed it forthrightly when he
questioned the sincerity of Pope's motives, first in writing and then
in withdrawing from political satire:

That he desisted from his attempts at reformation, is imputed by
his commentator to his despair at prevailing over the corruption of
the time. He was not likely to have been ever of the opinion that the
dread of his satire would countervail the love of power and money;
he pleased himself with being important and formidable, and gratifies
sometimes his pride, and sometimes his resentment, till at last he began to think he should be more safe if he were less busy.[1]

The comment is abundantly realistic. Of course Pope must have
known that his satire was ineffective in practice, but he needed the
solace of the illusion, and he must believe in the importance of his
role before he could arouse the excitement that inspired his poetry.
Johnson noticed this temperamental peculiarity when he wrote of
Pope's susceptibility to varying ideas and moods:

When Pope murmurs at the world, when he professes contempt of
fame, when he speaks of riches and poverty, of success and disappointment with negligent indifference, he certainly does not express his habitual and settled sentiments, but either wilfully disguises
his own character, or, what is more likely, invests himself with temporary qualities, and sallies out in the colours of the present.[2]

---

[1] Johnson, *Lives*, 'Life of Pope', vol. iii, p. 181   [2] Ibid., vol. iii, p. 212.

This is as just an estimate of the way Pope's genius and imagination worked as it is of his personality. His roles were indeed assumed, and his emotions 'feigned' to suit them, but the parts he played were always closely related to his circumstances and his real nature. Like Byron, he dramatized himself both as a personal solace and as a means of writing.

Some critics are instinctively repelled by this chameleon quality. De Quincey, for example, could not bring himself to believe that Pope's outbursts of rage or even of malice were genuinely felt. More often, doubts are cast on his moral professions. The difficulty arises because Pope speaks with ardent personal conviction about the most commonplace truths, while we associate these personal accents with unique and private experiences. To Pope such truths had the quality of intimate experience, however, because, as we have seen, he taught himself to look at his own life in their reflection, to see himself as retired and solitary, learning Horatian poise and Horatian temperance, exercising general benevolence and practising the virtue of friendship. He may have fallen short of many of these attributes, but to recognize how far short was part of the Horatian pose of wisdom. He can laugh with Bolingbroke at the inconstancy of his mind and the ease with which 'a fit of vapours clouds this demi-god'. Nevertheless, they were the beliefs by which he lived, in imagination even more than in fact.

Pope felt these truths and enjoyed the sentiments they aroused. He was, like most poets, delighted with his own feelings. Hazlitt recognized this power of enjoyment when he said of the *Epistles*: 'within this retired and narrow circle how much, and that how exquisite, was contained! What discrimination, what wit, what delicacy, what fancy, what lurking spleen, what elegance of thought, what pampered refinement of sentiment.'[1] 'Pampered refinement of sentiment', with its suggestion of self-indulgence, a luxury of feeling enjoyed for its own sake, shows Hazlitt's genuine insight. Self-indulgence is a moral danger, but, like so many pleasures, it warms the imagination. Whenever Pope is relishing his own feelings—his indignation at Sporus, his contempt for the young man on the

---

[1] Hazlitt, 'Lectures on the English Poets', *Works*, ed. P. P. Howe, vol. v (1930), p. 71.

Grand Tour, or his pride in his own part—the verse begins to reveal those compressions and subtleties which, so oddly mingled
with flowing eloquence, make up the texture of his best poetry.
Often he plays with his own anger, excusing it, or indulging it
openly, as in the Sporus passage, where the abuse begins as a half-
joking exaggeration between friends:

> Yet let me flap this Bug with gilded wings,
> This painted Child of Dirt that stinks and stings;
> (*Epistle to Arbuthnot*, ll. 309–10.)

Sometimes he reveals the 'lurking spleen' under the cloak of merriment:

> Who starv'd a Sister, who forswore a Debt,
> I never nam'd—the Town's enquiring yet.
> The pois'ning Dame—*Fr.* You mean—*P.* I don't. *Fr.* You do.
> *P.* See! now I keep the Secret, and not you.
> (Second Dialogue, Epilogue to the *Satires*, ll. 20–23.)

By playing with his interlocutor, provoking him, haranguing,
laughing at him, as Dryden did with his audiences in his prologues
and epilogues, Pope gives an impression of ease and control which
can even suggest good humour. There is nothing austere about his
moral satire.

The extreme subtlety of the style of the *Imitations* depended to
some extent on Pope's recognition of the dangers of the form. In the
Moral Essays he had been able to speak his mind with a rhetorical
fervour natural to didactic poetry, but the *Imitations* were more defensive than didactic, as Pope admitted when he explained their
origin: 'The Occasion of publishing these *Imitations* was the Clamour
raised on some of my *Epistles*. An Answer from *Horace* was both more
full, and of more Dignity, than any I cou'd have made in my own
person . . . .'[1] Like Oldham, he found the imitation a useful device
for making retaliation respectable. If he had been angry to find the
serious and traditional tone of the *Moral Essays* written off as personal spleen and malice, he was ready now to show what he could
do with these emotions. But merriment and anger (as he had

---

[1] *Satires, Epistles and Odes of Horace Imitated* (1733), The Advertisement.

promised Swift he would find them in his moral satire)[1] are mixed together, and with them the warm enjoyment of his own feelings of friendship, his love of virtue and of elegiac reflection. So completely are these strands woven together that the result cannot simply be described as poetic autobiography, and it is much more than abuse. The satirical monologue becomes, in Pope's hands, the perfect form for expressing intimacy and objectivity, and it helped him to express an attitude to life which was at once personal and characteristic of the spirit of the new poetry.

VI

Certain recurrent ideas and illustrations of Pope's moral system can be singled out as typical of his deepest convictions. The most important of these are often remarkably traditional. The vices attacked in the *Moral Essays* and the *Imitations* have one parent root —Pride. 'In Pride, in reas'ning Pride our error lies', Pope had written in the *Essay on Man*, continuing the familiar argument that Boileau and Rochester had already used between right and wrong reason. From the time of Temple's essay, the attack on the moderns had centred on this point of pride, and Pope recapitulated most of the themes of the battle in the fourth book of *The Dunciad*, where he makes his own case against philosophical presumption. But he is careful here to link it with other kinds of folly, to see it as only one branch of the great flourishing growth of pride. The pupils of the pedants, the virtuosi, the 'gay embroidered race', are all in varying degrees affected by the same egotistic blindness. All pay their homage to Dullness, 'Mother of arrogance, and source of Pride', but they are differentiated to this extent, that some fall under the heading of Pride of Letters, and others of Pride of Life. With the latter Pope is careful to make his picture as traditional and authoritative as possible.

He had chosen to attack avarice, covetousness, and sensuality in

[1] When Swift complained that the *Essay on Man* was 'too philosophical for me', and remarked that Young, who was generally supposed in Dublin to have written it, was 'not merry enough nor angry enough', Pope wrote at once, assuring him that if he came over and discussed his new satire with him, he would not make the same complaint. 'It will not want for Satire, but as for Anger I know it not; or at least only that sort of which the Apostle speaks, Be ye angry and sin not' (Sherburn, op. cit., vol. iii, p. 372).

various forms in the *Moral Essays* and the *Imitations*. These vices had been exposed so often that he treats them with all deference for the traditional preacher's view. The death-bed scenes at the end of *Moral Essay* I are meant to illustrate the ruling passion, but they could also be taken to represent some of the seven deadly sins. Lechery appears as the old man crawling to his wench on knocking knees; gluttony as Helluo; avarice as the crone who saves a candle with her last breath; pride in the milder form of Narcissa's vanity, and envy and avarice together in the brilliant brief dialogue between the miser Euclio and his lawyer. Anger, however, the inspiration of satire, is conspicuously absent.

Cobham, to whom Pope addressed this epistle, and who was startled, to say the least, by the 'extraordinary compliment' paid to his patriotism in the last four lines of the poem, was not pleased by this very traditional catalogue of vices. He complained that they were not ruling passions as he understood the term, and suggested cutting down the *exemplum* of the lecher, to which Pope agreed. But having seen his revision, Cobham wrote at greater length in a way which clearly shows that Pope had been too moral and not witty enough for him:

I like your Leachour better now 'tis shorter and the Glutton is a very good Epigram. But they are both appetites that from nature we indulg as well for her ends as our pleasure. A Cardinal in his way of pleasure would have been a better instance. What do you think of an old Lady dressing her silver locks with Pink and directing her Coffin to be lind with white quilted Satten trim'd with gold fringe Or Councelour Vernon retiring to enjoy himself with five thousand a year which he had got and returning back to the Chancery to get a little more when he could not speak so loud as to be heard? . . . I mean that a passion or habit that has not a natural foundation falls in better with your Subject than any of our natural wants which in some degree we cannot avoid pursueing to the last; and if a man has Spirits or appetite enough to take a bit of either kind at parting you may condemn him but you woud be proud to imitate him.[1]

This letter shows why Johnson felt that Pope 'derived little honour from the notice' of men like Cobham. The old sensualist would

---

[1] Sherburn, op. cit., vol. iii, p. 393 (8 Nov. 1733).

clearly have preferred to die in one of the more genial vices than breathing 'oh save my country, heav'n!' But he did not succeed in persuading Pope to return to the typical Restoration mode of satire. The old lady dressing for her coffin becomes the grimmer lesson of the young actress indulging her natural vanity at death. The lecher did not become a cardinal. The moral standard Pope assumes—that natural appetites raised to ruling passions become sins—remains as traditional as those of a sermon.

This is nowhere more apparent than in his treatment of gluttony. Gluttony appears to have been a form of intemperance that disgusted Pope particularly (though Johnson tells us that he loved too well to eat). Yet it is surprisingly rare as a general topic of satire in the period. Swift, for instance, has nothing to say of it. Horace, however, had made it the subject of one of his epistles which Pope chose to imitate, and besides the epigram in the first *Moral Essay*, there is a savage account of high living in the last book of *The Dunciad*. The ingenuities of French cooks are here made into a blasphemous parody of Christian dogma, and Pope's wrath rises as he describes the popularity of gamesters and South-Sea-Bubble speculators living in luxury in exile:

What cannot copious Sacrifice attone?
Thy Treufles, Perigord! thy Hams, Bayonne!
With French Libation, and Italian Strain,
Wash Bladen white, and expiate Hays's stain.
Knight lifts the head, for what are crowds undone
To three essential Partridges in one?

(Bk. IV, ll. 557–62.)

This has been called one of Pope's most scarifying images,[1] but if he was deliberately shocking, he was also deliberately recalling tradition. The comparison of the miracles of cookery to transubstantiation was a medieval commonplace—Chaucer had used it in *The Pardoner's Tale* (ll. 210–12):

Thise cokes, how they stampe, and streyne, and grinde,
And turnen substaunce in-to accident,
To fulfille al thy likerous talent!

[1] Maynard Mack, 'Wit and Poetry and Pope', in *Essays Presented to George Sherburn* (1949), p. 30.

Pope would have remembered this, as well as Dryden's blasphemous touches, when he wrote about his gourmet's trinity. In his treatment of sensual sins he evidently meant to retain the familiar attitude of the preacher, and to ally himself with common and Christian judgements.

But Pope was not content to examine human nature merely in terms of typical figures. His epigrams present us with types, his longer studies with characters. Having assured his readers of a traditional moral background and clarified the general issues, he proceeded to precise observations and the keen commentary of the satirist in his examination of human conduct, which is the real theme of the later poems. Character lies at their centre, his own and other men's, seen in a setting of history or of contemporary experience. Augustan literature is very much one of character. Dryden had admired Ovid and Chaucer for their painting of men and manners, and his school, inspired by a moral imagination and a realistic outlook, tried to show what men are by what they do.

It is valuable to consider the practice of these writers against the moral philosophy of some of the thinkers of the time, and much of what will be said about Pope's ideas of vice and virtue, and his technique for presenting them, can be illuminated by reference to one of the strictest and most severely logical philosophers of his age, Bishop Butler. In his second Dissertation, *Of the Nature of Virtue*,[1] Butler examines the whole subject in a way which makes clear some of the assumptions that lie beneath Augustan moral literature. He assumes a moral faculty—'powers of reflection and approval'— which is innate in man, and which he defines widely enough: 'Whether called conscience, moral reason, moral sense, or divine reason; whether considered as a sentiment of the understanding or as a perception of the heart; or, which seems the truth, as including both'.[2] The object of this faculty, he maintains, is actions:

those principles from which men would act, if occasions and circumstances gave them power; and which, when fixed and habitual in any person, we call his character. It does not appear, that brutes have the

---

[1] The two Dissertations *Of Personal Identity* and *Of the Nature of Virtue* were originally part of the *Analogy of Religion*, but Butler thought them not strictly relevant to the title of his larger work, and published them appended to it in 1736.

[2] J. Butler, *Works*, ed. W. E. Gladstone, vol. i (1897), p. 328.

least reflex sense of actions, as distinguished from events: or that will and design, which constitute the very nature of actions as such, are at all an object of their perception. But to ours they are: and they are the object, and the only one, of the approving and disapproving faculty. Acting, conduct, behaviour, abstracted from all regard to what is, in fact and event, the consequence of it, is itself the natural object of the moral discernment, as speculative truth and falsehood is of speculative reason.[1]

Butler's statement that the actions of men, abstracted from their consequences, are the proper objects of the moral faculty is a logical one introduced in order to clarify the point that, though the intention of these consequences may be taken into account, the fact that such consequences do not always result does not prevent judgement from being passed on the action: 'we have exactly the same sense of the action as if they did'. But the poet, and certainly the novelist, through the nature of his medium, is likely to display consequences. It is indeed part of the tradition of the satirist sometimes to upset the intended consequence—to show the money-lover stripped of his wealth at death, like Sir Balaam, or the proud man humbled, like Villiers. This is the preacher's licence, though, not the philosopher's exactness. Pope uses both.

Two of Butler's phrases in definition of the moral faculty—'a sentiment of the understanding' and 'a perception of the heart'—illustrate perfectly the way in which Pope approached his theme of human conduct. He assumed this innate faculty, on which his poetry depends, indeed, for its persuasive force, and also, like Butler, he exercised it upon character and actions. In the first *Moral Essay*, Pope's use of the ruling passion is only a clue; when he has unravelled his argument with it, and finds himself at the heart of the maze, 'the prospect clears, and Wharton stands confest'. In other words, the poem opens out into a character study, where Pope reveals his deepest interest in man himself as character and type. The portrait of Wharton is one of Pope's finest. Acute, relentless, yet oddly compassionate in its disentangling of the causes of Wharton's folly, it makes Dryden's Zimri look, for a moment, superficial. Pope seems to have felt a special interest in the young man of

---

[1] Butler, op. cit., vol. i, p. 329.

outstanding ability, corrupted by some 'vicious mole', or by a deep imprudence leading to folly. Perhaps something in this character reminded him of the qualities that so charmed him in Bolingbroke; he saw these talents as they would be gone sour, the prey of misdirected vanity:

> Shall parts so various aim at nothing new?
> He'll shine a Tully and a Wilmot too.
> Then turns repentant, and his God adores
> With the same spirit that he drinks and whores;
>
> (ll. 186–9.)

This brilliant catalogue is followed by a serious analysis of Wharton's character and a sober lament for his fate. Pope pitied him. In the last book of *The Dunciad* he appears again briefly, like some familiar ghost:

> Poor W—— nipt in Folly's broadest bloom,
> Who praises now? his Chaplain on his Tomb.
>
> (ll. 513–14.)[1]

But other characters of the same kind are treated more severely. The corrupt young man is one of the figures that touched Pope's moral imagination through the tragic irony of the most engaging qualities of youth, charm, and beauty turned to futility. Wharton had 'wanted nothing but an honest heart', and at the other end of the scale is Hervey (Sporus), 'the trifling Head, or the corrupted Heart', who possesses in perversion all the attributes of 'the great young man':

> Beauty that shocks you, Parts that none will trust,
> Wit that can creep, and Pride that licks the dust.
>
> (*Epistle to Arbuthnot*, ll. 332–3.)

How closely Pope observes his own world! Between these two extremes exists a whole tribe of the youthful, 'the gay embroidered

---

[1] It is difficult to decide why Professor Sutherland in his edition of the poem in the Twickenham Pope rejects the older identification with Wharton and prefers to suggest the young Earl of Warwick. The tomb and the panegyric on it are not the main point of the reference; the folly and the love of praise relate the character almost directly to the study of Wharton in the first *Moral Essay*, particularly since these attributes are not part of the general argument of the whole passage, but evidently apply simply to this one character.

race' of *The Dunciad*, whose presence helps to transform the last book from an attack on learned pride to an indictment of false values and false glamour in society at large. The idle Paridel, 'stretch'd on the rack of a too easy chair', is touched on lightly, but the Epicurean philosopher's corrupted pupil comes under the same condemnation as Sporus, almost in the same words: 'Bounded by Nature, narrow'd still by Art, A trifling head, and a contracted heart.'

The most brilliant of all these characters is the young hero of the Grand Tour, and Pope's genius for exposing the reality beneath the appearance shows to exceptional advantage in this long illustration. With something of Dryden's rapturous panegyric style, he exposes the youth's vulgarity—'Europe he saw, and Europe saw him too'. But it was Pope's own lyrical genius which inspired the description of the insidious beauty of Italy, and his ambiguous irony which dissolves the sweetness of the lines to dissipation:

> To Isles of fragrance, lilly-silver'd vales,
> Diffusing langour in the panting gales:
> To lands of singing, or of dancing slaves,
> Love-whisp'ring woods, and lute-resounding waves.
> (*Dunciad*, Bk. IV, ll. 303–6.)

The sponsor's enthusiasm too, as he recommends his pupil to the Queen of Dullness, is a familiar Augustan device for accentuating the poet's real contempt:

> So may the sons of sons of sons of whores,
> Prop thine, O Empress! like each neighbour Throne,
> And make a long Posterity thy own.
> (ll. 332–4.)

This is Restoration dandyism stripped of its romance and observed by the severe eye of the moralist. But the severity is never simple when the moralist is also a great poet. Pope pities Wharton; he creates a strangely beautiful image of perverted elegance in Sporus; he delights in the Acrasia's bower through which the hero of the Grand Tour blazes his way. Yet at the same time he exposes the folly, the vileness, and the vulgar insipidity that lies beneath each of them. He chose this sort of character as the butt of his attack for good reasons. These young men were unserious and hardened to insensitivity. Frivolous and insincere, they sinned against the qualities of honesty and sincerity which are the cardinal virtues of Pope's satire.

They sinned also against two of the most important virtues of the philosophy of the age—prudence and benevolence. They possessed neither a proper self-regard nor a regard for others. Pope seldom uses these two words, but his work shows that he was deeply convinced of the value of the qualities for which they stood, and acknowledged the results of neglecting them. A lack of prudence leads to folly; a lack of benevolence to that blind and hardened egotism which seemed to Pope the worst form of pride, and he showed how folly itself, though less culpable, could turn into the greater evil if it were persisted in. That is the lesson of these studies of 'the trifling head' and the 'contracted heart'.

Once again Butler is illuminating on the eighteenth-century attitude to these two virtues, prudence and benevolence. They are the only qualities with which he deals in any detail in his Dissertation, but he is careful to contradict the assumption that benevolence is the whole of virtue. When he accuses certain writers of misunderstanding the importance of benevolence he is presumably thinking of Shaftesbury, whose influence in the 1730s was already powerful, though in literature it is only in the 1760s that the full effect of the worship of benevolence becomes clear in the cult of sentiment and sensibility. Butler is anxious to separate the virtue as such from its possible result—just as he considered men's actions in themselves, as distinct from their consequences, to be the proper object of moral discernment. The sentimental philosophers maintained that benevolence was the supreme virtue because its exercise achieved an overbalance of happiness, whereas its opposite resulted in an overbalance of misery. Butler contests this view of virtue, which is oddly economic, as if one were to compare it to having a healthy balance in the bank to draw on, a sort of humanistic treasury of merits. His argument is that we do not indiscriminately approve benevolent acts. Our moral discernment is influenced by an absolute sense of justice which approves benevolence towards some but not to others. Similarly he observes, were treachery, violence and injustice, no otherwise vicious, than as foreseen likely to produce an overbalance of misery to society; then, if in any case a man could procure to himself as great advantage by an act of injustice, as the whole foreseen inconvenience, likely to be brought upon others by it, would amount to; such a piece of injustice would not be faulty or vicious at all: because it would be no more than, in any other case, for a man to prefer his own satisfaction to another's in equal degrees.[1]

Benevolence, though not a frequent word in Pope, occurs in *The Essay on Man* (Epistle IV), where 'self-love thus push'd to social, to divine' helps us to

> Grasp the whole worlds of Reason, Life, and Sense
> In one close system of Benevolence:
>
> (ll. 357–8.)

But although the notorious ease with which Pope concedes the principle of 'all partial evil, universal good' comes near to the fallacy Butler was attacking in his Dissertation, his *Moral Essays* are more alive to the dangers of assuming that an action producing happiness necessarily arises from a virtuous intention or nature, or that benevolence is always just. Pope was led to these observations by the satirist's keen eye for the particular instance, not by the logic of the philosopher. In speaking of the characters of men in the first epistle of the *Moral Essays* he warns us, with examples, that

> Not always Actions shew the man: we find
> Who does a kindness, is not therefore kind;
>
> (ll. 61–62.)

One of his favourite topics, the use of riches, to which he devoted two epistles, forced him to consider the two extremes of avarice and wanton extravagance. In the third epistle of the *Moral Essays*, 'pale Mammon', pining 'amidst his store' (whose stagnant reservoir contrasts with the Man of Ross's waterway), passes his wealth on to his ostentatious heir:

> This year a Reservoir, to keep and spare,
> The next a Fountain, spouting thro' his Heir,

---

[1] Butler, op. cit., vol. i, p. 335.

> In lavish streams to quench a Country's thirst,
> And men and dogs shall drink him 'till they burst.
>
> (ll. 175–8.)

Miserliness and prodigality equally are abuses of prudence and benevolence. In the same epistle, Pope invokes Bathurst 'yet un-spoil'd by wealth' to teach us

> That secret rare, between th'extremes to move
> Of mad Good-nature, and of mean Self-love.
>
> (ll. 227–8.)

Self-love in Pope has a variety of meanings. Sometimes, as in the second epistle of the *Essay on Man*, where he speaks of two principles, 'self-love to urge and reason to restrain', it has associations with the sense and instinct that Rochester opposes as right to wrong reason in his *Satyr Against Mankind*. But it is also a proper concern for man himself, which Pope sees as leading to social love, or general benevolence. In this sense it is very near the common philosophical meaning of prudence in the eighteenth century. Butler argues that 'the faculty within us, which is the judge of actions, approves of prudent actions and disapproves of imprudent ones', and though he admits that some would dispute it, he is prepared to maintain that 'prudence, or a due regard to our own welfare, is a part of virtue'. Traditionally, in classical and Christian morality, it has been re-garded as such; and the notion, as common as it is superficial, that the eighteenth-century admiration for prudence is a simple example of commercial and middle-class ethics leaves this out of account.

Pope uses the word once in combination with its opposite vice, folly. There is an ironic paradox when he says of the vain ageing beauties in the second epistle of the *Moral Essays*:

> At last, to follies Youth could scarce defend,
> It grows their Age's prudence to pretend;
>
> (ll. 235–6.)

What then did folly mean to him, in contrast to the prudence of self-love? If it implied no more than thoughtless or frivolous actions, his continuous attacks are like breaking a butterfly upon a wheel, and the topic seems hardly worth the indignation he lavishes on it. But to Pope a folly is not a foible, nor a fool the innocent victim of a corrupted world. The eighteenth century nourished a contrasting vein of comic satire, derived from Rabelais and Cervantes, which showed folly as an excess of benevolence, a happy imprudence, which the world, in its calculating way, regards as madness. It was this tradition, largely confined to the novel, that the romantics preferred. To Coleridge, Parson Adams (whom Hazlitt describes as the most romantic of Fielding's characters), and Sterne's Uncle Toby are recognizable heroes. But their folly is a superior wisdom, the wisdom of the heart. The grotesque fools of *The Dunciad*, on the other hand, the extravagant Wharton, the tittering mob of fops, are fools of another sort. Their folly, with which Pope is concerned, turns too quickly to actual vice.

Butler's definition of folly again illuminates what lies behind Pope's attack on them: 'From these things it appears, that prudence is a species of virtue, and folly of vice: meaning by *folly*, somewhat quite different from mere incapacity; a thoughtless want of regard and attention to our own happiness, which we had capacity for'.[1] Pope's anger at folly depends on his respect for prudence or self-love, the principle that urges a man to understand his own good. It is not only a love of order as opposed to disorder which impels him to attack bad writers, tasteless dillettantes, and frivolous courtiers. It is a belief in 'self-esteem, founded on just and right', a much more personal, less abstract consideration, and also an aesthetic one to the poet. For this reason Pope feels able to present himself in the role of the honest inquirer after true happiness, the guides to which are 'self love and social', prudence and benevolence, or a just understanding of the true position and capacities of man.

> Oh Happiness! our being's end and aim!
> Good, Pleasure, Ease, Content! whate'er thy name:
> That something still which prompts th'eternal sigh,
> For which we bear to live, or dare to die . . .
>   (Epistle IV, ll. 1–4.)

The whole of the last epistle of the *Essay on Man* is Pope's dissertation on happiness, and his conclusion, that virtue alone is happiness below, deserves to be treated as more than a well-worn cliché. The idea of virtue as self-love leading to social love has a cold ring to a modern reader, and little real attempt is made to discover what it

---

[1] Butler, op. cit., vol. i, p. 334.

means. But the way in which Pope insinuates his own feeling for virtue and its effects 'the soul's calm sun-shine and the heart-felt joy'—is more subtle and persuasive, and it is as essential a part of the material of the later satires as his attacks on folly and pride.

Friendship, the most intimate and personal form of benevolence, is the consistent standard of virtue Pope maintains in these works. He is said to have died with the words, 'there is nothing that is meritorious but virtue and friendship; and indeed friendship itself is only a part of virtue',[1] a remark which is entirely typical of Pope's habit of cultivating that good for which he was best fitted. What was most important to him in life becomes a recurrent theme of these poems; he warmly addresses Bathurst and Murray, shows his love for Bolingbroke and Swift, and by brief but pointed references he singles out for compliment Gay, Atterbury, Bethel. He presents his retired Horatian life as an ideal existence over which friendship and conversation preside:

> There *St. John* mingles with my friendly Bowl,
> The Feast of Reason and the Flow of Soul:
> > (*Imitations of Horace, Sat.* 2. 1, ll. 127–8.)

To his friends in particular he can speak of the sense of transience which distracts him even from his work:

> This subtle Thief of Life, this paltry Time,
> What will it leave me, if it snatch my Rhime?
> If ev'ry Wheel of that unweary'd Mill
> That turn'd ten thousand Verses, now stands still.
> > (*Imitations of Horace, Ep.* 2. 2, ll. 76–79.)

The same elegiac tone is as relevant when he is addressing them on public matters as on private:

> Alas, my BATHURST! what will they avail?
> Join *Cotswold* Hills to *Saperton's* fair Dale . . .
> Link Towns to Towns with Avenues of Oak,
> Enclose whole Downs in Walls, 'tis all a joke!
> Inexorable Death shall level all,
> And Trees, and Stones, and Farms and Farmer fall.
> > (*Imitations of Horace, Ep.* 2. 2, ll. 256–7, 260–3.)

---

[1] Spence, *Anecdotes*, p. 322.

This very transience makes friendship more precious, and it is in the face of 'the black fear of death that saddens all' that virtue takes on its brightest and most permanent aspect.

As well as friendship, Pope's independence is also a part of virtue in its honest self-respect. He is proud to be able to call himself 'un-plac'd, unpension'd, no man's heir or slave', and his devotion to his art is not only the personal peculiarity of the poet whose fate it is to write, but is justified by its wider function:

> O sacred Weapon! left for Truth's defence,
> Sole Dread of Folly, Vice and Insolence! . . .
> Rev'rent I touch thee! but with honest zeal;
> To rowze the Watchmen of the Publick Weal . . .
>   (Epilogue to the *Satires*, 2, ll. 212–13, 216–17.)

When he is proclaiming this function, Pope leaves behind the easy colloquialism of the Horatian style and allows the heroic note to enter. Here he turns to the favourite device of his grand style: the tableau. The opening scene of the fourth book of *The Dunciad*—a great allegorical set-piece—represents vividly those very values on which the epistolary style of the *Imitations* is a personal comment, even though it represents them in apparent defeat. Dullness in her triumph poses theatrically before her victims, Morality, Wit, reasoning (mad Mathesis), and Tragedy, who all appear in the atti-tudes of martyrdom, while only 'sober History' remains notably de-tached from the catastrophe. The description of the triumph of Vice which concludes the first Dialogue of the Epilogue to the *Satires*, which Hazlitt quotes as an instance of Pope's imaginative genius, and Savage singled out as one of his finest single passages, reads like an inspired summary of all his previous attacks on the abuse of wealth and the corruption of society:

> In golden Chains the willing World she draws,
> And hers the Gospel is, and hers the Laws:
> Mounts the Tribunal, lifts her scarlet head,
> And sees pale Virtue carted in her stead!
> Lo! at the Wheels of her Triumphal Car,
> Old *England's* Genius, rough with many a Scar,
> Dragg'd in the Dust! his Arms hang idly round,

His Flag, inverted trails along the ground!
Our Youth, all liv'ry'd o'er with foreign Gold,
Before her dance; behind her crawl the Old!
See thronging Millions to the Pagod run,
And offer Country, Parent, Wife, or Son!
Hear her black Trumpet thro' the Land proclaim,
That 'not to be corrupted is the shame'.

(ll. 147–60.)

The young dancing before Corruption are the 'gay embroidered
race' of the *Satires*; the old crawling behind her the misers, lechers,
and fools of the *Moral Essays*. It is part of the virtue of honesty and
independence to be moved to indignation by such a situation, where
'nothing is sacred now but villainy'. Pope concludes with a pride
that belongs to his role as the champion of virtue:

Yet may this Verse (if such a Verse remain)
Show there was one who held it in disdain.

(ll. 171–2.)

Virtue, as Pope shows it, has none of the effrontery and ostentation of Vice. The old magnificent terms in which panegyric had
exalted it are out of place in this world, where virtue is a modest intrinsic quality, shared alike by the great and humble:

Dwell in a Monk, or light upon a King,
She's still the same, belov'd, contented thing.

(ll. 139–40.)

The circumstances in which Augustan poetry had grown up led, as
we have seen, to a distrust of appearances and a growing awareness
of the easy corruption of the public world. Courtiers, writers,
statesmen alike were tainted by the scramble for power and place;
a situation in which the traditional idea of withdrawal takes on a new
importance. Honesty can only be judged by a man's actions, his
actual virtues and not his profession or his position, and 'the still,
clear mirror of retreat' reflects its qualities more truly than the
bustle of active life. The old contrast between the town and the
country was more and more associated with the contrast between
honesty and corruption.

Pope, in the first Dialogue to the Epilogue to the *Satires*, puts into

Fortescue's mouth the following warning that there are only certain things he can satirize if he wants to please the world:

> Why yes: with *Scripture* still you may be free;
> A Horse-laugh, if you please, at *Honesty*;
> A Joke on JEKYL, or some odd *old Whig*,
> Who never chang'd his Principle, or Wig:
> A Patriot is a Fool in ev'ry age,
> Whom all Lord Chamberlains allow the Stage:
>
> (ll. 37–42.)

The Augustans were beginning to find it easier to represent virtue as old-fashioned, awkward, unpolished in the eyes of the fashionable world. The stay-at-home country squire whom the wits had laughed at becomes Sir Roger de Coverley, the good old English gentleman. Innocence and unworldliness in themselves are regarded as the characteristics of the honest man in such later characters as Parson Adams and Uncle Toby. The honest old man has always been a figure in literature, but, if we look at Shakespeare, we find that he is sometimes only a minor figure—Adam in *As You Like It*, for instance; seldom a hero, and more often a servant. 'To be honest as this world goes is to be one in a thousand', but not necessarily to be on a level with the great, by virtue of this one quality. But to Pope and the Augustans, honesty itself was a quality of greatness.

Though, as we have seen, Pope does not portray 'foolish' or imprudent heroes of the sympathetic comic type, he does write at least one full-length study of the honest man who is also humble, obscure, old-fashioned. Sincerity and integrity are his great virtues, and a simplicity that scorns the disguises men assume for their advantage. Here he is in the figure of Pope's father, as he is described in the *Epistle to Arbuthnot*:

> Stranger to Civil and Religious Rage,
> The good Man walk'd innoxious thro' his Age.
> No Courts he saw, no Suits would ever try,
> Nor dared an Oath, nor hazarded a Lye:
> Un-learn'd, he knew no Schoolman's subtle Art,
> No Language, but the Language of the Heart.
> By Nature honest, by Experience wise,
> Healthy by Temp'rance and by Exercise:

His Life, tho' long, to sickness past unknown,
His Death was instant, and without a groan.
Oh grant me thus to live, and thus to die!
Who sprung from Kings shall know less joy than I.

(ll. 394–405.)

This character is inconspicuous and unheroic in spite of the magnitude of the virtue for which he stands. In the past, epic and panegyric with their elevated style had presented heroes of honour and chivalric worth, but when Pope substituted for these ancient forms his new genre of moral satire, he knew that by doing this he was celebrating a new kind of ideal. If it was not heroic in the old sense, neither was it purely stoical and rational. The honest man was not only, perhaps not often, the sage; but he was always the man of good feeling. A perception of the heart as well as a sentiment of the understanding, in Butler's words, is necessary for recognizing virtue, and the heart is often more important than the head in Pope's vision of honesty. His fools and villains are examples of the trifling head but even more of the contracted heart, while the good man, like the good poet, speaks 'the language of the heart', for which Pope complimented Cowley[1] and loved his father. He made a similar claim for himself in his own poetry, and what he said of the woes of Eloisa, 'he best can paint 'em who shall feel 'em most', was equally true of the sentiments of his moral song.

Thus, through the long and devoted practice of a lifetime, Pope created a style in which the conventions of satire and the traditions of morality could merge with a new and introspective sensibility; feelings were valued for their own sake, as well as for the persuasiveness with which they were expressed. He had begun to bring the actual writing of poetry into line with new ideas of truth to nature and of the authentic feelings of the heart. Both in temperament and style Pope is the most romantic of the Augustans. His verse is not essentially one of simple and forthright utterance, in spite of the importance he attached to assertion. Dryden, with his orator's aim of persuading the reader, cultivated the accents of honesty to en-

---

[1] Forgot his Epic, nay Pindaric Art,
But still I love the language of his Heart.
(*Imitations of Horace*, First Ep. of Second Book, ll. 77–78.)

hance his argument. Oldham exaggerated the rough tone of conviction to point a rage which was part of his sheer pleasure in writing
satire. But Pope, though on occasions he might share both attitudes,
was far more concerned with sincerity, with justifying his private
feelings, and with relating poetry and experience. For this reason,
even when his arguments are flimsy, they are presented with an
intensity which demands a positive response from the reader. For
this reason, too, his style often lacks the clear eloquence, the rhythmic inevitability, the simple revealing amplitude of Dryden's. It is
close, intricate, for all its deceptively smooth and polished elegance
full of concealments, hints, and surprises, and, more than that of any
other Augustan, figurative and metaphorical. His is such an individual interpretation of the new poetry that, in spite of all the admiration he aroused, it was scarcely possible to imitate him successfully or even to learn from him.

Nevertheless, his work epitomizes the attitudes and conventions
of the Restoration and early eighteenth-century school of poets. It
represents that strain of thought and feeling which we have traced
from Dryden, yet it transforms and develops all this material to such
an extent that, for the rest of the century, it was Pope's style, Pope's
moods, and Pope's subjects which became the objects of adulation
or attack. 'Every warbler has his tune by heart', Cowper complained, but not altogether justly. The external elegance of Pope's
style might be copied, his familiar attitudes of urbanity and wisdom
assumed, but the real strength of his manner, rooted in a tradition
where poetry and everyday life were closely wedded, was inimitable to poets whose circumstances had changed, however slightly,
and to whom even these recent conventions were growing thread-
bare. At Pope's death, the main stream of Augustan poetry was dry-
ing up, and the later poets of the eighteenth century began to draw
on new and different sources of inspiration. Yet at least one remained who was genuinely indebted to Pope for his subject-matter
and attitude. Johnson was the last figure of the age to whom the
traditions of the Honest Muse meant more than a mere literary pose,
and his work embodies some of the lasting qualities which passed
into later literature as the heritage of this school of writing.

VII

JOHNSON

I

JOHNSON's poem *London*, an imitation of Juvenal's third Satire, was published on 13 May 1738, probably the same day as Pope's first Dialogue of the Epilogue to the *Satires*, so that, as Boswell remarked, 'England had at once its Juvenal and Horace as poetical monitors'. Like Pope's, Johnson's poem was topical and political. It roused immediate interest and a second edition was published in about a week, a third being called for within two months. At this time Johnson was in a situation familiar to Augustan men of letters: he had thrown himself on the town in hopes of literary fortune, and was making a scanty living by journalism. Before he left Birmingham he had been in correspondence with Cave, the editor of the *Gentleman's Magazine*, and it is greatly to Cave's credit that he not only adopted some of the suggestions Johnson put forward in his first letter, but accepted the offer of his unknown correspondent to 'undertake, on reasonable terms, sometimes to fill a column'. Johnson had advised Cave to raise the tone of his journal above that of the common run of periodicals on these grounds:

that the Publick would not give You a bad reception, if beside the current Wit of the Month, which a critical examination would generally reduce to a narrow Compass, You admitted not only Poems, Inscriptions etc., never printed before, which he [Johnson] will sometimes supply You with; but likewise short literary Dissertations in Latin or English, Critical Remarks on Authours Antient or Modern, forgotten Poems that deserve Revival, or loose pieces, like Floyer's worth preserving. By this Method your Literary Article, for so it might be call'd, will, he thinks, be better recommended to the Publick, than by low Jests, aukward Buffoonery, or the dull Scurrilities of either Party.[1]

[1] Johnson to Cave, 25 Nov. 1734. *Letters of Samuel Johnson*, ed. R. W. Chapman, vol. i (1952), pp. 3–4.

Johnson's view of public taste was not absurdly idealistic. For some time journalism which was not simply party-inspired had changed its tone and was reflecting a new appreciation of light learning and politeness. In the 1690s, John Dunton, with his *Athenian Gazette* and *Athenian Mercury*, had helped to create an appetite for general knowledge which he satisfied in the palatable form of questions and answers. Addison, however, was much more influential in refining popular reading and taste. Johnson, in his *Life of Addison*, was to comment on the far-reaching effect *The Spectator* had had on social intercourse. After describing Addison's efforts to overcome the barbarous ignorance of an age when 'men not professing learning were not ashamed of ignorance', Johnson concludes: 'His attempt succeeded; enquiry was awakened, and comprehension expanded. An emulation of intellectual elegance was excited, and from his time to our own life has been gradually exalted, and conversation purified and enlarged.'[1] He was already aware of this influence in 1734 when he wrote to Cave, and of the new dignity which men like Addison and Pope had brought to the profession of author, both from the merit of their works and the independence and respectability of their lives.

This change that had come over Grub Street is illustrated by the kind of work in which Johnson found himself engaged when he arrived in London. Translations of biographies and histories, occasional Latin and English verses, and from time to time, before and after 1740, Parliamentary digests were what he produced for his living. But the rewards were as pitiful as they had been in the rougher Restoration period. Johnson tells us himself in his Life of Savage how he and the poet walked the streets at night for want of a lodging, and when that biography was published, the author, who had occasion to sign himself once to Cave, 'yours *impransus*', was still ashamed of his poverty-stricken appearance and obliged to his publisher for a meal. In a footnote to the Cave correspondence, Nichols relates the following story:

Soon after the publication of this life, which was anonymous, Mr. Walter Harte, dining with Mr. Cave at St. John's Gate, took occasion to speak very handsomely of the work. Cave told Harte, when

---

[1] Johnson, *Lives*, vol. ii (1905), p. 146.

they next met, that he had made a man very happy the other day at his house, by the encomiums he bestowed on the author of Savage's Life. 'How could that be?' says Harte: 'None were present but you and I'. Cave replied, 'You might observe I sent a plate of victuals behind the skreen. There skulked the Biographer, one Johnson, whose dress was so shabby that he durst not make his appearance. He overheard our conversation; and your applauding his performance delighted him exceedingly.'[1]

The literary profession was still precarious to a man too proud to hire his talents or court the great. But Johnson's satire was not written to order. It was his own serious and original work. Translation, which had been the mark of the gentleman amateur in the 1690s, was now the stock-in-trade of the hack, but imitation, since Pope, could still be used by a genuine poet.

Dodsley the bookseller bought the copyright of *London* from Johnson outright at ten guineas—a sum he himself stipulated for, as he told Boswell: 'I might, perhaps, have accepted of less; but that Paul Whitehead had a little before, got ten guineas for a poem; and I would not take less than Paul Whitehead.'[2] Dodsley was himself a very minor poet who had begun life as a footman, but never found himself a figure of scorn and envy as the dancing master Ogilby had done in less polite days. He was also a publisher of enterprise. He was in the habit of consulting Pope, some of whose works he had published, and Johnson in his Life of Akenside records how he accepted *The Pleasures of Imagination* for the high price of a hundred and twenty pounds, because Pope, having read it, 'advised him not to make a niggardly offer: for *this was no every-day writer*'. The ten guineas Johnson asked for hardly required any such consultation, but Pope's opinion of the poem is well known. When he was told that *London* was the work of an obscure writer called Johnson, Pope observed 'he will soon be déterré'.

Pope may well have been impressed by the power of *London*, but he must have noticed, too, how much it was the product of the tradition he himself had perfected. The tone of the Honest Muse—sincerity—is sustained throughout, and in spite of its topical

---

[1] J. Nichols, *Literary Anecdotes of the Eighteenth Century*, vol. v (1812), pp. 32–33.
[2] Boswell, *Life of Johnson*, ed. G. Birkbeck Hill, revised L. F. Powell, vol. i (1934), p. 124.

material *London* is both dignified and self-consciously literary. To remind the reader that this was a conventional imitation, the parallel passages from Juvenal were printed at the foot of the page; the echoes of Dryden's and Oldham's versions of the original were easy to recognize;[1] the political points themselves were of the kind Pope liked to make—attacks on Walpole's financial policy and on the stage licensing laws, which encouraged the taste for spectacle and the opera:

> With warbling eunuchs fill a licens'd stage,
> And lull to servitude a thoughtless age.
>
> (ll. 59–60.)

Pope's influence pervades the poem. Thales's indignation is Juvenalian, but his praise of retirement (for which Johnson had no personal sympathy) recalls Pope's use of a favourite theme. This idyllic picture, while it lacks Pope's lyrical touches, shares all his sentiments:

> There prune thy walks, support thy drooping flow'rs,
> Direct thy rivulets, and twine thy bow'rs;
> And, while thy grounds a cheap repast afford,
> Despise the dainties of a venal lord:
> There ev'ry bush with nature's musick rings,
> There ev'ry breeze bears health upon its wings;
> On all thy hours security shall smile,
> And bless thine evening walk and morning toil.
>
> (ll. 216–23.)

An even closer parallel is to be found in the moving passage on escape from poverty, where Johnson remembers the poor Indian from the *Essay on Man*, whose 'safer world' and 'happier island' are echoed in the lines:

> Has heaven reserv'd, in pity to the poor,
> No pathless waste, or undiscover'd shore;
> No secret island in the boundless main?
> No peaceful desart yet unclaim'd by SPAIN?
>
> (ll. 170–3.)

Though it has none of the free discursive pattern which allowed

---

[1] These imitations are recorded in *The Poems of Samuel Johnson*, ed. D. Nichol Smith and E. L. McAdam (1941), pp. 2–3.

Pope to vary and change his address so successfully, the style of
London owes some of its characteristics to the elder poet. The weight
of Johnson's language is never torpid; it is compact and muscular.
Like Pope he could use to full effect the terse devices, oxymoron,
zeugma, pun, and paradox, which give volume and depth to the
clear progressive development of the argument. One critic has said
that 'the closed couplet . . . tends to subdue images by putting them
into competition with other forms of complication',[1] and Johnson
understood the use of these forms. Not only images, but the kind of
brief descriptions which Pope loved, are subdued in Johnson. He
gives a mental picture, not a physical one. His account of the
dangers of the city of London is witty rather than vivid. Zeugma
makes the first point—'and now a rabble rages, now a fire'; then the
rhyme shows up an unsuspected resemblance between a physical
danger and a social menace:

> Their ambush here relentless ruffians lay,
> And here the fell attorney prowls for prey;
>
> (ll. 15–16.)

Monotony, however, suggests Johnson's limitation in contrast with
Pope, in his repetition of the same device in the next couplet:

> Here falling houses thunder on your head,
> And here a female atheist talks you dead.
>
> (ll. 17–18.)

London is not the work of a versatile stylist.

In his mature satire *The Vanity of Human Wishes* Johnson had
learned to be more sparing of these complicated witty practices,
recognizing that they convey a critical, ironic mood he did not
always want. But at those moments where they are needed they
lend tremendous power to his moral argument. The lines:

> Nor lute nor lyre his feeble pow'rs attend,
> Nor sweeter musick of a virtuous friend,
>
> (ll. 271–2.)

just stop short of zeugma, and even the compressed paradox

---

[1] Maynard Mack, 'Wit and Poetry in Pope', *Essays presented to George Sherburn*, ed.
J. L. Clifford and L. A. Landa (1949), p. 25.

> But everlasting dictates croud his tongue,
> Perversely grave, or positively wrong.
>
> (ll. 273-4.)

is so absorbed into the general tone that it might easily pass for a simple description. But these devices, though subdued, offer a continuous intellectual commentary on the situation. Mental powers control the physical, and all the ironic details are fitted into a generalized pattern which is only fully exposed in the fierce pun of the last line:

> Improve his heady rage with treach'rous skill,
> And mould his passions till they make his will.
>
> (ll. 281-2.)

This is Johnson's peculiar use of a style he found deeply congenial, which was directly derived from Pope. Yet though it was ready to hand in Pope's later satires, there could be few poets with the wit and formidable intellectual precision to develop it for themselves. Except in the most superficial sense it is absent from Savage, Young, or the later Churchill. Only Johnson had the ability and the inclination to use it for his own ends.

Though the originality of Johnson's genius is more strongly marked in *The Vanity of Human Wishes* than in *London*, the later poem is as clearly written under Pope's influence. At first glance Johnson's fondness for the unit of the long verse paragraph seems to look back to Dryden, but Pope, especially in the fourth epistle of *The Essay on Man*, had found a way of building up rhetorical and eloquent couplets to the climax of a bold assertion. This, in general, is the pattern of *The Vanity of Human Wishes*. In the two examples of the young scholar and Charles of Sweden, hypothetical clauses and rhetorical questions are piled up to maintain suspense for the final resolutions. The conclusion of the poem, too, is worked out on the same pattern. Johnson had admired the style of the *Essay on Man* in spite of his contempt for its argument, and innumerable traces of the poem appear in his work, which it would be tedious to detail. One or two examples will show how variously he used it. The whole passage on the vanity of ambition in the fourth epistle was in his mind when he wrote his later satire, and detailed images remained in his memory even from the rest of the poem. The suppliants of the great man, of whom, in a concealed image, Johnson says 'They mount, they shine, evaporate, and fall' (l. 76), recall the lines in the third epistle of the *Essay* where Pope speaks of the forms of nature—'Like bubbles on the sea of Matter born, / They rise, they break, and to that sea return' (ll. 19–20). Even on less serious occasions we find Johnson imitating the *Essay on Man*. A complimentary poem, *To Miss —— On her playing upon the Harpsicord in a Room hung with some Flower-Pieces of her own Painting*, contains the lines:

> Mark, when the diff'rent notes agree
> In friendly contrariety,
> How passion's well-accorded strife
> Gives all the harmony of life . . .
> (ll. 29–32.)

the source of which is this passage from the second epistle of Pope's poem:

> These mix'd with art, and to due bounds confin'd,
> Make and maintain the balance of the mind:
> The lights and shades, whose well accorded strife
> Gives all the strength and colour of our life.
> (ll. 119–22.)

Johnson's occasional poems, particularly his earlier ones, are full of imitation of the Augustan poets. That 'partial fondness' for the memory of Dryden to which he confessed later in his Life of Pope shows itself as an influence in *To Miss Hickman playing on the Spinet*, which is almost a parody of the rapturous style of Dryden's odes:

> When in your Eyes resistless Lightnings play, ⎫
> Aw'd into Love, our conquer'd hearts obey, ⎬
> And yield, reluctant, to despotick Sway. ⎭
> But when your Musick soothes the raging pain, ⎫
> We bid propitious Heav'n prolong your reign, ⎬
> We bless the Tyrant, and we hug the Chain. ⎭
> When old Timotheus struck the vocal String,
> Ambitious Fury fir'd the Grecian King:
> Unbounded Projects lab'ring in his Mind,
> He pants for room, in one poor World confin'd.
> (ll. 3–12.)

Rather less expected is his use of the lighter satirical conventions.

Before he came to London, Johnson had obliged some ladies at Lich-
field who were proposing to act Philips's *Distrest Mother* by writing
an Epilogue, and his manner here is a curious imitation of Pope's
social satire on women:

> Far hence are banish'd vapours, spleen, and tears,
> Tea, scandal, ivory teeth, and languid airs;
> No pug, nor favourite Cupid there enjoys
> The balmy kiss, for which poor Thyrsis dies;
> Form'd to delight, they use no foreign arms,
> Nor torturing whalebones pinch them into charms;
> No conscious blushes there their cheeks inflame,
> For those who feel no guilt can know no shame;
>
> (ll. 18–25.)

Only once again, in the verses *To a Young Lady on her Birthday*, did
Johnson attempt something in this vein, but there is a passage in
his tragedy *Irene* which reminds us of it and which looks back to an
even earlier source than Pope. Mahomet, overcome by Irene's arguments and example, admits that he has found in her one instance to
disprove his general rule about the nature of women:

> I thought, forgive my Fair, the noblest Aim,
> The strongest Effort of a female Soul,
> Was but to chuse the Graces of the Day;
> To tune the Tongue, to teach the Eyes to roll,
> Dispose the Colours of the flowing Robe,
> And add new Roses to the faded Cheek.
>
> (*Irene*, II. vii, ll. 61–66.)

The tone is naturally graver than in occasional verse, though it recalls Pope's Sylphs who 'early taint the Female Soul, / Instruct the
Eyes of young *Coquettes* to roll'.[1] Its more august original is, however, Book XI of *Paradise Lost*, where Michael points out to Adam
'a bevy of fair women, richly gay', and explains that 'this fair female
troop' is

> Bred only and completed to the taste
> Of lustful appetence, to sing, to dance,
> To dress, and troll the Tongue, and roll the Eye.
>
> (ll. 618–20.)

---

[1] *Rape of the Lock*, Canto I, ll. 87–88.

In writing his tragedy Johnson turned to the epic rather than the satiric source, but the odd connexion of these two passages with Pope indicates his instinctive recognition of what was most Augustan in Milton.

His serious and occasional poems equally show Johnson taking pains to establish himself as a self-conscious practitioner of the school of Dryden and Pope. Much of his poetry is imitation of theirs, and he was entirely characteristic of the Augustans in his feeling for verse writing as a social art and literary discipline. Though not a dedicated poet or a professional one in Dryden's sense, Johnson versified fluently and often. Boswell and Mrs. Thrale both record many instances of his gift for improvising, for his mind was so stocked with phrases, rhythms, and attitudes learned from the constant perusal of poetry that it was no labour for him to put his thoughts into verse. Possibly, had he been born in the next age, Johnson might not have attempted poetry, for this particular quality of the Augustan style—its availability to the man of letters—was quickly lost with the romantic movement. Johnson was a genuine poet, but he might not have discovered this without the encouragement of the convention in which he was working. Thus his most ephemeral verses are valuable even as an indication of the Augustan attitude towards the writing of poetry. Though it might not be a 'natural' expression in the sense of spontaneous or inartificial, yet writing verses on various themes and occasions was the common and proper exercise of a literary man. Those pieces on well-tried topics, written in a recognizable idiom which, to a reader ignorant of the tradition, may seem conventional and insincere, were rather an honest expression of respect for the craft, and of a sense of the occasions for which poetry was a suitable medium. The effect of this was often to dignify the occasion rather than the verse, or at least to give it its due. But the occasions were no longer necessarily public ones. Johnson's varied from the necessity of supplying a column to celebrating a birthday or the death of an old friend. He could do this effectively because his attitudes as well as his style had been carefully schooled by a discriminating study of the tradition he had chosen to follow.

Some of these attitudes coincided with Johnson's private convictions; others did not. The most interesting example of the latter is his treatment of the theme of retirement in verse. He gave no quarter to the common cant about solitude and retreat in private conversation, but he accepted its authority in literature. Juvenal had forced him to use it in *London*, but elsewhere, in his occasional poems, he develops the same idea gratuitously. In the Ode 'Stern winter now, by spring repress'd', printed in the *Gentleman's Magazine* in 1747, it inspired one of his finest stanzas:

> Teach me, thou venerable bow'r,
> Cool meditation's quiet seat,
> The gen'rous scorn of venal pow'r,
> The silent grandeur of retreat.
>
> (ll. 29–32.)

Johnson, in fact, was here recognizing the value of those commonplaces which possess a deep emotional appeal. He set about relating them, as far as he could, to truths of which he himself had no doubt. So, in his translation of Robert Freind's *Epitaph on Sir Thomas Hanmer*, which owes very little to its original, he linked the theme of retreat to that other Augustan commonplace, the dignity of the good man retired from active life. Constrained by necessity, Johnson, like Pope, had tested many of these commonplaces in his own life, though, unlike Pope, he had found many of them wanting. He told Boswell, 'I have thought of retiring and have talked of it to a friend; but I find my vocation is rather to active life'.[1] This theme, however, bore too close a relationship to moral ideas of which he approved to be entirely rejected in his poetry. In so far as it was bound up with respect for simplicity, integrity, and resignation, it was part of the vision of the good life which Johnson shared. In this epitaph he frequently looks back to Pope's 'Epistle to Harley', particularly when he is describing the uncorrupted public man, and these lines are as dignified and characteristic an example as any we possess of the Augustan ideal of honesty:

> This task perform'd, he sought no gainful post,
> Nor wish'd to glitter at his country's cost;
> Strict, on the right he fix'd his steadfast eye,

---

[1] Boswell, *Life*, vol. v (1950), p. 63.

With temp'rate zeal, and wise anxiety;
Nor e'er from virtue's path was lur'd aside,
To pluck the flow'rs of pleasure or of pride.
   Her gifts despis'd, corruption blush'd and fled,
And fame pursu'd him, where conviction led.
   Age call'd at length his active mind to rest,
With honour sated, and with cares opprest;
To letter'd ease retir'd, and honest mirth,
To rural grandeur, and domestick worth;
Delighted still to please mankind, or mend,
The Patriot's fire yet sparkled in the friend.
   Calm conscience then his former life survey'd,
And recollected toils endear'd the shade;
Till nature call'd him to the gen'ral doom,
And virtue's sorrow dignify'd his tomb.

(ll. 27–44.)

As so often in Augustan poetry, and particularly in Johnson, the epithets carry the full weight of the underlying conception. If we isolate them we find that they constitute a list of qualities which Dryden and Pope had each singled out for praise, and which had begun to represent an ideal but familiar character: steadfast, temperate, wise, active, lettered, honest, rural, domestic, calm. They create an image of the Horatian countryman, the retired politician, the man of letters, the hero of the private life who, like Bolingbroke, has first lived actively. Johnson repeats the traditional Augustan argument for retirement in one line: 'And recollected toils endear'd the shade.'

This is the last large-scale example we shall find in verse of that characteristic hero of the Honest Muse, the great man retired from active life, and it is one of the most complete. Like many of Johnson's better passages, it is a powerful summary of the previous ideals and attitudes of the Augustans. It illustrates, too, that extraordinary reversal which had taken place from the earlier conception of the hero who blazes out like a comet from obscurity into the world. Marvell in *Upon Appleton House* had praised Fairfax for preferring horticulture to the Wardenship of the Cinque Ports, but he was nevertheless compelled to compliment him for his soldiership as much as for his pacific virtues. Even more characteristic of the old high way of panegyric are his lines on Cromwell in the *Horatian Ode*:

> And, if we would speak true,
> Much to the Man is due,
> Who, from his private Gardens, where
> He liv'd reserved and austere,
> As if his highest plot
> To plant the Bergamot,
> Could, by industrious Valour climbe
> To ruine the great Work of Time,
> And cast the Kingdome old,
> Into another Mold.

In Marvell a peculiarly private love of rural retirement adds poignancy to his praise of heroic action without invalidating it, but industrious valour and its great effects of ruin and change held little appeal for the Augustans. To them Cromwell, 'damn'd to everlasting fame', was an example of how 'all that rais'd the Hero sunk the Man'; had he never left his private garden he might have remained guiltless of his country's blood, like the obscure heroes of Gray's *Elegy*. All he stood for—revolution, enthusiasm, inordinate ambition—seemed as dangerous to the poets of the age as it did to Hume when he came to write his *History of England*. For the caution which professional poets had learned from insecurity and privation, and statesmen from diplomacy, had made honourable survival rather than glory the enviable crown of a man's career. The old hero, with all his tragic potentialities, had dwindled to a name 'to point a moral or adorn a tale'.

This does not seem a hopeful attitude for literature. But as old ways died, new approaches to ideas and emotions which were so far-reaching in the work of the philosophers of the age provoked writers also into reassessing virtue in the light of mundane circumstances, and this, in its turn, gave rise to a vivid realization of private, individual man, surrounded by his social responsibilities, no longer a tragic hero but a figure alternately ironic and comic. It was the peculiar art of the Augustan poets to endow this figure with dignity, which the sober realism of their attitude, and the refined Horatian pastoralism of their mood, successfully effected. But

Johnson was the last poet of his time strictly to avoid developing any of the inherent lyricism of this ideal. He refused to touch on the pleasures of introspective reflection which solitude could excite, or on the grandeur and power of nature herself. Being melancholy and hypochondriac by temperament, he found no pleasure in introspection, and he had a townsman's indifference to the country. Simply by virtue of this natural bent he was well suited to carry on the more rigid Augustan notion of retreat as the dignified and quiet conclusion to a life of useful and active virtue, a sort of symbol of the honest and prudent self-sufficiency of the wise man.

There is in Johnson's poetry another typical Augustan attitude with which he had close personal sympathy—the distrust of the scholar who shuts himself off from the world. The long example of the young enthusiast in *The Vanity of Human Wishes* sadly points to the fallacious hopes of the learned while yet acknowledging the dignity of the pursuit. In a more severe spirit, Johnson attacks Gelidus the mathematician in *Rambler* No. 24, as a man who forfeits all human regard for want of remembering 'that though there are hours which may be laudibly spent upon knowledge not immediately useful, yet the first attention in due to practical virtue'. Gelidus's fault is his insensibility, the pride and folly of a man whose sense of proportion is so wholly lost that he can neglect 'the endearments of his wife, and the caresses of his children to count the drops of rain, note the changes in the wind, and calculate the eclipses of the moons of Jupiter'.[1]

Distinguishing between right and wrong reason, useless and useful knowledge, was, as we have seen, one of the favourite exercises of the Augustan moralist. The battle of the ancients and the moderns lay behind his mistrust of the specialist and the professed man of learning, while a new ideal of politeness encouraged him to be intolerant of austere scholarship. Johnson commented with approval on the increase in polite knowledge since Addison's time, but it carried with it a new danger. In *The Adventurer*, No. 139 (1754), an attack was made on the superficiality of modern criticism and learning and the absurd fears of pedantry which had encouraged it. Though Johnson had touched on this subject in *Rambler* No. 173,

---

[1] *Rambler* No. 24, 'Works of Samuel Johnson', vol. ii (1825), p. 120.

'Unreasonable fears of pedantry', he more often repeats the earlier Augustan attitude, but does so entirely for his own reasons. Eight of the *Rambler* essays are devoted to reminding the scholar of his precarious position; two of them describe the embarrassments of an unpolished student in society for the first time, and in one of these (No. 170) Johnson openly declares that such a man must learn to live with others on their terms if he hopes to be happy, or, what is more important, useful. He himself was proud of his own manners, which, on formal occasions, were courtly almost to excess, and of his knack of mixing with all sorts of men. These qualities seemed to him matters of moral responsibility. Yet his attitude is not exactly the same as that of his predecessors. He comments finally on the famous dispute between Bentley and the wits in his Life of Swift: 'But Wit can stand its ground against Truth only a little while. The honours due to learning have been justly distributed by the decision of posterity.'[1] Nor did he join in ridiculing the virtuosi. In *Rambler* No. 82 he mildly laughs at their follies, but in the next essay he points out that the passion for collecting is a harmless occupation which passes a man's time innocently and may lead to useful discoveries.

What distinguishes Johnson's attitude in this from Pope's or Swift's is a greater sympathy for and understanding of learning, and a more comprehensive moral sense. Pope's protective attitude to literature had fostered his prejudice against critics; the partial critic with his microscopic eye and the self-important pedant are the natural enemies of the poet. Since Temple and Swift and King had already launched the attack on scholarship and science under the guise of a moral intention—to expose pride, he found that he too could range these adversaries in *The Dunciad* under the colours of 'reas'ning pride' and folly. The figure of the awkward student only raised in him good-natured contempt,[2] but his real wrath was reserved for the pedant as dullard, the spoil-sport of literature:

> in closet close y-pent,
> Of sober face, with learned dust besprent. . . .

---

[1] Johnson, *Lives*, vol. iii, p. 11.
[2] See *Imitations*, Ep. ii. 55, ll. 116–22.

To future ages may thy dulness last,
As thou preserv'st the dulness of the past!
(*Dunciad*, Bk. III, ll. 185-6, 189-90.)

Johnson, who understood the solaces as well as the temptations
of learning, had no personal axe to grind in taking over this convention. To him it was not so much a convention as part of his conviction that any pursuit which dominated a man's life to the exclusion
of common duties was immoral. Supported by his own claims to
know what it was really about, he turned a new argument against
scholarly detachment, and, without prejudice to learning, he cast
doubt on the ultimate wisdom of the learned. In contrast to the
solitary scholar, whom, Mrs. Thrale tells us, 'he hated in his heart',
he set up the man who understood how to enjoy life innocently and
to use it well.

Because there was already an established convention in satire for
regarding the strict pursuits of scholarship as a branch of pride, it
was easier for Johnson to use the topic for his own purposes. What
Dryden, in his translation of Juvenal's tenth Satire, called 'the
windy satisfaction of the brain', was a much more serious matter to
Johnson. The whole of the first part of the example of the young enthusiast in *The Vanity of Human Wishes* is a direct encouragement to
the youth to sacrifice all trivialities to his great aim, but it concludes
with the famous warning:

> Yet hope not life from grief or danger free,
> Nor think the doom of man revers'd for thee:
> Deign on the passing world to turn thine eyes,
> And pause a while from letters, to be wise;
>
> (ll. 155-8.)

Scholarship is a solitary pursuit, and something of his own terror of
solitude prompted Johnson to feel as he did. He had a horror of
the ideas that steal unsolicited into the vacant mind. 'Remember',
Mrs. Thrale recalled his saying, 'that the solitary Mortal, is certainly luxurious, probably superstitious and possibly mad.'[1] In
spite of his partiality for the Roman Catholic faith, he had little
sympathy for the contemplative life, remarking that mortification

---

[1] *Thraliana*, ed. K. C. Balderstone, 2nd ed., vol. i (1951), p. 180.

was a simple necessity in an enclosed order, since 'a convent is an idle place, and where there is nothing to be *done* something must be *endured*.'[1] The scholar's life was subject to the same dangers: scholarly retirement might easily lead to idleness, to morbid introspection, and to self-indulgence. It always pleased him when he was able to say of a poet that he had achieved scholarly excellence and yet rejected the scholar's life, as he observed approvingly of Tickell: 'Tickell was not one of those scholars who wear away their lives in closets: he entered early into the world, and was long busy in publick affairs.'[2]

Here a personal bias supported his use of one of the satirical conventions of Augustan verse, and gave him frequent occasions— though more often in his prose than his poetry—of using it. Johnson loved the movement of life, the little ceremonies of society, ordinary amusements, conversation and friendly intercourse, anything that forced a man to exert himself for others and to fulfil his own capacities. It is scarcely surprising that he felt a natural sympathy for the kind of poetry which takes conduct and ways of living as its main subject. Yet he spent remarkably little time describing the surface of life in his own verse. No one comes away from reading Johnson's poetry with a clearer idea of what it was like to be alive in the middle years of the eighteenth century. If anything his verse retreats from the present into a timeless world of common experience and abstract truth which is reflected in his style. Even when he is using examples in the manner of Pope, he makes no attempt at dramatic vividness of character study. Wolsey and Charles of Sweden are not conceived of as personalities. They are rather presented in such a way that, though we learn nothing new about them, we understand more clearly and comprehensively the situation each illustrates. Johnson's power and relevance were quite as exact as Pope's, but they were directed towards different ends. When he names Harley, Wentworth, Hyde, or more recent figures like Swift, Marlborough, Anne Vane, or Catherine Sedley, he is giving specific application to the universal truth of the poem, but that truth does not itself depend on individual evidence. It is beyond

---

[1] *Johnsonian Miscellanies*, ed. G. B. Hill, vol. i (1897), p. 210.
[2] Johnson, *Lives*, vol. ii, p. 304.

proof in a way that is not true of, say, Pope's argument for the Ruling Passion.

This brings us to the originality of Johnson and of his contribution to the poetry of the Honest Muse. Closely as he adhered to the conventions in style and attitude, his genius required this discipline only as a support for a predominant cast of mind, a preoccupation which was by no means out of key with the school of poetry in which he had been bred, but which, in its intensity and depth, imposed certain limitations on a kind of verse that was already conservative and not easily susceptible of development. Johnson was not a wide-ranging or versatile poet: his devices are limited, his style tends to monotony. His principal concern was not for the craft, nor for self-expression, nor for poetry as a social art. He was almost exclusively interested in truth. The word to him was absolute, not to be interpreted as poetic truth, or truth of experience, or truth of vision, though it might involve all these. At the heart of his life the revealed truth of Christianity held a secure place, and it was never challenged from the moment when, as a young man, he sat down seriously and rationally to consider the grounds for his faith and the nature of his doubts, and decided for the former. Everything he wrote or thought about was related to the guiding principles of his faith, and he judged his own and other men's experience of life against this standard. He recognized those qualities in the Augustan style which were available to a poet whose main concern was both so profound and so deliberately limited. Two in particular he made entirely his own: the elegiac mood which matched his convictions and his peculiar sensibility, and the idiom, in so far as it demanded a formal and definitive use of language. In his use of these two qualities Johnson stands out as original, and as a valuable contrast to those other poets of the middle of the century whose talents were already leading them in other and newer directions.

II

The subject of *The Vanity of Human Wishes* is the main theme of all Johnson's imaginative work. He treated it in *Rambler* Nos. 204 and 205 as the history of Seged, Emperor of Ethiopia, in his search for happiness, and it distinguishes *Rasselas* from the two other great philosophical romances of the age, *Gulliver's Travels* and *Candide*. It gives depth and shape to his greatest work, the *Lives of the Poets*, that monument to Augustan achievement and to the humanity of the author, for throughout the series of biographies Johnson carefully relates the individual lives to this universal theme.

In the earlier Life of Savage he had pointed the moral unambiguously at the conclusion: 'This relation will not be wholly without its use if those who languish under any part of his sufferings shall be enabled to fortify their patience by reflecting that they feel only those afflictions from which the abilities of Savage did not exempt him.'[1] Johnson reminds us that these afflictions are inevitable. In the Life of Pope one of the most moving and perceptive passages illustrates his view that men, as they grow old, must be content with what they have, however imperfect, and conform to the inevitable. Describing the supposed indifference of Martha Blount to the poet in his last days, Johnson concludes with this subtle speculation on the reasons for Pope's continued fondness:

Perhaps he considered her unwillingness to approach the chamber of sickness as female weakness or human frailty; perhaps he was conscious to himself of peevishness and impatience, or, though he was offended by her inattention, might yet consider her merit as over balancing her fault; and, if he had suffered his heart to be alienated from her, he could have found nothing that might fill her place: he could only have shrunk within himself; it was too late to transfer his confidence or fondness.[2]

Often a brief account of the death of one of the poets is prefaced by an ironic reminder of the shortness of life or happiness. Of Thomson he says, 'he was now at ease, but was not long to enjoy it';[3] of Philips, 'having purchased an annuity for four hundred pounds, he now certainly hoped to pass some years of life in plenty and tranquillity; but his hope deceived him';[4] of Dyer, 'he did not indeed long survive that publication, nor long enjoy the increase of his preferments'.[5] In the Life of Collins, for whom he felt great pity, he

---

[1] Johnson, *Lives*, vol. ii, p. 434.   [2] Ibid., vol. iii, p. 190.
[3] Ibid., p. 294.   [4] Ibid., p. 323.
[5] Ibid., p. 345.

sadly observes: 'But man is not born for happiness. Collins, who, while he "studied to live", felt no evil but poverty, no sooner "lived to study" than his life was assailed by more dreadful calamities, disease and insanity.'[1]

This elegiac refrain runs through all serious Augustan poetry, and with Johnson it was an acute personal response to the conditions of existence. His *Lives* are more than biographies and pieces of literary criticism. They are memorials to human activity, achievement, and merit, and to human folly, uncertainty, and mortality. 'Fate and gloomy night' encompass their subjects, while the author is performing the same duty in prose as Dryden and Pope in verse, of celebrating human worth and recalling its inevitable fate.

Tragic irony had been as strong an element in Pope as comic irony in Dryden. In Johnson it is the inspiration of his greatest satire, and he surpasses his predecessors by his concentrated and pervasive awareness of the theme. Everything is measured against the fact of death and the movement of time towards that final end. He felt the physical and mental horror of death more acutely than Dryden or Pope, and he could understand the terror that often ruffles the surface of a stoical resignation. Yet again, he felt more strongly than any other Augustan the ultimate truth of the Christian revelation, and in the union of these two powerful factors—the emotion and the conviction—lay all that was most characteristic in his poetry.

Underneath the facts and observations that appear on the surface of Johnson's verses we recognize something irregular and disorderly, forces outside our control against which hope and ambition struggle in vain. The young enthusiast cannot escape; the virtuous man and the luxurist are equally subject to time and death.

> Year chases year, decay pursues decay,
> Still drops some joy from with'ring life away;
>
> (ll. 305–6.)

he writes in *The Vanity of Human Wishes*, recalling Pope's lines:

> Years foll'wing Years, steal something ev'ry day,
> At last they steal us from our selves away;

---

[1] Johnson, *Lives*, vol. iii, p. 337.

In one our Frolicks, one Amusements end,
In one a Mistress drops, in one a Friend:
(*Imitations of Horace, Ep.* 2. 2, ll. 72–75.)

But Johnson's tone is more intense than Pope's:

Time hovers o'er, impatient to destroy,
And shuts up all the passages of joy:
(*Vanity of Human Wishes*, ll. 259–60.)

For him the provinces of joy border on those of despair:

In groundless hope, and causeless fear,
Unhappy man! behold thy doom,
Still changing with the changeful year,
The slave of sunshine and of gloom.
(*Winter's Walk*, ll. 13–16.)

Johnson's personal experience of the changes of fortune and his fear of death disposed him to feel keenly these commonplace topics. He made no lengthy meditation on death in his own poems, but lurking melancholy and open fear often return him to this theme. Since men seldom live to enjoy the rewards of their toil (though Johnson himself was fortunate in this), the old tradition of reminding them of their neglect of genius took on a special meaning for him:

See nations slowly wise, and meanly just,
To buried merit raise the tardy bust.
(*Vanity of Human Wishes*, ll. 161–2.)

There were enough instances in the period to make this point specifically as well as generally true. Garth had complained of the obscurity of Dryden's grave, and Pope and Sheffield had contrived epitaphs for it. William Mason had raised subscriptions for a monument to Milton in the Abbey (and had been ridiculed by Pope for putting his own name on it), and there were enough reminders in satire of poets society had starved and not commemorated, like Cowley and Butler. These are only the commonest instances of how, through their concentration on it in poetry, the Augustans had made the little world of letters into a microcosm of the larger world, which gives a certain poignancy to their use of the traditional commonplaces in such a context. Johnson's experience as a professional writer coloured even his moralizing on life and death. In the Prologue to *A Word to the Wise* he asks the audience to be generous to a dead man's work:

> To wit, reviving from its author's dust,
> Be kind, ye judges, or at least be just:
> Let no resentful petulance invade
> Th'oblivious grave's inviolable shade.
>
> (ll. 7–10.)

The familiar rallying tone of the Prologue is given a new turn by his touch of grim irony:

> Where aught of bright, or fair, the piece displays,
> Approve it only—'tis too late to praise.
> If want of skill, or want of care appear,
> Forbear to hiss—the Poet cannot hear.
>
> (ll. 15–18.)

Inevitably he follows this by a moral reminder of the final futility of criticism:

> By all, like him, must praise and blame be found;
> At best, a fleeting gleam, or empty sound.
>
> (ll. 19–20.)

This close connexion between the world of letters, the conventions of poetry, and the professed morality of the age gives a cumulative power to the best Augustan verse. It seems to belong to a complete civilization, and to provide a coherent philosophy of existence—unadventurous, unmysterious in comparison with others, but authoritative, realistic, and instinct with dignity. Johnson is the last important writer to possess it in quite this characteristically Augustan way. As literary society and the conventions of poetry changed, this particular coherence was lost. The appeal of the elegiac did not weaken, but graveyard musings lack the peculiar laconic power of this deliberately restricted and literary treatment of the theme. Where it lingers, even in the least expected places, it still conveys a tone of sober and realistic tragedy that is unlike anything else. Isaac D'Israeli's catalogue of literary misfortunes, *The Calamities of Authors*, for instance, has something more

than a purely scholarly or antiquarian interest because it was
written with this tradition in mind, under the shadow of Johnson's
Lives.

But Johnson's treatment of the elegiac was not coloured only by
his attitude to life. It was affected by his feelings for the end of life—
for faith and religious reassurance. Though we often feel in his
poetry the oppression of a temperament in which

> Scarce frighted love maintains his fire,
> And rapture saddens to despair.
>
> *(Winter's Walk*, ll. 11–12.)

we are always aware of the control he exerts over it, the effect of
a faith which is itself an act of will, and which can answer the elegiac
questions with those affirmations that conclude *The Vanity of
Human Wishes*. To be capable, at one and the same time, of conveying
deep pessimism and fervent conviction requires a style and a vocabulary of quite remarkable concentration and compression, and every
critic has noticed Johnson's exceptional power over the defining and
connotative qualities of words. But the tone of Johnson's poetry as
much as his style is peculiarly suited to the dual conception of the
transience of this world and the steadfastness of the next. In the
first place it is authoritative, monumental, and detached. The
Augustan poetry with which we have been dealing shows a new
realization of the relationship between the writer and his audience
which mirrors actual social circumstances. Dryden's various moods
of tolerance, genial contempt, warm approval, and forthrightness
continually remind us of the people he is addressing and his attitude
towards them. Pope is so concerned to persuade, to dazzle by his
emotional vivacity, to make us like him, that we infer the kind of
audience he is writing for by our own warm response to his brilliant
discourse. But whilst Johnson's poetry is undeniably public and
aimed at an audience, we have no idea what that audience consists
of or even what it is like. No allowances are made, no hints dropped,
no shifts of tone adopted. Though this is didactic poetry, seldom obscure and often fervent, it is not in any sense argumentative. Just as
it gives us no display of personality, so it suggests no particular
relationship with the reader. It is the kind of utterance which might

be prophetic if it were not for the care with which every attitude is presented through the conventions and commonplaces of the thought of the time. Nor does this suggest any timidity on Johnson's part, any more than his consistent preference for the abstract word (though often animated by an epithet of feeling or passion) suggests frigid insincerity. The latter gives the curious impression of a formal, expert, but common language. The former—the use of conventional attitudes—implies solidarity with his audience, a feeling of community, of a man writing for men, not from any professional or social relationship but from a recognition of their common humanity and its deeper concerns.

Johnson's intention seems to be to define and incite certain states of mind in which truth can be more easily and fully received. In this he shares a great deal with the hymn writers of his age. Addison's hymns, which had been published in *The Spectator*, were not devotional works but exhortations to virtue and songs of praise. That neat exactitude of language which had developed through the practice of translation and the poetry of persuasion and argument was admirable for conveying restrained enthusiasm and accurate definition:

> Yet then from all my Griefs, O Lord,
> > Thy Mercy set me free,
> Whilst in the Confidence of Pray'r,
> > My Soul took Hold of Thee.

> > (*Spectator* No. 489, ll. 21–24.)

In this common metre of the old metrical psalms, which provided a traditional religious framework, a great deal of secular lyric poetry had already been written.[1] It was at once conventional, capable of expressing sentiment, and sufficiently regular to throw into relief the powerful effects of individual words. Personal sincerity is as much the aim of the religious writer as of the love poet, and his readers must be able to assume it, but originality is scarcely required of him. The material of the hymn writer is revealed truth, which he cannot interpret freely, but only decorate, expound, and enjoy. Johnson, speaking of devotional verse in his Life of Waller,

---

[1] Oldmixon in his Preface to the *Poems on Several Occasions* (1696) commented on the suitability of the measure for lyric verse.

was to make this same point to the disadvantage of religious poetry. 'The topics of devotion are few'; they are not susceptible of variation; the poet is limited in his manner of address since he is writing to God, a being not capable of passions, and his subject is too lofty and awful to be treated with the detached pleasure of the craftsman: 'Repentance, trembling in the presence of the judge, is not at leisure for cadences and epithets.'[1]

But the eighteenth-century hymn writer was addressing a congregation and inciting it to praise. He was free to use fervent rhetoric for this purpose, and he had, too, the preacher's duty of expounding. Isaac Watts, in the Preface to *Hymns and Spiritual Songs* (1707), describes his intention of appealing to both the feelings and the intellect of his congregation:

The most frequent Tempers and Changes of our Spirit, and Conditions of our Life, are here copied, and the Breathings of our Piety express'd according to the Variety of our Passions, our Love, our Fear, our Hope, our Desire, our Sorrow, our Wonder, and our Joy, as they are refined into Devotion, and act under the Influence and Conduct of the Blessed Spirit.... I have avoided the more obscure and controverted Points of Christianity, that we might all obey the Direction of the Word of God, and *sing his Praises with Understanding*. Psalm xlvii. 7.[2]

Watts's material is scriptural and credal; his phrases are taken from the Gospels and Epistles, or from the theological language of religious teaching, and they serve to illustrate some clear and basic point of doctrine. The effect of these scriptural phrases and theological terms in Watts's hymns corresponds roughly to that of the classical allusions and poetic diction in the secular poetry of his time. Like Johnson's abstract diction, they provide a sort of common language, an idiom which is in no sense personal, but which possesses the qualities of power derived from an authoritative source and suggests disciplined fervour combined with strict truth and accurate definition.

The hymn could express sentiment and arouse feeling. In the lucid stanzaic form and the context of familiar theological terminology,

---

[1] Johnson, *Lives*, vol. i, p. 292.
[2] I. Watts, *Hymns and Spiritual Songs* (1707), the 17th ed. (1751), p. vii.

conventional images strike home with the clarity of more detailed descriptions, as in Watts's 'A Prospect of Heaven makes Death easy':

> Sweet Fields beyond the Swelling Flood
>   Stand drest in living Green;
> So to the *Jews* old Canaan stood,
>   While Jordan roll'd between.
>
> (ll. 9–12.)

The simple words 'sweet' and 'living', and the conventional 'swelling flood', attract to themselves all the reader's power of brief visualization, and they are instinct with the traditional sentiment of pastoralism. Into such kinds of hymn writing the familiar elegiac themes of secular poetry could also be introduced, as in the well-known 'Man Frail and God Eternal', which has lasted as well as Gray's *Elegy*:

> A thousand Ages in thy Sight
>   Are like an Evening gone;
> Short as the Watch that ends the Night
>   Before the rising Sun. . . .
>
> Time like an ever-rolling Stream,
>   Bears all its Sons away;
> They fly forgotten as a Dream
>   Dies at the opening Day.
>
> (ll. 17–20, 25–28.)

Johnson, admirer though he was of Watts the man, has nothing to say in praise of his hymns—except those for children, which he recommended as an example of humility: 'A voluntary descent from the dignity of science is perhaps the hardest lesson that humility can teach.'[1] In spite of this it is a fact that he was attracted to the stanzaic form, not for trifling love lyrics or pastoral fancies, but for serious moral themes. His early *Ode on Friendship* has much in common with Watts, from its use of apostrophe:

> Directress of the brave and just,
>   O guide me through life's darksome way,

---

[1] Johnson, *Lives*, vol. iii, p. 308.

And let the tortures of mistrust
On selfish bosoms only prey,

(ll. 13–16.)

to the note of formal rapture in these verses:

When Virtues kindred Virtues meet,
And sister souls together join,
Thy pleasures, permanent as great,
Are all transporting, all divine.

Oh, must their ardours cease to glow
When souls to blissful climes remove?
What rais'd our Virtues here below,
Shall aid our Happiness above.

(ll. 21–28.)

It is easy for anyone familiar with eighteenth-century hymns in their proper congregational setting to recognize this as the language of sincerity adapted to a public audience and an incontrovertible theme. Johnson's *Ode*, like a good hymn, assumes that a certain state of mind will be excited by the subject, and sets out to confirm it through the style.

One unexpected fact emerges from a study of this style in the hymn—that abstractions and definitive language acquire a precise effectiveness and a curious simplicity in the lyric measures. The heroic couplet may suggest monotony and a sort of heavy grandeur which can blur the clarity of such devices unless the syntax and the pointing is as agile as Pope's at his best. But the lyric stanza, regular yet varied, has a lightness and an orderly movement which combines exactness with the tone of sincerity that lucid statement, however generalized, tends to produce. The verse from Johnson's *Ode*, 'Stern winter now, by spring repress'd', which we have already quoted,[1] on 'the silent grandeur of retreat' is an excellent example of this. The lovely phrase makes up a single line, perfect as a whole, in which every word has its peculiar distinctness thrown into greater relief by the brief metre. The stanzaic measure and the fervour of the great dissenting hymn writers of the eighteenth century did much to encourage lyricism and simplicity in a diction which still remained classically formal.

[1] See above, p. 233.

John and Charles Wesley, the sons of the minor poet and man of letters Samuel Wesley, who, like Watts, had first been included in *The Dunciad* and then, after mild complaint, removed again by Pope, understood the full force of Augustan compression and terseness, but they practised a new simplicity of diction and syntax. Charles, the truer poet of the two brothers, writes at his best with a Wordsworthian purity that comes from the chaste theological accuracy of his language and the syntax of open and uncomplicated statement or address. In his powerful and mysterious poem *Wrestling Jacob* he creates a sense of brooding awe and struggle by the most restrained devices, relying on the symbolic force of the story and telling it in direct and personal tones:

> Come O thou Traveller unknown,
>   Whom still I hold but cannot see,
> My company before is gone,
>   And I am left alone with thee.
> With thee all night I mean to stay,
> And wrestle till the break of day.
>
> I need not tell thee who I am,
>   My misery or sin declare,
> Thyself hast called me by my name;
>   Look on thy hands and read it there!
> But who, I ask thee, who art thou?
> Tell me thy name, and tell me now.

This demand is reiterated at the end of each stanza until the climax is reached and the revelation made through a full and final definition—a familiar theological statement:

> My prayer hath power with God; the grace
>   Unspeakable I now receive?
> Through faith I see thee face to face,
>   I see thee face to face and live!
> In vain I have not wept and strove,
> Thy Nature and thy Name is Love.[1]

In *Wrestling Jacob* the hymn comes very close to the personal

---

[1] Charles Wesley, 'Wrestling Jacob', in *Poetical Works of John and Charles Wesley*, ed. C. Osborn, vol. ii (1869), pp. 173–6.

lyric. Uncomplicated though the style is, the movement of thought and the completeness of the experience conveyed convince us of the wider possibilities of the form. Cowper's tragic *Castaway* has the same restraint combined with keen poignancy of feeling, and Cowper, too, had learned the art from his practice in hymn writing. But Johnson's only attempt at the hymn—an early poem *Upon the Feast of St. Simon and St. Jude*—is an entirely different kind of work, written in the enthusiastic style of the Pindaric ode, and he never repeated it. Nevertheless, and in spite of his contemptuous parodies of Percy's ballads, he was drawn to the form of the stanzaic lyric, and towards the end of his life he wrote one poem, perhaps his most moving, which displays the best stylistic qualities of the hymn and the grave elegiac tones that pervades his own work. The elegy, *On the Death of Dr. Robert Levet*, composed in 1782 when Johnson was at greater distance from the high Augustan tradition of his youth, is a poem which shows the influence of others written in the meanwhile. The style and mood of some of the stanzas is not unlike Watts; the ideas in others recall Gray's *Elegy*; yet it is entirely characteristic of Johnson in its sober authenticity and its sincerity.

Johnson's attack on *Lycidas*, though it might have seemed unduly severe to an eighteenth-century reader, would not necessarily have appeared wrong-headed. The pastoral tradition of questioning and apotheosis and the old mode of panegyric had gradually died. The new idea of elegy was that it should be more concerned with the honest achievements of the dead than with the mystery of death itself. To the Augustans death was a fact to be accepted, not the subject for poetic meditation, and the death of a good man seemed rather to level him with others than to distinguish him with unique glory. The natural tendency to brood over the melancholy circumstances of time and transience, indulged almost excessively in the work of poets like Young and Blair, was firmly restrained in true Augustan poetry by a strict sense of context and relevance. Nor did Dryden and Pope ever use death as the occasion for the kind of impassioned reflection on mortality and fame that Milton made of it in *Lycidas*. The great elegies in English poetry fall roughly into two groups—those which tell us as much about the poet himself as about the dead, and those which are more carefully restricted to their nominal subject. The first group contained undeniably greater individual poems—*Lycidas*, *Adonais*, *In Memoriam*—because of the greater freedom the poet assumes in trying to answer the questions raised by death and loss. The second group is composed largely of works written in the Augustan period and tradition, which contain either direct expressions of grief or sober eulogies of the dead, and which answer no questions but merely state the melancholy fact of mortality.

Johnson approved only of those elegies which were written from the same conviction as his own of the need for unaffected sincerity of feeling towards the dead, and purity of style. His criticism of Cowley's verses on the death of Hervey shows him cautiously distinguishing between what he admired and what he disliked in elegiac composition, and, to justify his coolness towards the poem, he hints that the merits Cowley ascribes to his friend are not of the highest order, and that he displays no genuine feeling in describing them:

> In his poem on the death of Hervey there is much praise, but little passion, a very just and ample delineation of such virtues as a studious privacy admits, and such intellectual excellence as a mind not yet called forth to action can display. He knew how to distinguish and how to commend the qualities of his companion, but when he wishes to make us weep he forgets to weep himself. . . .[1]

Dryden's sober note of epic lament in the *Lines to the Memory of Mr. Oldham*, though it achieved more simplicity and directness than the pastoral convention, seems not to have struck Johnson as valuable. He does not mention the poem in his Life of Dryden. No doubt its pagan fatalism repelled him, just as the Christian sentiments of the *Ode to Mrs. Anne Killigrew* disposed him to enjoy the enthusiasm of the poem—'undoubtedly the noblest ode that our language has produced'. But of *Eleonora*, with its metaphysical echoes of Donne, he was more dubious, on the ground that 'Dryden confesses that he did not know the lady whom he celebrates. . . . Knowledge of the subject is to the poet what durable materials are to the architect.'[2]

Knowledge of the subject lies behind Cowley's elegy on Hervey,

---

[1] Johnson, *Lives*, vol. i, pp. 36–37.   [2] Ibid., pp. 441–2.

but Johnson could not believe that those qualities the poet praises in his friend could ever have aroused real love. His own favourite elegy, Tickell's *To the Earl of Warwick on the Death of Mr. Addison*, praised the active and positive qualities of the dead man and was based on Christian principles and beliefs. At the time of its composition there was already a common assumption that sincerity naturally speaks simply, and Tickell, who had claimed accuracy for his panegyric on George I, openly declared in the first lines of his elegy that sincere grief has no time for poetic ornament:

> What Mourner ever felt poetic Fires!
> Slow comes the Verse that real Woe inspires:
> Grief unaffected suits but ill with Art,
> Or flowing Numbers with a bleeding Heart.
>
> (ll. 5–8.)[1]

The result of this unaffected grief seems oddly stilted and formal when read today, but to compare it with Dryden's elaborate odes is to see how far poetry had moved towards the direct expression of sentiment. It was this—sentiment expressed simply and with restraint—that Johnson admired in elegiac verse. His own poem *On the Death of Dr. Robert Levet* demonstrates how he himself achieved it.

> Condemn'd to hope's delusive mine,
>   As on we toil from day to day,
> By sudden blasts, or slow decline,
>   Our social comfort's drop away.
>
> Well tried through many a varying year,
>   See LEVET to the grave descend;
> Officious, innocent, sincere,
>   Of ev'ry friendless name the friend.
>
> Yet still he fills affection's eye,
>   Obscurely wise, and coarsely kind;
> Nor, letter'd arrogance, deny
>   Thy praise to merit unrefin'd.
>
> When fainting nature call'd for aid,
>   And hov'ring death prepar'd the blow,
> His vig'rous remedy display'd
>   The power of art without the show.

---

[1] *Minor Poets* (1751), vol. ii, p. 272.

In misery's darkest caverns known,
  His useful care was ever nigh,
Where hopeless anguish pour'd his groan,
  And lonely want retir'd to die.

No summons mock'd by chill delay,
  No petty gain disdain'd by pride,
The modest wants of ev'ry day
  The toil of ev'ry day supplied.

His virtues walk'd their narrow round,
  Nor made a pause, nor left a void;
And sure th'Eternal Master found
  The single talent well employ'd.

The busy day, the peaceful night,
  Unfelt, uncounted, glided by;
His frame was firm, his powers were bright,
  Tho' now his eightieth year was nigh.

Then with no throbbing fiery pain,
  No cold gradations of decay,
Death broke at once the vital chain,
  And free'd his soul the nearest way.

'The power of art without the show' exactly defines the effect of this poem. Johnson makes no superior claim for Levet, but he describes his qualities in a style which suggests the poet labouring for accuracy in conveying the moderate talents of the old man, yet, at every turn, drawing a general truth from the individual quality. Only one allusion is permitted, introduced by the unexpected colloquialism which increases its effect of sincerity, but it is the highest compliment Johnson can pay:

> And sure th'Eternal Master found
> The single talent well employ'd.

The figures of reticent and conventional personification which sustain the dignity of the style seem so natural that Johnson can move imperceptibly from them to the Wordsworthian simplicity of

> His frame was firm, his powers were bright,
> Tho' now his eightieth year was nigh.

When Johnson describes the innocence of the old man's later days, something of the hymn writer's fluent and tender directness touches his style. He was once maintaining that no one could honestly claim to have passed a life free from uneasiness, when a member of the company quoted against him his own verses:

> The busy day, the peaceful night,
> Unfelt, uncounted, glided by . . .[1]

But these were part of his necessary tribute to the good man; poetic justice rather than poetic licence inspired them, the belief that peace is reserved for the virtuous and a quiet death removed from all suspicion of fear. They recall forcibly the lovely opening verses of Watts's hymn, *The Pleasures of a good Conscience*:

> Lord, how secure and bless'd are they
> Who feel the Joys of pardon'd Sin!
> Should Storms of Wrath shake Earth and Sea,
> Their Minds have Heav'n and Peace within.
>
> The Day glides swiftly o'er their Heads,
> Made up of Innocence and Love;
> And soft and silent as the Shades
> Their nightly Minutes gently move.[2]

Levet's virtues, though obscure, were not those of a retired man, and Johnson could praise them for their positive merits through a simple but dignified account of the surgeon's activities. The Christian tone which is explicit in the allusion to the parable of the talents is implied throughout the preceding description of Levet's life. Johnson's own close knowledge of his subject justifies the simple and moving account of the old man's death in the two concluding stanzas. In the direct Augustan tradition, there is no finer elegiac tribute than this to the 'sort of necessary *Man*, or Surgeon to the wretched Household he held in Bolt Court; where Blind Mrs. Williams, Dropsical Mrs. Demoulines, Black Francis and his White Wife's Bastard with a wretched Mrs. White, and a Thing that he called Poll, shared his Bounty, and increased his Dirt'.[3]

---

[1] Boswell, *Life*, vol. iv (1934), p. 274.
[2] Watts, *Hymns*, Bk. II, Hymn 57, p. 180.   [3] *Thraliana*, vol. i, pp. 531-2.

On the Death of Dr. Robert Levet is the logical conclusion of the Augustan taste for truth to nature in style and subject. Behind the poem lies the conviction that the topic—a good man's life and death—is its own justification, and that nothing must be allowed to obscure it. The idea of Levet celebrated in a pastoral elegy, Levet raised by an apotheosis, is unthinkable and absurd. Johnson's poem reminds us that the Augustan style at its most honest had discovered a way of celebrating the obscurely virtuous as well as the public man.

The development of the elegy from the 1720s to the time of Johnson's is an interesting illustration of this. Simplicity in style and directness of approach went together with a growing popularity of character description in verse. It was becoming common for the elegiac poet to single out in his subject those virtues that aroused immediate admiration and recognition: social qualities and moral uprightness were as much the theme of elegy as death or grief. Even aesthetic tastes could be celebrated in this form. A curious example of Miltonic imitation, the blank verse poem by the Revd. Dr. Shipley, *To the Memory of a GENTLEMAN, who died on his Travels to Rome*, 'written in 1738' and later included in Dodsley's *Collection*,[1] provides a touching picture of the unhappy conclusion to a modest Grand Tour:

> LANGTON, dear partner of my soul,
>   Accept what pious passion meditates
> To grace thy fate. Sad memory
> And grateful love, and impotent regret
>   Shall wake to paint thy gentle mind,
> Thy wise good nature, friendship delicate
>   In secret converse, native mirth
> And sprightly fancy; sweet artificer
>   Of social pleasure; nor forgot
> The noble thirst of knowledge and fair fame
>   That led thee far thro' foreign climes
> Inquisitive: but chief the pleasant banks
>   Of Tiber, ever honour'd stream,
> Detain'd thee visiting the last remains
>   Of ancient art; fair forms exact

[1] Dodsley, *Collection*, vol. v (1758), pp. 239–40.

In sculpture, columns, and the mouldering bulk
    Of theatres. In deep thought rapt
Of old renown, thy mind survey'd the scenes
    Delighted, where the first of men
Once dwelt, familiar: Scipio, virtuous chief,
    Stern Cato, and the patriot mind
Of faithful Brutus, best philosopher.
    Well did the generous search employ
Thy blooming years by virtue crown'd, tho' death
    Unseen oppress'd thee, far from home,
A helpless stranger. No familiar voice,
    No pitying eye cheer'd thy last pangs.
O worthy longest days! for thee shall flow
    The pious solitary tear,
And thoughtful friendship sadden o'er thine urn.

For all its obtrusive mannerisms this is a quiet, private poem, and
the intention of the style is to recall the sober, formal, yet intimate
compliments Milton paid to the subjects of his sonnets at a time
when panegyric was the more common mode of celebrating virtue.
But the kind of virtue celebrated here is in keeping with the melancholy tone of the poem. Langton's character is mild, gentle, good-
natured, and delicate; an amiable and retiring young man, he is
more a figure of sentiment than a characteristic Augustan hero.

    In 1742 the death of the young poet Richard West was the
occasion for a number of elegies of which the best known is Gray's
Sonnet. Here again the tone is restrained, though, in spite of Wordsworth's notorious attack on the insincerity of its 'gaudy and inane'
phraseology, the emotion is genuine, particularly in the quiet
concluding lines;

    I fruitless mourn to him, that cannot hear,
    And weep the more because I weep in vain.

But the poem by Thomas Ashton, included in Shenstone's
Miscellany, shows more clearly how an elegy could also become
a typical Augustan example of character. It is written in an
almost jauntily satirical vein and suggests no personal grief. Ashton,
a personal friend of West's, is almost inconceivably composed; his

intention is not to bury West but to praise him, and he produces
a recognizable picture of the moral poet in contemporary terms:

> While surfeited with Life each hoary Knave
> Grows *here* immortal and eludes the grave
> Thy virtues prematurely met their Fate
> Crampt in the Limits of too short a date
> Thy mind, not exercis'd so oft in vain
> In health was gentle, and compos'd in pain
> Successive trial still refin'd thy soul
> And plastic Patience perfected the whole
> A friendly aspect, not suborn'd by art
> And eye which look'd the meaning of the heart
> A tongue which simple truth and Freedom fraught
> The faithfull Index of thy honest Thought
> Thy pen disdain'd to seek the servile ways
> Of partial censure or more partial praise
> Thro every tongue it flow'd, with nervous ease
> With sense to polish, or with wit to please
> No lurking venom from thy pencil fell
> Thine was the kindest satyr—living well
> The vain, the loose, the base might wish to see
> In what thou wert, what they themselves should be.
> Let me not charge on Providence a crime
> Who snatch'd thee blooming to a better clime
> To raise those virtues in a higher sphere
> Virtues, which only could have starv'd thee here.[1]

Gray himself accepted this poem when it was sent to him and
wrote it down in his commonplace book,[2] and it seems likely that
even the terms in which it is written—conventional Augustan
notions of literary integrity and stoical resignation—produced an
effect of respect and admiration to which someone unacquainted
with the idiom would fail to respond. The familiar qualities of
healthful temperance, simple truth, honest thought, plastic
patience, and the common sentiment that the good life is a moral
example, 'the kindest satyr', even the reminder of society's neglect,
all these mark the very indifferent verses as consciously within the
tradition. As we read them we cannot help observing that it is

---

[1] *Shenstone's Miscellany*, ed. I. A. Gordon (1952), p. 47.   [2] Ibid., p. 147.

much harder to write well in this dignified, formal, yet social idiom, which Johnson triumphantly managed in his elegy on Levet, than in the gentler and more private language of sentiment which Shipley's poem and Gray's *Sonnet* represent in their different ways.

Johnson's elegy was written forty years later than this, and though it stands above all the others that have been mentioned, it had one greater predecessor—Gray's *Elegy Written in a Country Churchyard*, a poem so completely classical in the best sense that it seems outside period or school, but which, in fact, draws so widely on the associations of Augustan and post-Augustan elegy, that Johnson himself, no friend to the rest of Gray's work, admired it and was influenced by it.

The *Elegy Written in a Country Churchyard* is, like those other elegies we have noticed, a poem of praise. It celebrates secluded lives cut off from the chance of fame. Retirement was a rich subject, capable of various developments. To the Augustans it had appealed as the quiet conclusion of a useful life, but later eighteenth-century writers began to court the idea of obscurity for its own sake, of a life led entirely out of the world which was nearer to the old pastoral conception of *otium* and innocence. The pure Horatian ideal of the country life had never been more gracefully and persuasively presented than by Cowley in the previous century:

the pleasantest condition of Life, is *in Incognito*. What a brave Privilege is it to be free from all Contentions, from all Envying or being Envyed, from recieving and from paying all kind of Ceremonies? . . . Upon the whole matter, I account a person who has a moderate Minde and Fortune, and lives in the conversation of two or three agreeable friends, with little commerce in the world besides, who is esteemed well enough by his few neighbours that know him, and is truly irreproachable by any body, and so after a healthful quiet life, before the great inconveniences of old age, goes more silently out of it then he came in, (for I would not have him so much as Cry in the *Exit*). This Innocent Deceiver of the world, as *Horace* calls him, this *Muta persona*, I take to have been more happy in his Part, then the greatest Actors that fill the Stage with show and noise, nay, even then *Augustus* himself, who askt with his last breath, Whether he had not played his *Farce* very well.[1]

[1] Cowley, *Essays, Plays and Sundry Verses*, ed. A. R. Waller (1906), pp. 398-9.

This picture of a civilized country existence occurs in Cowley's essay *Of Obscurity*, but it is a slightly different form of obscurity from the one described in Gray's *Elegy*. For meanwhile the opinion had begun to grow that a life cut off from the world must, by its very nature, be better than one spent in it. Johnson laughed the idea out of court, but the sentimental appeal of simplicity and quietness was too strong to be overcome by reason.

William Melmoth, who had repeated the conventional poetic theories of the value of retirement in his *Epistle on Active and Retired Life*,[1] had other and more general things to say on the subject. The *FitzOsborne Letters*, with their easy tone of moral chit-chat, contain a number of essays on the charms of retirement. In one Melmoth goes so far as to make a general observation about the superiority of obscure lives:

Perhaps the true measure of human merit, is neither to be taken from the histories of former times nor from what passes in the more striking scenes of the present generation. The greatest virtues have, probably, been ever the most obscure; and I am persuaded in all ages of the world more genuine heroism has been overlooked and unknown, than either recorded or observed.[2]

It is safe to assume that anything Melmoth says on a moral or literary topic was already a firmly established commonplace when he was writing. That an obscure life was likely to be the most virtuous is an idea implicit in the Horatian poetic convention which had gradually been recognized and accorded a definite sentiment of its own. It was related also to the older pastoral ideal, and Shenstone, who had retired to the country to distinguish himself as a poet by his devotion to this one slender topic, rang all the possible changes on it. At its simplest, the old contrast between town and country is repeated in his *Inscription near a Sheep-cote* (1745):

> Shepherd would'st thou here obtain
> Pleasure unalloy'd with pain?
> Joy that suits the rural sphere?
> Gentle shepherd! lend an ear . . . .

---

[1] See above, p. 159.

[2] [William Melmoth], *Letters . . . by the late Sir Thomas FitzOsborne Bart.* (1748), Letter XLIII, p. 191.

If thou canst no charm disclose
In the simplest bud that blows;
Go forsake thy plain and fold,
Join the crowd and toil for gold.

But the traditional shepherd and the apologetic satirist or poet, justifying his flight from the town, had been joined by yet another figure, the real countryman himself. In Georgic nature poetry like Thomson's, the countryman had grown from a simple figure introducing the necessary human detail into a landscape and developed into a character in his own right, a man experiencing pleasure or tragedy. His day-to-day occupations are lovingly recorded and his life appears as a moral ideal. The death of the swain caught in the snow-drifts is depicted as a lesson to the 'gay licentious proud' to remind them of their suffering fellow men. The honest country labourer teaches them that he, like the Horatian poet, enjoys a true contentment. When Thomson repeats Horace's and Cowley's prescription for happiness, he puts the young labourer with the poet as an equal example of rural virtue:

Oh! knew he but his happiness, of men
The happiest he! who far from public rage
Deep in the vale, with a choice few retired,
Drinks the pure pleasures of the rural life. . . .
Here too dwells simple truth, plain innocence,
Unsullied beauty, sound unbroken youth
Patient of labour—with a little pleased,
Health ever-blooming, unambitious toil,
Calm contemplation and poetic ease.

(*Autumn*, ll. 1235-8, 1273-7.)

Gray's idea in the *Elegy* was to record the inconspicuous virtues of obscurity exemplified in this new character, and to spread over the whole poem the ideal atmosphere of country life and the philosophic melancholy which Thomson had already invoked, and which suited both his own temperament and the elegiac theme. Because this new pastoralism was so bound up with the Augustan moral ideal, there was no problem for Gray in repeating the commonplaces of formal funereal poetry in a country setting. They were by now as appropriate here as in the more elevated context of public lament. A man who reads the inscriptions on country gravestones can feel the same emotions he experiences in looking at the epitaphs in Westminster Abbey: he may even feel them with greater poignancy; his emotions may be stirred more tenderly. To be reminded of death in this calm and innocent setting is to recall not honour and nobility but the essential virtues of bare humanity. Gray's use of landscape, then, is not simply inspired by his romantic sensibility to the moods and appearances of nature. It is intended to create a moral image with all the authority of the Augustan tradition behind it.

How easily the Augustan conventions blend into the quiet picture of a country evening! Like Pope, Gray names historical examples to recall nobility and point the familiar theme—'the paths of glory lead but to the grave'. The privations of the rude forefathers of the hamlet he concedes:

> Chill Penury repress'd their noble rage
> And froze the genial current of the soul,
>
> (ll. 51–52.)

but he turns them to advantages. Again like Pope, he recalls how all that raised the hero sunk the man, and takes this to be the justification for their harder, simpler lives. Their lot precluded greatness,

> nor circumscrib'd alone
> Their growing virtues, but their crimes confin'd;
> Forbad to wade through slaughter to a throne,
> And shut the gates of mercy on mankind. . . .
>
> (ll. 65–68.)

> Far from the madding crowd's ignoble strife,
> Their sober wishes never learn'd to stray;
> Along the cool sequester'd vale of life
> They kept the noiseless tenor of their way.
>
> (ll. 73–76.)

Pope had praised the merit of this obscurity when, speaking of the Man of Ross's memorial, he wrote:

> Go, search it there, where to be born and die,
> Of rich and poor make all the history;

Enough, that Virtue fill'd the space between;
Prov'd, by the ends of being, to have been.

(*Moral Essay* III, ll. 287–90.)

The parish register with its simple statement of a man's existence
is the best monument, so long as his survivors remember his virtues.
But Gray's countrymen have no outstanding virtues to be remembered by. It is the nature of their lives—'the noiseless tenor of their
way'—which soothes the sentiments and also recalls the familiar
theme of the vanity of ambition. The terms in which Gray describes their retired lives echo indirectly many of the passages we
have already quoted from Dryden and Pope in praise of 'the silent
grandeur of retreat'. They depict a mood of reserved tranquillity
which lies at the centre of the Augustan moral vision. Dryden
writes of seeking repose 'in the cool shades of wit' and of the quiet
and content of mind which 'only in the shades, like laurels grow'.
Pope sees himself 'in life's cool evening, satiate of applause', and observes his friends 'in the clear, still mirror of retreat'. The image was
already formed by the time Gray came to write the *Elegy*, and the
full connotation of 'the cool sequestered vale of life' and 'the noiseless tenor of their way' can only be felt against the background of
shade and silence with which the earlier Augustans had associated
their ethos.

The gravity of the theme had moved Gray originally even to imitate the style of the hymn. The Eton MS. version of the poem contains this stanza:

Hark! how the sacred Calm, that broods around
  Bids ev'ry fierce tumultuous Passion cease,
In still small Accents whisp'ring from the Ground
  A grateful Earnest of eternal Peace.[1]

He relinquished it in the final version, perhaps because the fervour of the style attracts too much attention to itself in this
diffused and muted atmosphere of reflective melancholy. But that
he had attempted it at all suggests what we have already tried to
demonstrate in this chapter—the closeness of the hymn writing of
the period to the temper and style of Augustan elegiac verse.

---

[1] *An Elegy . . . The Three Manuscripts*, ed. R. Fukuhara and H. Bergen (1933), p. 6.

Johnson's admiration for Gray's poem came from his response to these familiar sentiments, and to the consciousness behind the style of the whole tradition of non-satiric Augustan verse. It is not surprising to find some influence on his own elegy, where the verses

> Nor, letter'd arrogance, deny
> Thy praise to merit unrefin'd
>
> (ll. 11–12.)

recall Gray's

> Let not Ambition mock their useful toil,
> Their homely joys and destiny obscure;
> Nor grandeur hear with a disdainful smile,
> The short and simple annals of the poor.
>
> (ll. 29–32.)

It is a far cry from Puttenham's belief that exemplary history must be taken from the lives of the great and never from those of the obscure or simple to this moral reverence for 'the short and simple annals of the poor'. Donald Stauffer in his *Art of Biography in Eighteenth Century England* points out that the spiritual confessions and autobiographies of the Methodists did much to confirm this respect for the poor and unlearned.[1] Even earlier, Richardson's first novel had already shown that the experiences of a servant girl could be as complex and absorbing and more exemplary than those of a princess. Wordsworth's rustics spring from a tradition which was already established, though dominated by a mood and a moral convention with which he had little patience.

Johnson, in his own life, showed that perfect sympathy with the poor which had become a matter of sentiment and imagination in the new convention. He did not need the added attraction of a rural setting to convince him of the intrinsic value of every individual life, and he refused to idealize poverty or obscurity. In the divergence of attitude between him and his contemporaries we can see something of the development of different aspects of the Augustan point of view. The Horatianism and the cult of sincerity which had played such an important part in Pope's sensibility grew easily into this new pastoralism in which, though the artificiality of the older

---

[1] Donald Stauffer, *The Art of Biography in Eighteenth Century England* (1941), chapter v.

mode had been modified, shepherds exchanged for labourers and Arcadia and the golden age for an actual contemporary landscape, the idyllic mood remained. On the other hand, the realism, the objective honesty, sometimes sceptical and ironic, had proved less susceptible of development outside satire. A personality like Johnson's, a passion for truth and accuracy, and a deep emotional response to absolute ideas were needed still to discover in it a source of genuine poetry.

Johnson's early career had been passed in circumstances so like those of the professional Augustans that they left a lasting mark on his outlook and supported his natural tendency to imitate rather than to experiment or develop in verse. Yet the two elegiac pieces he wrote which commemorate individual lives—his translation of Friend's *Epitaph on Sir Thomas Hanmer* and the poem *On the Death of Dr. Robert Levet*—show, in their differences, that he was capable of a range which reflects something of the development of the convention. The earlier *Epitaph* stands squarely in the earlier tradition, both in the type of character it depicts and in the style which relates every point to a moral aim. This is the idiom Thomas Ashton attempted with such little success in his poem on West. It needs the mastery and discipline of Pope to be fully effective, but Johnson, though he does not achieve this, shows a genuine understanding of the mode. The elegy on Levet, on the other hand, with its unadorned description of the old man's qualities and his death, while it shares with the earlier work a formal idiom of personified abstractions that elevate and generalize, yet contrives to give an effect of much greater simplicity. This simplicity has more in common with the hymn writer's mood than the satirist's. The syntax is notably direct, which, as we have seen, was common practice in this stanzaic form, and had already been used in paradoxical combination with formal diction in the hymn. The repeated inversions of the *Epitaph on Hanmer*, which recall its Latin original, are entirely absent. As a result the verses move at a quiet narrative pace which emphasizes the authenticity of the emotions and the facts recorded. This effect of simplicity is new to Johnson's poetry: *London* and *The Vanity of Human Wishes* do not attempt it. But the new kind of subject demanded it. The simple and honest hero, an obscure old man,

could only be celebrated in what Pope had called 'the language of
the heart'. Johnson adopted the style of the hymns and of a work
like Gray's elegy because its restraint carried with it the fluent
natural ease of the lyric, and the lyric was the form for poetry of
feeling. Boswell tells us that Johnson could not repeat the verses on
Levet without tears. He wrote them in a style that might arouse
the same response in his readers.

III

Though Johnson could vary the mode or form of his poems
according to their subject, he made little or no change in diction and
language, and, within the couplet, he allowed no new variations.
Looking back over a period of general improvement in the arts of
civilization, he was not dismayed by the idea that perfection had
been reached in verse with Pope, and that though 'new sentiments
and new images' might be introduced in future, 'to attempt any
further improvements in versification will be dangerous'.[1] He seems
to have felt that a strict standard of technique left the mind freer to
develop new sentiments and images. At any rate, he was certain
that too much refinement of verse style could be a bad thing. In the
first draft of *Irene* he himself had written the line 'Fenc'd from the
Sun and sheltered from the Breeze', corrected it to 'Fenc'd from
the Summer breeze, and vernal show'r', and scribbled in the margin
against the last, 'polish'd into weakness'.[2] He was referring here
both to the diction and to the softening effect on the metre when
the strict antithetical division marked by a heavy pause after the
fourth syllable was eliminated. Any development from Pope's
normal practice in diction or versification seemed to him likely to
encourage this sort of precious refinement.

Such a view inevitably makes a poet nervous of innovation: it
may even attract him to the greater freedom of prose as a medium.
Nevertheless, innovations had been made in the heroic couplet by
the time Johnson was writing the *Lives*, of which he could not have
been unaware. These lines of Goldsmith's, for example, have a completely different metrical effect from anything in Pope:

[1] Johnson, *Lives*, vol. ii, p. 251.
[2] Johnson, *Poems*, ed. Nichol Smith and McAdam, p. 363.

Sweet was the sound, when oft at evening's close
Up yonder hill the village murmur rose;
There, as I pass'd with careless steps and slow,
The mingling notes came soften'd from below;
The swain responsive as the milkmaid sung,
The sober herd that low'd to meet their young;
The noisy geese that gabbl'd o'er the pool,
The playful children just let loose from school:
The watchdog's voice that bay'd the whisp'ring wind,
And the loud laugh that spoke the vacant mind.
These all in sweet confusion sought the shade,
And fill'd each pause the nightingale had made.

(*The Deserted Village*, ll. 113-24.)

Goldsmith's verses have a winding, easy flow, and though the end-stopped rhyme is there we are hardly aware in reading them of the normal regular beat of the traditional couplet. For one thing, the caesura is hardly marked at all in the catalogue of 'mingling notes' so that they do, in fact, 'come soften'd'. The inversion of normal poetic stress in favour of normal speech stress—'sweet was the sound', or 'these all in sweet confusion sought the shade'—was not itself new. Dryden and Pope had often used it, but almost always followed by a gently marked pause. By contrast, Goldsmith's lines lack the feeling of an intricate rhythmic pattern; the complications have all been smoothed out, except for an occasional lyric irregularity, rather like Dryden's 'Fair Galatea with thy silver feet', in such verses as 'There as I past with careless steps and slow', though here again Goldsmith's device is so subdued as to be scarcely noticed.

The whole effect of Goldsmith's verses is of a murmurous flow of associations—individual pictures sliding into the memory—and for this effect he needed a new metrical treatment of the couplet. The important unit is the paragraph, but the paragraphs are not sections in a logical argument; they read rather like inner monologues, the poet reminding himself of the past. Sometimes he interrupts the flow with a familiar Augustan apostrophe to his muse—'Dear charming nymph, neglected and decried' (l. 411), or an open address to the reader in didactic style—'Ill fares the land, to hast'ning ills a prey, Where wealth accumulates, and men decay' (ll. 551–2), but these are interpolations rather than an essential part of the rhetoric of the poem. The conventions are still there, but they have begun to look slightly different in this new context. Even the character studies are transformed by their setting; they are not so much moral *exempla* as parts of a narrative, figures in a story. Goldsmith's mood, so different from Dryden's or Pope's, required a new technique; his intention forced him to modify the traditional style.

Johnson was to some extent Goldsmith's poetic mentor. He corrected *The Traveller* and *The Deserted Village* and added lines to both, and we must assume that he had noticed these innovations. If so, he was sufficiently pleased by the total effect to approve of Goldsmith's work; the presence of the old conventions, however modified, the 'truth to nature' of the whole poem with its detailed descriptions and its passages of reflective commonplace, were Augustan enough to please him. He may even have observed the occasional touch of humorous parody Goldsmith allows himself in his treatment of the old traditions. The idyllic description of the 'parlour splendours' of the village inn is made up of many of the same details he had already used in his burlesque 'heroical description of nature' which the poverty-stricken poet reads to the assembled club in Letter XXX of *The Citizen of the World*. The whole of this passage shows from the ease of the parody how perfectly well Goldsmith was acquainted with the Augustan traditions of style and subject:

> Where the Red Lion flaring o'er the way,
> Invites each passing stranger that can pay;
> Where Calvert's butt, and Parson's black champaign,
> Regales the drabs and bloods of Drury lane;
> There in a lonely room, from bailiffs snug,
> The muse found Scroggen stretch'd beneath a rug.
> A window patch'd with paper lent a ray,
> That dimly shew'd the state in which he lay;
> The sanded floor that grits beneath the tread;
> The humid wall with paltry pictures spread;
> The royal game of goose was there in view,
> And the twelve rules the royal martyr drew;

The seasons fram'd with listing found a place,
And brave prince William shew'd his lamp-black face:
The morn was cold, he views with keen desire
The rusty grate unconscious of a fire;
With beer and milk arrears the frieze was scor'd
And five crack'd tea-cups dress'd the chimney board,
A night cap deck'd his brows instead of bay,
A cap by night—a stocking all the day.

With this last line he seemed so much elated that he was unable to proceed. 'There gentlemen!' cries he, 'there is a description for you; Rabelais's bed-chamber is but a fool to it:

A cap by night—a stocking all the day!

There is sound and sense, and truth, and nature in the trifling compass of ten little syllables.'[1]

The sanded floor, the tea-cups, the pictures all reappear in *The Deserted Village*, there transformed by their context into details of domestic comfort. Even the familiar antithetical balance of the final couplet is repeated:

The chest contrive'd a double debt to pay,
A bed by night, a chest of drawers by day;

(ll. 229–30.)

But here it is so absorbed into the descriptive texture of the style that it becomes a mere statement of fact; there is no pretence at a witty point. Whereas Scroggen's night-cap, which roused its author to such raptures of Augustan apologetics, is a humorous parody of the neat paradox to which the heavy dividing pause lends itself so easily. Under all the good-natured burlesque humour, it is hard not to suspect Goldsmith of impatience with the traditional notion of 'sound and sense, and truth and nature in the trifling compass of ten little syllables'. His own compass was wider. He preferred the range of the paragraph and the casual ease of a loose, rambling recollection of detail.

Johnson was not so aware of the limitations of the style. It had served him well in his own poetry. He preferred discrimination to

---

[1] O. Goldsmith, *The Citizen of the World*, ed. A. Dobson (1934), pp. 81–82.

association as a poetic principle, and in this he was at one with earlier Augustan poets and critics. If he seems often to reproduce the characteristic diction, the grammatical idiom and pattern of the earlier Augustans, it was not the result of timid unoriginality but of a genuine acceptance of a style which seemed fully to convey the kind of reality with which he was concerned. His pronouncements on style reflect this. He was not primarily a technical critic; he was more interested in judging what a writer had to say than the way in which he said it. Like Dryden and Pope, he had no inbred respect for the rules as rules, and if we want to discover what the common technical assumptions of the Augustans were we would be better advised to read Gildon and Dennis than Pope or Johnson. But his attitude to subject-matter was closely associated with his view of style and language.

General conformity to certain conventions of idiom within a period can never be simply attributed to critical precepts. It is always nearly related to the modes of thinking and feeling of the time. This is evident even in private letters, particularly in earlier periods when the act of writing, of putting ideas and feelings into words, is seen as an occasion of some formality in itself. When Sir Thomas More, reminding his children that he has been an indulgent father, says that he has 'chastised them with peacock's feathers', he uses an image we would more easily associate with poetry than with private correspondence. The girls who went to Richardson when he was a boy to ask him to write their love-letters had no doubt that a more elegant and literary style than they could command would perfectly reflect their feelings. Similarly, a literature which to us seems 'unnatural' in its style may well have struck contemporaries as entirely persuasive and realistic. Mrs. Thrale's proof of the 'strong Feelings of Nature and Passion' of *Eloisa to Abelard*—that it was the favourite of the kept mistresses of the town, who could not possibly have appreciated its poetic ingenuity[1]—illustrates this. The extremely stylized expression of the poem bore a real relation to the way in which these women liked to think of the nature of love. They felt that in some recognizable and quite unliterary way it was 'like' Pope's poem. Very probably this is always true to some

---

[1] See above, p. 165.

extent, and there may be many people today who think that love is 'like' the language of popular songs or the terse understated dialogue of a contemporary novel.

Before the romantic period, this inevitable connexion between life and language was supported and emphasized by an attitude towards experience which tended to formalize and discriminate. Experience was not purely or entirely a personal matter, but rather a recognizable reaction to some truth the value of which had already been established. It could therefore be expressed in terms which reflected that evaluation. This is clear if we look at Johnson's remarks on the language proper to poetry in his Life of Dryden, and notice that they refer to the function of poetry and to a particular view of reality rather than to a simple and isolated theory of diction:

> There was before the time of Dryden no poetical diction, no system of words at once refined from the grossness of domestick use and free from the harshness of terms appropriate to particular arts. Words too familiar or too remote defeat the purpose of the poet. From those sounds which we hear on small or coarse occasions, we do not easily receive strong impressions or delightful images; and words to which we are nearly strangers, whenever they occur draw that attention to themselves that they should transmit to things.[1]

The first of Johnson's points—that the language of poetry is not an everyday language—is not the same as Gray's view that the language of poetry is never the language of the age. Johnson was not a literary archaist. If a poet was to write 'to common degrees of knowledge', as he praised Waller for doing, he must use the language of the age and of the spirit of the age. To the Augustan age language, and poetic language especially, must be true to nature. The problem is, of course, what they understood by this.

By nature the Augustans meant more than that common reality which everyone perceives rationally and with his senses. They would have agreed with Sir Joshua Reynolds's later definition, when he maintains that nature comprehends 'not only the forms which nature produces, but also the nature and internal fabrick and

---

[1] Johnson, Lives, vol. i, p. 420.

organization, as I may call it, of the human mind and imagination'.[1]
The human mind and imagination are not bound by the superficies
of things; they obey their own laws and search for the essential
nature of reality. To Reynolds this was not a matter for unique and
individual apprehension, 'for how can that be the nature of man, in
which no two individuals are the same?'[2] Behind this lies the
Aristotelian idea of nature always working towards perfection and
continually deflected by accident. It is the province of the mind to
conceive of that perfection; so much was good Renaissance aesthetic doctrine, and it remained true of the neo-classicism of the
Augustans. They were acutely observant of the accidents, and
eager to present them, but only in a way which would make perfectly clear their relation to perfection. In the old doctrine of the
kinds, satire, for instance, was a rough informal mode to indicate its
distance from the ideals of tragedy and epic. This doctrine remained only in vestigial though respected form in the eighteenth
century; but even when Pope expanded the satirical style, allowing
it a much greater range of effects than had traditionally been
granted to the genre, he still took care to underline the contrast
between the perfect and the accidental, the ideal and the real.

To do this, he did not noticeably vary his diction. The Elizabethans had often marked the difference between the kinds by using
a different sort of language for each. Bucolic dialect was introduced
into pastoral, colloquial and technical terms into satire, while the
polysyllabic mellifluous diction of the aureate style was reserved
for the more serious forms. Language to them was capable of
innumerable variations; it was a growing thing on which neo-
logisms, new coinages, strange developments could be grafted at
will. The Augustans would not accept the same freedom. More
even than Dryden, who shared something of the experimental spirit
of his predecessors, Pope chose a diction which conformed to a certain common simplicity. This he took as his standard: a clear and
unambiguous form of expression. Detail, local characteristics,
material fact—the accidents, as it were—required simple statement.
Nothing could be more precise than Pope's picture of the mean inn

---

[1] Reynolds, *Discourses*, ed. R. E. Wark (San Marino, 1959), Discourse 7, p. 124.
[2] Ibid.

where Buckingham lies dying in the third of the *Moral Essays*. The ideal, on the other hand, might demand a more heightened effect, but this is often achieved by an intensified rhythm and a simplification of the syntax rather than by a deliberate change to lofty vocabulary. Periphrasis of a sort does occur, but it is not the familiar formal kind we find in the *Pastorals* and the translation of Homer. Here, in the satires, Pope distinguishes his high style from his low by substituting for simple enumeration of fact and thing (which is characteristic of his satiric descriptions) a kind of expansive allusiveness. In the description of the inn he selects the relevant objects and names them. But in the passage on the Man of Ross in the same epistle, as we have seen, the reference to the fountain and the waterfall—'Not to the skies in useless columns tost, nor in proud falls magnificently lost'—is deliberately oblique. The things are not named here, they are translated into wider descriptive and associative terms which allow the poet at one and the same time to depict and to comment. This is a form of periphrasis or writing round which, while it elevates the tone of the passage, never forces the poet to sacrifice precision and point. It carries with it an effect of statement and evaluation combined, being at once precise and yet intellectually removed from the particular. A very careful discrimination in the use of epithets, adverbs, and verbs is necessary in this style, and the descriptive word is as often an adverb as an adjective, since its function is not primarily to heighten or intensify the effect of the noun. But in this elaborate technique of skilfully avoiding the name or synonym of a thing while yet fully referring to it, the actual diction is seldom of an intrinsically different kind from that which Pope uses in his more direct satirical passages.

Johnson, with less spontaneous imagination than Pope and a more academic approach to language, naturally tended to develop this kind of style. He was less interested in moving from the particular to the general, and he shows none of the brilliance in handling transitions of mood and purpose which makes Pope's style so dazzlingly vivid. But he learned from Pope how to manage the word-game in such a way as to stick to the facts without sacrificing his moral point. His own peculiar device is an example of conciseness where the general and the particular unite in a sort of narrow paradox.

Everyone has noticed his love of the abstract word as an agent. It is seldom a full-blown personification, but a word with partly metaphorical force, standing for the mental quality itself, and indicating its unique vitality. Three examples will show us some of the ways in which he uses it:

> Whose night *congratulating Conscience* cheers.

> Now *lacerated Friendship* claims a tear.

> How, when competitors like these contend
> Can *surly virtue* hope to fix a friend,

In the first of these Conscience is merely conscience, the mental or spiritual state, and because it is normally conceived of as having active power (conscience pricks or goads us), the modifying adjective 'congratulating' and the verb 'cheers' only reinforce the natural liveliness of the word without transforming it. In the second, the greater force of the adjective 'lacerated' makes Friendship a more sensitive and vivid conception, and this is even more true of the last example, where 'surly' transforms virtue into a character, a sort of oblique representation of the Johnsonian personality itself. In each case we can see how Johnson, unlike Pope, limits himself to epithets to refer us almost entirely to the noun, and that the effect of this is to solidify and fix the original impression of the abstract substantive. Pope's love of movement and change is reflected in his emphasis on the verb and adverb, which accounts for the feeling his best poetry always gives of vitality and potentiality, of freedom within the limits of a conservative diction. He was not naturally attracted to the abstraction, whereas Johnson's passion for it is characteristic of his genius. But to Johnson the abstract word is as alive as the attribute for which it stands. When he uses it the effect is not of a vague and amorphous impression of the ideal, but of a substantial world of mental qualities, fixed and invariable, which constitute his view of reality. By the careful contrivance of his style he rigorously excludes from his poetry anything except that nature and truth which he was capable of conveying with sincerity. The interplay between the general and the particular, the tragic discrepancy between the perfect and the accidental, which underlies

the irony of life for Johnson, might be presented with the breadth
and diversity of Dryden or Pope, but it could also find powerful
expression in this more limited and concentrated range.

As to Johnson's view of language, I suppose hardly anyone today
would agree with him that 'from those sounds which we hear on
small occasions we do not easily receive strong impressions or delightful images', but, for better or worse, we have lost the sense of
occasion in life and literature. All our activities, large or small,
seem to us to have much narrower and more comparable ranges of
significance. To Johnson and his contemporaries this was not so.
The discrimination he recommended in the use of language was of
the same sort as he supposed operated in our experience of life. Degrees of effectiveness in words related to the comparative importance of the things and events to which they refer. We can see how
nearly this attitude relates to the discrimination in selecting relevant details, commonly applicable examples, and specific themes
which makes up such a large part of the Augustan manner, and how
this itself is the result of a view of reality which presupposes some
fixed standard of truth in thought and of goodness in conduct, the
result, in fact, of that ethos which inspired the best of Dryden's
and Pope's poetry as well as Johnson's. Johnson's distrust of remote
words which 'defeat the purpose of the poet' arises from the same
point of view, for his purpose is to define and present that ethos.
Words must clarify and never obscure the truth. In the *Essay on
Criticism* Pope had written:

> But true *Expression*, like th'unchanging *Sun*,
> *Clears*, and *improves* whate'er it shines upon,
> It *gilds* all Objects, but it *alters* none.
>
> (ll. 315–17.)

Johnson repeated the same idea in a different way when he said in
the Preface to his Dictionary, 'I am not yet so lost in lexicography as
to forget that words are the daughters of earth and that things are
the sons of heaven'.[1]

The terms in which the Augustans speak seem to mark a division
between the thing and the word, the subject and the expression,
which the romantics came to consider typical of a vicious and faulty

---

[1] Johnson, *A Dictionary of the English Language*, vol. i, 1755, Preface, A2v.

approach to the nature of poetry. Any study of Johnson, the last Augustan publicly to profess this view, must lead to a serious consideration of what was meant by it, and since it can even be maintained that some of the assumptions of Augustan poetry were absorbed into the new sensibility and to a certain extent affected romanticism, it is important to try to discover where, on this particular issue, the difference lies. That honesty which had reduced the possible subject-matter of poetry to 'truth' in the sense of factual reality lay behind the Augustans' point of view. They derived from the Renaissance their idea of the poet's duty of imitating nature's perfection, but their notion of that perfection was very different from the Elizabethans'. Imagination did not so often mean invention to them, for, deprived of the aid of myth and fable, they could no longer feel that the poets delivered a golden world nearer to truth than the brazen world of fact. Facts themselves, and the common reason which perceives them, were the medium through which the Augustans were left to discover perfection, and thus history or tradition (the facts of past and tried experience) on the one hand, and morality (a clear-sighted, honest assessment of the present) on the other, made up the most important part of their vision. But this deprivation affected their style. They hesitated to play with language, because language is the common means of communicating truth, and it is dangerous to meddle with it. Instead they felt it their duty to fix and purify the literary language so that its precision and its clear referential qualities should be preserved. Neither Dryden nor Pope openly deplored or contradicted this theory, though the one exuberantly broke through its restrictions, and the other was fired to extraordinary feats of syntactical agility and subtlety by its very limitations. We find Johnson, in the Preface to the Dictionary, recognizing the shifting nature of language—that one word is budding and another fading as he goes to press—but he does so to regret it, not to seize it as an opportunity for creative experiment. Just as he resigned himself to the transience of life, so he believed that the mutability of language must be admitted, but that words should be used as durably as possible, since the poet's duty is to impose on his medium some of the permanence of truth. From this we can see why Johnson praised Dryden for having found the language brick and left it marble; he was thinking not only of its decorative but of its lasting qualities. Johnson's own belief that truth was not relative or dependent on purely rational speculation, but absolute and revealed, helped, too, to draw him to the theory of a fixed language for literary use.

The romantics' quarrel with this attitude was both literary and philosophical. De Quincey in his essay on style puts forward the literary argument: 'if language were merely a dress, then you could separate the two; you could lay the thoughts on the left hand, the language on the right. But, generally speaking, you can no more deal thus with poetic thoughts than you can with soul and body. The union is too subtle, the intertexture too ineffable.'[1] A new conception has entered here, however; that of poetic thoughts. This suggests a peculiar truth proper to poetry, which Johnson would never have admitted. To him truth was one and indivisible, and though it might be comprehended in varying degrees, it was not susceptible of a variety of modes of perception. The poet himself, to the Augustans, was man like others. His view of reality could never be radically different from theirs. Behind De Quincey's words, on the other hand, lies the romantic assumption that poetry is a particular way of experiencing life, and the best way, too, combining as it does in 'ineffable intertexture' the spiritual and the material. These two opposites are no longer distinguished and put against each other like the old alternatives of perfect and accidental, or general and particular. They are seen in the unity of the poetic vision by a nature so constituted as to possess a greater degree of insight than is permitted to ordinary men.

To understand more completely the particular development and effect of this change of view, it is worth considering the attitude of the greatest and most revolutionary of the romantics, Wordsworth, to see how a poet who directly inherited an eighteenth-century diction and style could completely reverse the eighteenth-century position. Pater says this about Wordsworth's language, illuminating the whole romantic conception of style: 'His words are themselves thought and feeling; not eloquent or musical words merely, but that sort of creative language which carries the reality of what it

---

[1] De Quincey, *The Collected Writings*, D. Mason, vol. x (1897), p. 230.

depicts, directly, to the consciousness'.[1] This sort of creative language is the aim of the romantic poet. It is evidently at the opposite extreme from the rhetorical Augustan style, even when that claims to be 'the language of the heart'. But no change of style or conception ever occurs without preparation, and we can find connexions between the romantics and their predecessors not only in eighteenth-century nature poetry, but even, unlikely as it may seem, in the stricter Augustan tradition. Wordsworth's confessed intention, for instance, of using the language of men for the purpose of conveying truth and sincere experience, and his desire to be thought of as a teacher or nothing, would have seemed natural and proper to Johnson. These are close to the aims of the Honest Muse, and even though, in the meantime, new developments of sensibility had brought inevitable changes, points of contact remain. When Wordsworth invites us to 'come forth into the light of things' he is not speaking vaguely, but with an exact sense of things as objects, palpable reality, in Johnson's words, 'the sons of heaven'. These are the given material of each poet. But there is no question in Wordsworth of choosing a style which will improve or clarify the original subject so that it exists unobscured but gilded by the play of eloquence and expression. Things are still the source for Wordsworth, but they are not the end.

In the *Lyrical Ballads* Wordsworth is scrupulously careful to claim authenticity for almost every incident with which his poems deal. He himself talked to the heroine of *We Are Seven* in the grounds of Goodrich Castle; he knew Simon Lee at Alfoxden; the words of the Idiot Boy were reported to him by a friend. In each case actual circumstance, literal fact, is the groundwork of the poem, and it is as if Wordsworth, in his own way, were confirming the Augustan contention that 'the mind nauseates what she can't believe'. The claim is not made in the poem itself, however, but included in the notes as an additional guarantee of the reality and truth these works are meant to convey. It is the mode of conveyance that has changed from the Augustan. Wordsworth is rooted in the physical and actual, even more strongly than his predecessors, particularly than Johnson. For, unlike Johnson, he will not take anything on

[1] W. Pater, 'Wordsworth' *Appreciations* (1889), 4th ed. (1910), p. 58.

trust; it must all be put to the test of personal experience. Where Johnson is deliberately conservative, and anxious to accept common standards and the common view whenever he can, Wordsworth is instinctively radical. Nature for him is the root and origin, not the perfection to which everything tends, and his poetry continually refers back to this source. Memory and rediscovery, leading us back to 'the hiding places of man's power', are the great forces in his work, not that intellectual power which rationalizes experience into terms of the absolute. The assumptions which Johnson accepted, and on which he based his distinctions between greater and less significance, were no longer verifiable in the same way to Wordsworth, and thus no longer important for his poetry.

For the same reason Johnson's carefully discriminated choice of words was to Wordsworth like a veil coming down between the reader and reality. Wordsworth's reality included the poem itself, or at least, the whole original conception of which the poem was the articulate sign. Often he speaks as if the process of composition were spontaneous—the imagination, or power of perception, and the words coming simultaneously. Writing to Sir George Beaumont, he admits the excessive length of *The Prelude* but adds that it may well be impossible to reduce it, since 'the fault lies in the original conception'[1]—an apology no Augustan could ever have thought of making. The process which Dryden and his followers had described sequentially as the invention, or finding of the thought, followed by the clothing of it in well-chosen words and eloquent expression, is, as it were, telescoped into one action by Wordsworth. His new idea of the imagination included at one and the same time the recognition of fact or actuality, the perception of its significance, and the prophetic power of the word to convey this.

But we should notice that one point of contact with the Augustan view still remains here. The words the romantic poet uses are no more meant to transform the reality they convey than to embellish it. Pater says they carry the reality of what they depict directly to the consciousness, and that reality, however complex, was not susceptible of the witty transmutations to which the Elizabethans and the metaphysicals subjected their material. In other

---

[1] C. Wordsworth, *Memorials of William Wordsworth*, vol. i (1851), p. 306.

words, the romantic's respect for nature as the *fons et origo* of his genius is nearer to the Augustan's respect for fact or literal reality than it is to the Renaissance attitude towards a world which the poet, with his divine prerogative of making, can transform from brazen to golden.

We have left out of account here the enthusiasm and passion involved in Wordsworth's conception of style, and the supremely important role of the imagination, without which it would have been impossible to translate such an 'honest' matter and manner to the extraordinary heights of intensity Wordsworth achieves, because these elements are so foreign to Johnson that they have no place in this chapter. But we can, to some extent, compare the solution each poet found to a not entirely dissimilar problem—how to convey at one and the same time authentic fact and higher truth. Wordsworth's habit of picking his way through the quicksands of language by the use of a pedestrian and literal diction, until he reaches the point at which 'the light of sense goes out', is his answer to the problem of finding words which neither alter nor obscure the facts but which, through the unique agency of the imagination—the modifying and associating power acting upon the original perception—in the moment of truth themselves become that truth. Like Johnson he struggles for accuracy. The same careful labouring for words which mean no more or less than he can say with honesty, which was evident in Johnson's poem on Levet, is present in Wordsworth's strange power of conveying elementary impressions, even abstract ideas.

Wordsworth, however, has no wish to fix and substantiate these impressions and ideas as Johnson has. The whole point of his poetry is to convey them as intimations, hesitant, fugitive, and negative suggestions: 'an obscure sense of possible sublimity', 'blank misgivings of a creature moving about in worlds not realised'. Here language is striving to convey what the poet admits to be beyond communication, since, of its very nature, it is imperfectly perceived and apprehended. But Wordsworth does not move into myth or image to express this meaning: he seldom, even, has recourse to metaphor. Like his Augustan predecessors, he respects the defining power of the word and keeps to that. Direct description and direct statement are the staple elements of the Wordsworthian style at its greatest, and these are to some extent an inheritance from the Augustan attitude to truth and to language. Wordsworth rejected their absolutes and their ideals of perfection, but he retained their obstinate reliance on what can be perceived and then defined by the power of the word.

Between Johnson's view and De Quincey's lies a whole way of writing which with revolutionary completeness had carried out the remotest implications of sincerity, truth to nature, and the direct expression of experience; yet, as we have seen in Wordsworth, it bears some traces of the ancestry against which it claimed to rebel. It is fruitless to regret that the Augustans themselves never went so far. It was impossible that they should. Their whole view of reality was limited by a desire to conserve what was best in tradition, and to secure literature and society from the dangers of extravagant innovation. Enthusiasm in the early part of the century and sentiment in the later were equally outside the bounds Augustanism set itself, and equally opposed to that moderation on which literary as well as moral prudence depended. If the collapse of the old ways of thought in the latter part of the seventeenth century had set a problem in clarification and definition, the new eighteenth-century philosophy of perception, and its contention that morality, taste, judgement, ideas themselves derived from perception alone, set an equally severe problem of control which philosophers felt as keenly as poets. Berkeley argued back to the original perception of God to justify the revealed truth of Christianity as a principle of belief and conduct. Hume, rejecting this, was still aware of the practical need for rules to govern those sentiments of the heart and mind which for him constituted morality and taste, and in his private views clung with Augustan conservatism to a practical *status quo*. It takes perhaps a poetic rather than a rational temperament fully to accept the revolutionary conclusions of the theory of perception, and a poetic temperament which must also have faith in the infallibility of that peculiar instrument of perception, the imagination. Johnson did not accept these new theories. Dedicated to the rational and the traditional, an orthodox Christian, believing in absolute truth, he inevitably took his position with that literary attitude which was conservative and critical in its moral view of the dangers of excess. The most conservative element in this attitude was its view of poetic language. But Johnson recognized the fact that a way of saying something in itself amounts to an idea or attitude. If he limited the possibilities of language it was in order to define and embody a view of reality which he held with a passionate conviction of its truth.

A valuable and sincere expression of experience can be received from poets who use language in the way of Johnson and the Augustans, and do not carry it to the lengths which enabled the later romantics to effect a revolution in sensibility. Older notions of the particular function of poetry had lingered with the Augustans, and the feat of reconciling these with a pressing sense of newer experiences of truth produced a kind of literature which has certain peculiar qualities of equilibrium. They preserved a breadth and catholicity which, in the work of their greatest poets, seldom lapses into emptiness because of their concern for reality and their curiosity about ways of living. Their poetry is both grave and graceful, weighty and witty. What it lacks is any sense of vision or wonder. But it did not entirely lack the possibility of growth, in spite of its intention to limit and perfect. Johnson himself, wary of innovation or improvement in diction and versification, was always ready to praise something new in sentiment or an originality of approach, as long as it seemed to him to come nearer to the truth. As we shall see, his attitude to genres and kinds was as radical and irreverent as his attitude to language was authoritarian.

IV

At the beginning of the eighteenth century the old idea of distinct kinds of poem with a decorous style appropriated to each, though it was retained to some extent in critical precept, was rapidly losing its attraction to the practising poet. Dryden, the earliest of the Augustans, was naturally the most influenced by this theory, but even Dryden made his variations of style not only according to the form, but also within the one mode, so that he ex-

tended the range of satire, for instance, beyond anything that had
been thought of by those earlier critics who had defined it as of the
rough and savage kind. Pope developed this tendency yet further.
In his mature satiric style the elegiac, the witty, the elevated, and
the idyllic all combine; he moves from grave to gay, from lively to
severe in the same poem, and the mingled influence of the epic, the
pastoral, and the epistle make up a mixed style which, though it is
characteristic of Pope's genius, is also typical of the eclecticism of
his school. It reflects a new idea of poetry as consisting not in kinds
but in the direct communication of varied experience, eloquently
expressed but not distinguished by traditional genres.

Johnson's attitude towards genre is the natural outcome of this
movement. Even his attack on *Lycidas* owes something to the
gradual loss of interest in the pastoral form throughout the eighteenth century. Rapin in 1659 and Fontenelle in 1688 had argued
the case for the 'ancient' and the 'modern' interpretation of pastoral
respectively—Rapin being a conservative imitator of Virgil and
Fontenelle maintaining a realistic and descriptive approach to the
form. This dispute gave an artificial stimulus to the writing of
pastoral in the Restoration and the early eighteenth century which
it sorely needed to survive at all. A crop of pastoral elegies had
appeared at the death of Rochester (Oldham's and Mrs. Aphra
Behn's being the best and the best known of these), but these
modish extravagances, for the most part unmoving and frigid, show
how little intrinsic life was left in the genre. The love poems of the
wits had masqueraded with pastoral names and settings, but they
too lacked any touch of the innocence and purity associated with
the original manners of the form. In the next century Philips and
Pope vied with each other in giving a practical demonstration of the
principles of Fontenelle and Rapin, but the liveliest example of
pastoral at this time is to be found in Gay's *Shepherd's Week*. Gay's
eclogues were originally intended as parodies of the 'modern' attitude and burlesques of Philips's style, but as Johnson was quick to
observe in his Life of Gay:

the effect of reality and truth became conspicuous, even when the
intention was to shew them groveling and degraded. These Pastorals
became popular, and were read with delight, as just representations

of rural manners and occupations, by those who had no interest in the rivalry of the poets, nor knowledge of the critical dispute.[1]

When parody begins to be more delightful than actual contemporary examples, we can safely assume that the form itself is in process of dying. The rough bucolic realism of *The Shepherd's Week*, for all its burlesque humour, is getting close to the direct descriptions of nature which, if classical analogies are needed, were more Georgic than pastoral.

Two of the *Rambler* essays, numbers 36 and 37, deal with the pastoral, and in them Johnson appears to make a compromise between the ancient and the modern position. He admits that Virgil, imitating Theocritus, brought the form to perfection, and that no one since has improved on him. At the same time he emphasizes the descriptive nature of the form and obviously looks on it as country poetry. A pastoral is 'a poem in which any action or passion is represented by its effects upon a country life',[2] and it pleases us because we are familiar with the images of nature and associate them with tranquillity and ease. But the pastoral form as it has been used by the moderns comes under attack for a new reason; these writers have 'filled their productions with mythological allusions, with incredible fictions and with sentiments which neither passion nor reason could have dictated since the change religion has made in the whole system of the world'.[3] False fabling and paganism seem peculiarly associated with the form to Johnson, and he dismisses contemptuously the technical discussion as to whether the sentiments and language of pastoral shepherds should be idealized or realistic: 'In pastorals as in other writings, chastity of sentiment ought, doubtless, to be observed, and purity of manners to be represented, not because the poet is confined to the images of the golden age, but because, having the subject in his own choice, he ought always to consult the interest of virtue'.[4] Dispute over the kind of language to be used, and the convention of a rough bucolic style, seemed to him even more futile; he makes excellent fun of Spenser's pedantry on this point in *The Shepheard's Calendar*.

[1] Johnson, *Lives*, vol. ii, p. 269.
[2] *Rambler*, No. 37, 24 July 1750, *The True Principles of Pastoral Poetry*.
[3] Ibid.　　　　　　　　　　　　　　　　　　　　　[4] Ibid.

Spenser begins one of his pastorals with studied barbarity:

> Diggon Davie, I bid her good-day,
> Or Diggon her is, or I missay.
> *Dig.* Her was her while it was day-light
> But now her is a most wretched wight.

What will the reader imagine to be the subject on which speakers like these exercise their eloquence? Will he not be somewhat disappointed to find them met together to condemn the corruptions of the church of Rome? Surely, at the same time that a shepherd learns theology, he may gain some acquaintance with his native language.[1]

On the whole, then, Johnson shows little interest in pastoral as a genre. *Rambler* No. 36 and the later Life of Phillips each contain brief histories of its development, but in the latter the account is so terse as to suggest contempt, and the tone easily slips into irony:

> Petrarch entertained the learned men of his age with the novelty of modern Pastorals in Latin. Being not ignorant of Greek, and finding nothing in the word *Eclogue* of rural meaning, he supposed it to be corrupted by the copiers, and therefore called his own productions *Aeglogues*, by which he meant to express the talk of goatherds, though it will mean only the talk of goats.[2]

His implication is that behind such discussions and considerations in adapting an ancient form to modern literature is the bigotry of learning for which he blames Milton in choosing the strict Greek model for *Samson Agonistes*. Johnson's impatience with such academic experiments grew stronger as he grew older, and it is striking to find alongside his general conservatism a sort of moral radicalism which looks at literature from the point of view of virtue and reality. If he criticizes Milton, he criticizes Milton's critics more severely for their formal arguments about the kind and structure of *Paradise Lost*: 'The questions whether the action of the poem be strictly *one*, whether the poem can be properly termed *heroick*, and who is the hero, are raised by such readers as draw their principles of judgment rather from books than from reason'.[3] It would certainly have confirmed him in his contempt to know that such

---

[1] *Rambler*, No. 37.   [2] Johnson, *Lives*, vol. iii, p. 317.
[3] Ibid., vol. i, pp. 175–6.

questions have become the stock-in-trade of later literary examiners. Is *Paradise Lost* an epic? Johnson was satisfied to take Milton's word for it with no further argument: 'Milton, though he intituled *Paradise Lost* only a "poem", yet calls it himself "heroick song".'

Johnson's position is made unequivocally clear when he turns on his favourite Dryden for doubting that Adam is the hero of a true epic: 'Dryden, petulantly and indecently, denies the heroism of Adam because he was overcome; but there is no reason why the hero should not be unfortunate except established practise, since success and virtue do not go necessarily together'.[1] A whole time-honoured mode of criticism crumbles like the walls of Jericho at this statement of literal fact. That Milton had shown Adam unsuccessful and unfortunate, had, in fact, in technical terms, substituted a tragic for an epic hero, seemed to Johnson matter for congratulation, not because it was an interesting experiment, but because Milton had put truth before the requirements of convention, because he had followed nature rather than art. Johnson could scarcely have chosen a better example of the pressing needs of truth in a poet's subject-matter affecting his whole procedure, for Milton himself was entirely aware of what he was doing and why. In *The Reason of Church Government* he had already mentioned two possibilities of epic composition: 'whether the rules of Aristotle herein are strictly to be kept, or nature to be followed, which in them that know art and use of judgment, is no transgression, but an enrichment of art'. In Book IX of *Paradise Lost* he devoted a whole passage to explaining why he had chosen the second method and to contrasting his own conception of the heroic with that of 'established practise':

> Not sedulous by Nature to indite
> Wars, hitherto the only Argument
> Heroic deem'd, chief maistry to dissect
> With long and tedious havoc fabl'd Knights
> In Battles feign'd; *the better fortitude*
> *Of Patience and Heroic Martyrdom*
> *Unsung*; or to describe Races and Games . . .
> The skill of Artifice or Office mean,
> *Not that which justly gives Heroic name*

---

[1] Johnson, *Lives*, vol. i, p. 176.

To Person or to Poem. Mee of these
Nor skill'd nor studious, *higher Argument*
Remains, sufficient of itself to raise
That name . . .
(Bk. IX, ll. 27–33; 39–44.)[1]

'That which justly gives heroic name to person or to poem' was Milton's quest, and the Augustans, while their aim was less confidently elevated, shared his impatience with the trappings of appearance and rhetoric, the swelling epithets he was to attack in *Paradise Regained*, 'thick laid / As varnish on a Harlot's cheek' (4. 343–4). They intended to strip off the glittering figurative dress in which the older way of interpreting reality had been clothed, in hopes of finding a new face of truth underneath. Johnson's famous injunction, 'clear your mind of cant', fitted his literary as well as his moral views, and it matched the Augustan distrust of too rigid and formal an adherence to purely technical standards of composition. Even that correct and conventional poem Pope's *Essay on Criticism* contains a passage which reminds us how he liked to emphasize the proviso, implicit in all rules, that they may justly be broken in a good cause:

> Some Beauties yet, no Precepts can declare,
> For there's a *Happiness* as well as *Care.*
> *Musick* resembles *Poetry*, in each
> Are *nameless Graces* which no *Methods* teach
> And which a *Master-Hand* alone can reach. . . .
> Great Wits sometimes may *gloriously offend,*
> And *rise* to *Faults* true Criticks *dare not mend*;
> From *vulgar Bounds* with *brave Disorder* part,
> And *snatch* a *Grace* beyond the Reach of Art,
> Which, without passing thro' the *Judgment*, gains
> The *Heart*, and all its End *at once* attains.
(ll. 141–5, 152–7.)

The effect of these touches of nature is instantaneous, according to Pope, and appeals to the feelings, not the reason. He believed that a poet should write on what he knew, must write about it naturally, and would then inevitably move his reader. Johnson, it is not so

[1] Italics mine.

often realized, shared these assumptions. The poet, a man writing for men, offering them truth, diversion, and consolation, can scarcely fail to produce an emotional effect which is not so much the result of style or convention, but rather of a close, sincere knowledge of the subject and a just assessment of its value. If he does not know intimately and well what he chooses to write about, the effect will be as Johnson described it in his criticism of *Eleonora*: 'the praise being therefore inevitably general, fixes no impression upon the reader, nor excites any tendency to love, nor much desire of imitation . . .'.[1] The poem, in fact, is neither moving nor persuasive. We may be surprised to find Johnson here implying that general statements will not produce a powerful emotional response, unless we recall that to him, as to Pope, general ideas could only be valuable if they were drawn from and justified by actual experience.

Johnson uses the term 'truth to nature' which we have glanced at in its stylistic sense, more often with regard to the sentiments and themes of a work. 'The heart naturally loves truth', he wrote, and truth to nature is often synonymous with 'affecting' in his criticism in the *Lives*. Of a simple and tender passage in Shenstone's *Pastoral Ballad* he says it is one 'to which if any mind denies its sympathy it has no acquaintance with love or nature', and he praises Shenstone's style in 'light and short compositions' because there 'we are entertained at once with two imitations, of nature in the sentiments, of the original author in the style, and between them the mind is kept in continual employment'.[2] From this we can see how nature to Johnson did not mean a poet's peculiar attitude to life, but rather his power of touching on the common chords of experience, and it is this nature which, in the thought of the period, is as often associated with passion as with quiet reflective sentiment.

Eighteenth-century critics were encouraged in their liberal interpretation of the rules and their search for nameless graces by the example of Shakespeare, the outstanding 'natural' genius, whose supremacy in his own country had never seriously been challenged.

---

[1] Johnson, *Lives*, vol. i, pp. 441–2.
[2] Ibid., vol. iii, p. 356.

In his 'Preface to Shakespeare' the only distinguished name Johnson can cite as one of those who 'form their judgment on narrower principles' than nature is Voltaire. With him are ranged Dennis and Rymer; against them Dryden, Pope, Johnson himself, and a long race of critics, editors, and literary men. Writing in defence of Shakespeare's apparent irregularities, Johnson refers constantly to nature. 'There is always an appeal open from criticism to nature', 'Shakespeare is above all writers, at least above all modern writers, the poet of nature, the poet that holds up to his readers a faithful mirror of manners and of life'; his plays exhibit 'the real state of sublunary nature, which partakes of good and evil, joy and sorrow, mingled with endless variety of proportion and innumerable modes of combination'; his 'violations of rules merely positive become the comprehensive genius of Shakespeare'. The comparison Johnson makes between Voltaire's favourite, *Cato*, and Shakespeare's plays reads like a summary of the critical points we have enumerated in considering the Augustans' neglect of convention in their pursuit of authenticity:

Voltaire expresses his wonder, that our authour's extravagances are endured by a nation, which has seen the tragedy of *Cato*. Let him be answered, that *Addison* speaks the language of poets, and *Shakespeare*, of men. We find in *Cato* innumerable beauties which enamour us of its authour, but we see nothing that acquaints us with human sentiments or human actions; we place it with the fairest and the noblest progeny which judgment propagates by conjunction with learning, but *Othello* is the vigorous and vivacious offspring of observation impregnated by genius. *Cato* affords a splendid exhibition of artificial and fictitious manners, and delivers just and noble sentiments, in diction easy, elevated and harmonious, but its hopes and fears communicate no vibration to the heart; the composition refers us only to the writer; we pronounce the name of *Cato*, but we think on *Addison*.[1]

The neat and odd distinction between the language of poets and the language of men that Johnson makes here recalls the peculiarities of the Augustan attitude towards style, expression, and words. With their view of utility and order in experience and terminology it was necessary to insist on the distinction, but, in fact, critically, the

---

[1] Johnson, 'Preface to Shakespeare', in D. Nichol Smith (ed.); *Eighteenth Century Essays on Shakespeare*, 2nd ed. (1963), pp. 124–5.

whole point of Johnson's argument is that the language of men produces the greater poetry. Here is the familiar point reiterated —that literature, to be moving, must be true, and that style, skill, judgement, and learning alone can never communicate any vibration to the heart. What can is observation, an accurate, authentic, and loving record of fact, 'impregnated by genius'.

Johnson had his own conception and his own definition of genius: 'that power which constitutes a poet; that quality without which judgment is cold and knowledge inert; that energy which collects, combines, amplifies and animates'.[1] Vigour, nervous energy, and a comprehensive sensibility—these are not terms we would quarrel with, though Johnson himself felt, perhaps, the futility of trying to define the nature of genius, as he suggests in Rasselas's ironic reply to Imlac's rhapsodic account of the character and function of a poet: 'Enough! Thou hast convinced me, that no human being can ever be a poet.'[2] Yet this touch of self-deprecating scepticism does not contradict the fact that Johnson believed the power of genius and its operations to be susceptible of rational definition. Though he rejected the old terms of rhetoric and the conventions for which they stood, he was as anxious to distinguish, define, and limit the irregular and boundless nature of genius as he was prepared to discriminate between the various kinds of experience that go to make up nature itself. His admiration for Shakespeare did not lead Johnson to any sense of the mystery of an inspiration which made such poetry possible. Other critics, many of them writing before Johnson produced his last work, the Lives, had begun to develop a peculiar theory of poetry which derived from a sense of wonder at the uniqueness and comprehensiveness of genius. Joseph Warton in The Adventurer, No. 93 (1753), writing on The Tempest, observes, 'the poet is a more powerful magician than his own Prospero'. Edward Young in his Conjectures on Original Composition (1759) claimed that the poet, from the point of view of his inspiration, is more a magician than an architect, and in his Essay on the Dramatic Character of Sir John Falstaff (1777) Maurice Morgann developed this idea and presented it as an aesthetic theory, in which

[1] Johnson, Lives, vol. iii, p. 222.
[2] Johnson, Rasselas, ed. R. W. Chapman (1927), p. 52.

the romantic apprehension of the poet's control over 'the hiding places of man's power' is already apparent when he writes: 'True Poesy is *magic* not *nature*: an effect from causes hidden and unknown. To the Magician I prescribe no laws; his law and his power are one; his power is his law. Him, who neither imitates, nor is within the reach of imitation, no precedent can or ought to bind, no limits to contain.'[1]

But to Johnson true poesy was still nature. It could be observed, analysed, understood. It followed general laws and principles, but laws of human experience and truth as understood by his age, not those of pedantry and learning. It spoke the language of the heart, not the language of the kinds or the language of prophecy and inspiration; and if poets were, as Imlac maintains, 'the legislators of mankind', they could never be, as Shelley was to assume, 'unacknowledged'. The poet's duty to teach and to delight, to communicate truth and to imitate nature, compels him in every age to look for the most honest, comprehensive, and persuasive way of doing this. If he fails here he cannot fulfil his responsibilities.

I have tried to show in this book how such a search led the Augustans to reject, among other things, many of the old genres and conventions; to relinquish fable and to distrust figurative language. The common idea of their poetry and criticism as artificial and dominated by rules and distinctions of kind is still misleading, though true to the extent that they did not want to break wholly with the past and were prepared to effect a conservative compromise. The work of minor poets and critics of the early eighteenth century often holds timidly to academic standards, but the characteristics of the great Augustans, Dryden, Pope, Swift in prose, and later Johnson, are an expressive realism of tone and manner, an ideal of simplicity, candour, and sincerity which preserved the dignity of the old and established, while reflecting and recording the new shift in sensibility that had been gradually taking place since the Restoration.

Johnson shared all these qualities, and he held to them with a force and an unapologetic confidence which indicates how perfectly they

---

[1] Maurice Morgann, 'Essay on the Dramatic Character of Sir John Falstaff', in D. Nichol Smith, *Eighteenth Century Essays on Shakespeare*, p. 235.

suited his own temperament and how they illustrated a genuine vein of feeling in his age. By the time he was writing the *Lives of the Poets* men had already ventured further and speculated more widely in aesthetic theory and in the practice of direct self-expression. But Johnson repeated the older principles of the Honest Muse in terms that suggest the deep emotional appeal they still held for him. What he says of Pope's choice of story in *Eloisa to Abelard* reveals the importance that a genuine Augustan attached to emotion, to originality, and imaginative freedom: 'So new and so affecting is their story, that it supersedes invention, and imagination ranges at full liberty without straggling into scenes of fable.'[1] Yet from this, too, we can see how he felt that such qualities were best served by the narrow principles of realistic truth and nature which his predecessors had established. Limits were to be set to the freedom of poetry, but they were the limits of truth and experience, not of convention and rule.

> Truth fails not; but her outwards forms that bear
> The longest date do melt like frosty rime . . .
> *(Ecclesiastical Sonnets*, 3. 34, ll. 7–8.)

Johnson would have understood and approved these lines of Wordsworth's. The outward forms of past convention were already melting when Dryden began to write, and Johnson, looking back over the whole period, found that many of them had disappeared altogether. No one would ever again write an epic, though it had already given life to other kinds of verse, and bequeathed an attitude which the Augustans treated with reverence. But when Johnson writes on Milton he is interested in *Paradise Lost* as a poem in its own right, not in the epic as a kind. The old form had been quietly laid aside, and wits like Walpole could be flippant at its expense: 'Epic poetry is the art of being as long as possible in telling an uninteresting story; and an epic poem is a mixture of history without truth and of romance without imagination.'[2] The great aim of the new age was history with truth. As a substitute for the epic it had created new modes of narrative and story-telling: written history itself, and that great modern form, so wide that it can scarcely be

---

[1] Johnson, *Lives*, vol. iii, p. 235.

[2] Walpole, *Correspondence*, ed. W. S. Lewis, vol. xxix, Part II (1955), p. 255, to the Revd. W. Mason, 25 June 1782.

called a kind in the old sense, the novel, in which the hero may be tragic or comic, the narrative ironic or sincere, subjective or objective, and in which the intention is clearly 'to exhibit the true state of sublunary nature which partakes of good and evil, joy and sorrow, mingled with endless variety of proportion and innumerable modes of combination'. In poetry the epistolary style which the Augustans had devised, together with the discursive poem as a free and less formal mode than the old ones for expressing truth and sentiment, was already dissolving into that yet freer form, the rambling essay in verse of which the prevailing mood is reflection and the stress is on feeling. A new idea of inner coherence, rising from this concentration on feeling, had also led to the elevation of one of the most neglected of the old kinds, the lesser lyric, or song, which was now again valued for its power of expressiveness, its simplicity and poignancy. Everywhere the movement was towards a gradual dissipation of the stricter outlines, the distinctions and proportions, those limitations within which the Augustans themselves had worked out new modes of expression.

Johnson, who had looked back with satisfaction at the gradual cultivation of society since the time of Addison, noticed another development which he viewed with less favour. In the *Adventurer*, No. 115 (1753), he observes:

The present age, if we consider chiefly the state of our own country, may be stiled with great propriety THE AGE OF AUTHORS; for, perhaps, there never was a time, in which men of all degrees of ability, of every kind of education, of every profession and employment, were posting with ardour so general to the press. The province of writing was formerly left to those, who by study, or appearance of study, were supposed to have gained knowledge unattainable by the busy part of mankind; but in these enlightened days, every man is qualified to instruct every other man; and he that beats the anvil, or guides the plough, not contented with supplying corporal necessities, amuses himself in the hours of leisure with providing intellectual pleasures for his countrymen.[1]

Johnson does not pretend to give any reason for this sudden burst of

---

[1] Johnson was the author of *Adventurer*, No. 115, signed T. See L. F. Powell, 'Johnson's part in *The Adventurer*', R.E.S., vol. iii (1927), pp. 420–9.

literary activity. He concludes his paper with a series of injunctions to the would-be writer which give us a curious picture of the old Augustan benevolently attempting to regulate the flood of potential romanticism and self-expression. The first qualification is 'a perfect knowledge of the subject'; the next, mastery of the language, and this is to be learned by a perusal of the best authors ('no man is a rhetorician or philosopher by chance'). But these traditional heads of advice could have little effect on such a situation as he describes. The concept of realism and sincerity which the poetry of the Honest Muse had insinuated so successfully into literature, the notion of writing genuinely about what one knows and understands, is a short step from writing about what one feels—from self-expression, in fact. The man who is writing about himself and for himself has little use for rhetoric, which is the art of persuading others. But the Augustans had never lost their sense of the writer's duty of persuasion and exposition. To write for themselves would have seemed to them a breach of literary etiquette; besides, they had been bred in a society where those who lived to please must please to live. But their successors, amateurs where they had been professionals, were under no such pressure to adapt themselves to an audience. They were influenced rather by the subtle ways in which Dryden's persuasive tone had been transformed into Pope's more private monologue of self-justification; they had been convinced by his insistence on touching the heart. It had become difficult to see why, if a poet must write to the heart, he should not write from it and about it. An age of polite readers had turned gradually into the age of amateur authors which Johnson saw with half-serious dismay, and literature to them inevitably became a mode of self-expression. As soon as this had happened, true Augustanism, which rose from a union between the old and the new, a temporary compromise, was dead. Johnson alone remained to remind his contemporaries in his old age of all it had stood for. For this reason, any study of Augustan literature must conclude with him. In his own life he seems to epitomize the principles, the experience, and the genius of the Honest Muse.

APPENDIX

THE following two poems, Dorset's *On the Countess of* DORCHESTER and Halifax's *On the Countess Dowager of* * * * are markedly characteristic of the witty tradition of satire against women, and each directly influenced Pope. They are reprinted here in full as they are hard to come by in modern anthologies or collections.

I

On the Countess of DORCHESTER, *Mistress to* King JAMES *the Second. Written in* 1680

I

Tell me, *Dorinda*, why so gay,
  Why such embroid'ry, fringe, and lace?
Can any Dresses find a way,
To stop th'approaches of decay,
  And mend a ruin'd Face?

II

Wilt thou still sparkle in the Box,
  Still ogle in the Ring?
Canst thou forget thy Age and Pox?
Can all that shines on Shells and Rocks
  Make thee a fine young Thing?

III

So have I seen in Larder dark
  Of Veal a lucid Loin;
Replete with many a brilliant Spark,
As wise Philosophers remark,
  At once both stink and shine.

II

On the Countess Dowager of ✻ ✻ ✻

Courage, dear *Moll*, and drive away Despair,
Mopsa who in her Youth, was scarce thought fair,
In spite of Age, Experience, and Decays,
Sets up for Charming, in her fading Days:
Snuffs her dim Eyes to give one parting Blow.
Have at the Heart of ev'ry ogling Beau!
This goodly Goose, all feather'd like a Jay,
So gravely vain, and so demurely gay,
Last Night t'adorn the Court, did overload
Her bald buff Forehead with a high Commode:
Her steps were manag'd with such tender Art,
As if each Board had been a Lover's Heart.
In all her Air, in ev'ry Glance was seen
A Mixture strange, 'twixt Fifty and Fifteen.
Admiring Fops about her crowding press;
H—bd—n himself delivers their Address,
Which she, accepting with a nice Disdain,
Owns 'em her Subjects, and begins to reign:
Fair Queen of *Fopland* is her royal Stile;
Fopland! the greatest Part of this great Isle!
Nature did ne'er so equally divide
A Female Heart, 'twixt Piety and Pride:
Her Waiting-maids prevent the Peep of Day,
And, all in Order, on her Toilet lay
Pray'r-books, Patch-boxes, Sermon-notes and Paint,
At once t'improve the Sinner and the Saint.
Farewel, Friend *Moll*, expect no more from me,
But if you would a full Description see,
You'll find her somewhere in the *Litany*,
With Pride, Vain-glory, and Hypocrisy.

INDEX

PRINTED IN GREAT BRITAIN
AT THE UNIVERSITY PRESS, OXFORD
BY VIVIAN RIDLER
PRINTER TO THE UNIVERSITY